MAKE NO MISTAKES™
ABOUT…
BUYING REAL ESTATE

Third Edition

MELISSA WALTERS & RUDY SILMON

For more information contact:

Mill City Press, Inc.,
212 3rd Avenue North, Suite 570
Minneapolis, MN 55401
Or
info@millcitypress.net

ISBN 10: 0-9795604-2-X
ISBN 13: 978-0-9795604-2-2

www.MakeNoMistakes.com

TABLE OF CONTENTS

Section II:
Understand Your Home Loan
Before You Start House-Hunting

Section V:
Successfully Navigating
The Loan Process to Closing

Section VI:
What To Do After You Move In

Section VII:
How To Keep Your House,
And Other Tips

Mistake # 57: *Facing foreclosure with no plan*
Mistake # 58: *Giving up too easily when the answer is no*
Mistake # 59: *Not understanding your foreclosure prevention*
 options
Mistake # 60: *Not taking advantage of free mortgage counseling*

Mistake # 61: *Trusting too easily*

Section IIX:
Pass The Knowledge On

DEDICATION

To our fathers, Winston E. Walters and Lonzo Silmon, who passed on to be with our Lord and Savior. They are still in our hearts, minds and souls.
To our mothers, Maritza Walters and Ruby Silmon, for their guidance and support.

AUTHORS' ACKNOWLEGMENTS

We would first like to give thanks to our Heavenly Father for the Make No Mistakes™ idea and His support. Next, to our families, whose lives were disrupted by our busy schedules as we wrote this book. Special thanks to Rudy's wife, Janet, and daughter, Rachel, for their encouragement and sacrifice.

Thanks to our editor, Lori Zue of Lori Zue Editing Services, www.LoriZueEdits.com, and to our graphic artist who designed our cover, Scot Hester, of Number Eight Design, www.no8design.com.

We would also like to give thanks to our dedicated team at One Call – One Team, LLC, and to our clients for all the many experiences we've shared.

Our appreciation goes to our friends and associates who've worked behind the scenes and have given us their valued input along the way.

And a special thanks goes to Regina Calloway Simmons of West Palm Beach, Florida for her input on wills and living trusts.

Melissa Walters
Rudy Silmon

Note About This Information

This book was written for informational purposes only. We believe all information presented here is accurate as of the date of publication, however, some information may change at any time. Readers should consider this information a starting point. We encourage everyone to fully research any topic discussed herein.

If you have conflicting or updated information for this reference guide, please contact us so we can present that information in our blog, located on our website at www.MakeNoMistakes.com.

Preface

The *Make No Mistakes*™ concept began for us years ago in our daily interaction with our clients and the people who came to our seminars. We found that most people had enough real estate knowledge to be dangerous. Or they relied heavily on their friends and loved ones for advice to help them through a process that they knew very little about. Most people insisted on diving head first into uncharted waters with unknown obstacles which they had no knowledge or expertise to effectively deal with. As a result, they made costly mistakes during their real estate transactions.

Knowing a bit about real estate is not enough. Most people don't deal with real estate transactions on a regular basis or don't know which experts to turn to when they know they need more help. We have also witnessed people deciding to take short cuts, or tossing aside experts' advice – only to regret their choices when the outcomes were stressful, expensive or avoidable.

We believe having the right knowledge and putting it into action will make the real estate process an enjoyable one and – most importantly – one that does not cost unnecessary dollars. In fact, this knowledge will *save* people money. And in today's market, every penny counts!

Our goal in writing this reference guide was to pass necessary knowledge on to you by providing the information, tools and checklists which will properly drive this process to a successful and profitable conclusion.

It all starts with you. While many people are involved throughout the real estate process, you are the most important one. **In reality, *YOU* are the only one who can truly look out for your best interest. And when the transaction is complete, you are the one who is *ultimately* responsible for the property and for paying the mortgage loan!** So do your homework and make decisions that meet your needs. Use this information wisely and don't be intimidated by the complexity of the real estate business or the amount of information presented. Remember, buying real estate can be an emotional purchase and you may find yourself making compromises or decisions under pressure, which leads to *costly mistakes*. This reference guide will arm you with *information, knowledge* and *checklists* to help you. Don't end up like millions of people who have lost their homes – or never had one to start with – due to lack of knowledge!

This is the third edition of our *Make No Mistakes™ About ... Buying Real Estate* guide. Our series of *Make No Mistakes™* guides are designed to help and inspire you on a variety of topics to learn and profit from other people's mistakes. We wrote this particular reference guide, *About ...Buying Real Estate*, because we truly love the "game" of real estate. Together, we have more than 40 years of practical experience. As investors, owners of a real estate company and a mortgage brokerage firm, we see other people's successes and failures every day. In this reference guide, we share our mistakes, stories, inside secrets and tricks of the trade. Most importantly, we hope to encourage you to take action, to educate you along the way, to give you the insight to avoid the pitfalls and to achieve huge success!

No matter how useful it is, however, this reference guide is only a vehicle for people who are interested in real estate, successful transactions and personal growth. We ask you to join us in our belief that sharing important knowledge will help everyone achieve more and improve the quality of their lives. We do this by passing our knowledge on, and believing it spreads outward from there. If you "Pass The Knowledge On," you'll accomplish a great deal since little is truly accomplished without others moving to the next level *with you*.

Use this information to begin your journey. *Make No Mistakes*™ *About ... Buying Real Estate,* and then *Pass The Knowledge On!*

Section I:
Getting Started

CHAPTER 1

LACKING KNOWLEDGE CAN COST YOU!

A lack of knowledge during a real estate transaction often leads to a mistake, which will nearly always cost you money. Did you know that almost every single real estate transaction has a mistake, and it can go *unnoticed*? Often times the mistake is in the *smallest* of details and it's left to the buyer to find them! This impacts not only your savings when you buy - but your *profits* when you later sell! It's extremely unfortunate, because many times people have a hard time bouncing back from a costly real estate experience. This reference guide was written to help you quickly and easily understand the process of buying real estate and to help ensure you make no costly mistakes.

Mistake # 1: *Buying real estate unprepared because you lack the right knowledge*

Though we encourage you to seek professional guidance throughout the real estate purchasing process, we'll also tell you not to depend *solely* on these professionals. They're human, and humans make mistakes! By all means, establish a good relationship with a professional, but do your own research too, so you understand what he or she is recommending. You can start by reading this reference guide and noting the real estate mistakes we've covered. You might also follow up with a seminar to further educate or refresh your memory on the buying process. It's not every day you purchase real estate!

Throughout this reference guide you'll find descriptions and explanations about the mistakes other buyers have made. You'll also find the tools and checklists to help you *Make No Mistakes™ About…Buying Real Estate,* ***even when you work with professionals.*** We provide this information because it's our goal to level the playing field between the *haves* and the *have not's* – the people with real estate knowledge and those who have little or none. Here are just a few examples of what you'll gain from this reference guide:

- Examine your present and future financial goals to ensure you don't buy too much house even when a loan officer says you can afford more
- Determine which mortgage loan is best for you when you're presented with more than one option
- Choose the best property based on your budget, "must haves" and desires in a home
- Learn the specific contractual language you should have in your earnest money contract (which isn't included in the standard contracts)
- Know which elements will help you negotiate the best deal
- Read and understand the HUD-1 (Settlement Statement), which itemizes the financial details at closing
- Know what to do after you close in order to best protect your investment

In reality, *YOU* are the only one who can truly look out for your best interest. And when the transaction is complete, you are the one who is *ultimately* responsible for the property and for paying the mortgage loan! That's why, in addition to this reference guide, we have devised a **Make No Mistakes™ System**. In the event you don't have time to thoroughly read all the chapters in this reference guide, the **Make No Mistakes™ System** will provide you with email reminders telling you what you have to do next in the real estate purchasing process. Like what to look for and what to avoid. In addition, you'll be provided with your *Make No Mistakes™ Home Buyer's Checklist Workbook*, which will assist you in completing each task to ensure that all parties involved in your real estate deal are doing what they are supposed to do on your behalf. ***Remember, you need to be the one driving this ship since you are the one who will ultimately be responsible for it.*** You can get more information on this system by going to **www.MakeNoMistakes.com**, clicking on the **Make No Mistakes™ System**. Follow the directions on the first page to begin receiving your automatic emails.

Have you ever made a decision – consciously or unconsciously – that cost you dearly? Most of us have, and it's just part of the journey called *life*. To our chagrin, we've learned how costly those decisions can be when we made them ourselves, without spending time to *gather the facts* or *align ourselves* with the right people. Worse yet is finding out, months or years later when it's too late to do anything about it, we were taken advantage of! At other times, we just go through life, not knowing what we don't know. The costly and painful mistakes are the ones we remember the most.

But what if we told you mistakes in real estate can be avoided? That you don't need to learn it the hard way, and that you can look back on your real estate transactions with pride and pleasure? Would you then be as excited to read this reference guide as we were to compile the information and share it?

We designed this reference guide to include the 50+ most common key real estate mistakes. Not only will you learn how and why these mistakes happen, you'll also discover the solutions for fixing the problems or, better yet, how to avoid them in the first place. For just that reason, we included 17 checklists so you and your chosen professional know exactly what to do to avoid costly and time-consuming mistakes.

Use these checklists, available at www.MakeNoMistakes.com, to create a smooth process and a more profitable transaction:

	CHECKLIST		PURPOSE
1	Budget Spreadsheet		Determine how much house you can truly afford, keeping in mind your current costs and future financial expenses.
2	Home Search Criteria		Determine what features are important to you. What you "must have" vs. what you desire.
3	Make No Mistakes™ Home Buyer's Checklist		Review the process of a real estate transaction. Use this to track all parties' tasks involved in your real estate transaction.
4	Things Not To Do When Applying for a Mortgage		Avoid costly mistakes that could negatively impact your loan or interest rate.
5	How to Identify a "Good" Real Estate Agent		Identify the characteristics of a "good" real estate agent, who will help with one of the largest investments of your life.
6	How to Identify a "Good" Loan Officer		Identify the characteristics of a "good" loan officer who will have your best interests at heart.
7	Borrower's Paperwork		List of all the items you need to provide your loan officer in order to find the best loan for you.
8	Lender Comparative		Compare financial options presented by varying loan officers to determine which mortgage loan program is best for you!

	CHECKLIST	PURPOSE
9	**Property Viewing**	Use this checklist to focus on other aspects of the property besides aesthetics. Also, use this tool to draft your offer.
10	**Identify Your Leverage**	Determine which items are negotiable, in your opinion, and where your leverage lies.
11	**Utility Checklist**	Ask questions about the cost to run and maintain the property so you're sure you can afford the house and then budget correctly.
12	**Pre-Inspection**	Prepare to meet the inspector, and understand the results of his findings.
13	**Murphy's Law**	Know what to expect on the day you close and prepare for the unexpected.
14	**Moving Checklist**	Plan your move so it goes smoothly!
15	**Things to Ask For At Closing**	Important items to collect at the closing table from the seller.
16	**After Closing Checklist**	Complete and protect your investment with this list of tasks and final forms.
17	**Taking Possession of Your Home**	Items necessary to address in order to make your home safe upon taking possession from the previous owner.

These checklists are the primary tools you'll use to understand your responsibilities as well as your opportunities. Don't be caught unaware or overlook a key step. Visit our website to print the checklists referenced in this reference guide. Keep the checklists with other papers you accumulate during your real estate search and property purchase. It may be helpful to put them in the same order they're listed here. If you glance ahead to see the next few lists, you'll know what to expect and you'll be prepared. And being prepared is often all it takes to turn a profitable transaction into a *very* profitable transaction.

Mistake # 2: *Failure to use the easy-to follow checklists and tools already prepared for you*

The checklists often have more extensive information than what we cover in this book. Here, we focus on fixing mistakes if you've already made them, or how to avoid them in the first place. The checklists, however, show the items you'll need to know, do or gather so you can successfully complete a particular part of your real estate transaction. For example, in the *Property Viewing Checklist*, we suggest you take pictures of the home you're interested in buying. You're only in the home a few times before it might actually become yours. When the sellers move out, the property will look different to you. You'll want to compare the empty house to the pictures you took – if only to make sure it's not too empty! We've seen a seller remove closet shelving, hoping the buyer wouldn't notice. It's easy enough to deal with this situation if you have the pictures in hand. You might also enjoy showing family and friends the pictures of the house before you're able to take possession of it. Pictures also help you decide where furniture might fit, for example, or if you want to change the window treatments.

The checklists, which *we regularly update*, are on our website, www.MakeNoMistakes.com. You can access them anytime you're considering a real estate transaction, even if it's years from now. As the real estate purchase process changes and improves, *so will our checklists and our website. This means you will always have the latest tools and information you can reference again and again.*

For some reason, *Murphy's Law* makes a regular appearance in real estate transactions. The law, which says, "Whatever can go wrong, will go wrong, and at the worst possible time, in the worst possible way," is all too often true. We prefer to call it, "life throwing us an unexpected challenge." It's inevitable. This is one reason we created this reference guide, its tools and checklists. They will provide real solutions you can quickly implement, and they'll help you to better understand the process and stay focused on the goal.

Mistake # 3: *Becoming emotionally attached to the property*

We see buyers who want a particular property and let their *emotions* get in the way of making a rational, logical decision. This often becomes a costly mistake, and it's a hard one to recover from, especially if you buy too much house, for example, and are now facing foreclosure.

A bad real estate decision is costly. It can quickly impact your credit, your savings, your retirement and your ability to pass wealth on to your family. What's scary is when the American Dream of homeownership is so strong; people create equally strong reasons to justify their mistakes. Some homeowners disregard the possibility of future pain and consequences, and simply hope the poor decision will somehow work out.

In reality, success in real estate is like success in life. Those who are most successful have the right plan; they work hard on it and try to avoid making too many mistakes. Having the right plan means making good decisions along the way. Good decision-making comes from being diligent, from practical experience and from the ability to tap into the necessary resources to help identify problems and provide solutions. In turn, this will create a higher level of success in buying real estate.

Being diligent means pursuing your goals with *conviction*, *persistence* and *dedication*. Practical experiences are *lessons learned* – perhaps through the process of trial and error – over time. It can also come from simply asking questions when uncertain. Resources are *the means* you use to get your goal accomplished (e.g., cash, good credit scores, and information via the internet, books, tapes, or people who can help you). Lacking something in these areas or trying to cut corners can quickly increase your chances of failure -- *big time*!

Over the years we have witnessed many people, including ourselves, succeed and fail in real estate. Many people feel they have enough knowledge because they read books, listened to CDs or watched other people making money by buying and selling real estate. This is a great start, but it's only that: a start.

Most people know someone who has purchased real estate in the past. In fact, when you let others know that you are thinking about purchasing real estate you'll get advice from everyone. Keep in mind most people have enough knowledge about real estate to be *dangerous*! The stories and advice they'll share come with good intentions, but unless the advice-givers deal with real estate *everyday,* be careful. This is why *Make No Mistakes™...About Buying Real Estate* was created!

On every successful journey there is a first step. This reference guide helps you take that step and puts you on the right path. The information will guide you to saving thousands of dollars, improving your credit score and choosing the right people to help you. Take advantage of our tools and checklists in this reference guide and on our *website* to be sure that happens. Use a highlighter to focus your attention on important points, making it easy to return to them later. You can also turn to the index in this back of the reference guide for a quick reference. The 50+ key **Mistakes** are printed in **bold letters** so you can easily find them, and are listed in the table of contents. *Our blog, which you can access through our website, discusses various subjects, updates and current events related to real estate. It also shares other mistakes we've come across since writing this edition of our book. Our goal is to always keep you current.*

Remember, a lack of knowledge can hurt you, but having the knowledge and not using it is much worse! We also encourage you to *"Pass the Knowledge On."* You'll find this statement at the end of each chapter. The reason we repeat it has to do with our company's vision. "Our Vision is to increase homeownership and revitalize America's communities for future generations through real estate literacy and by creating a grassroots movement to *'Pass The Knowledge On.'"* Which means, if you feel the information in this reference guide offers real value, pass the information on to someone else. Consider getting your children involved in the process. You'll be surprised how teaching them about real estate will help you learn more too. Children often see things we, as adults, don't. So consider making it a family affair and pass the knowledge on!

Pass The Knowledge On!

CHAPTER 2

IS THIS A GOOD TIME TO BUY?

In this chapter, you will learn the advantages and disadvantages of owning your own home, and if it makes sense to buy in a changing market.

In the first few years after 2000, we saw low interest rates and loose lender requirements. This time period offered many Americans the opportunity to do the following:

a. Own a home for the first time
b. Purchase a second home
c. Invest in real estate
d. Refinance a property
e. Take cash out, in the form of a home equity line of credit[1] (HELOC)
f. Construct a new home

---

[1] A *home equity line of credit (HELOC)* or an equity loan is a second loan that you take out on your house, often on top of your existing mortgage loan. While your mortgage went toward purchasing your home, a home equity loan is cash that the lender gives you to spend as you please. It's usually a percentage of the house's appraised value, minus the existing mortgage.

Today, we're seeing foreclosures and fear driving people *out* of the market. Depending on what TV channel you watch or newspaper you read, everyone has an opinion on why this is happening. In fact, there is so much on the topic of the slowing and demise of the real estate and mortgage industries that many people choose to do nothing.

Mistake # 4: *Allowing fear to stop you from buying*

Fear and the inability to make a decision are causing many would-be homebuyers to rent instead. While doing nothing is always an option, fear drives emotions and these emotions could cause you to miss out! ***Great opportunities may pass you by because you are unable to read between the lines of all the information coming at you.*** All of which means you need to make your decision based on *facts,* not emotions, because people delivering these messages may have their own motives. Don't sit on the fence and try to time the real estate market. That's like trying to time the stock market. If people could truly time their entry and exit, as well as every transaction in between, they would all be rich. And that just doesn't happen. In fact, one of our seminar attendees asked us, "When is the best time to buy?" Our answer was, "When you find the right deal!"

As defined in Maslow's hierarchy of needs, two of the primary physiological necessities of humans are food and shelter. In other words, people *will always need* a roof over their heads, so they have to either rent or own. This is a fact that will remain as long as you live. Therefore, there will always be benefits to owning real estate in any market. The key is to understand what these benefits are and what's going on in the *local* market *you're* in, as opposed to what's going on anywhere else. If you live in Houston, Texas, it is unrealistic to base your buying decision on information about Austin or Dallas, even though they're in the same state.

Mistake # 5: *Making a buying decision based on national trends*

Residential real estate is a local product, not a national one. What's happening in your local market is the only thing that really matters when you are looking to buy. And it's an easy decision when you understand the current trends and how they'll affect your purchase.

This is why it's important to work with people who can help you find good opportunities, who have access to the market trends and who understand the local market because they're in it every day. There are only two types of real estate purchases: good buys and bad buys. This holds true for any market, whether it is a buyer's market or a seller's market. The keys are to not expect unrealistic property appreciation[2] and to take the time to understand *your* real estate market.

Key Questions to Ask Yourself Before Buying in Any Market:

Are you at a point in your life where you want AND need to own a home? *Want and need are two different things,* and have two distinct meanings. How you answer this question dictates how long you are willing to wait to find the right property. Is there something driving you to own? Is your lease up next month? Did your family size suddenly increase? Do you need a tax write-off? Do you need more space? Obviously, if you *want to own* as opposed to *need to own,* you can approach the decision with less pressure.

However, if time is working against you because your lease is up, for example, consider leasing on a month-to-month basis to avoid any time pressure. We often hear the comment that renting month-to-month is too expensive and renters would prefer not to do this. ***Our response to this is making a mistake due to time pressure is even more costly.***

---

[2] *Appreciation* is the profit you make from the sale of a property. It's the difference between what you paid for the property vs. what you sold it for, minus expenses.

So, whether you *want* or *need* to purchase a home, start the process sooner rather than later. Gather the right information, ask questions, attend free seminars, read the local paper and get yourself prepared.

How long do you plan to live in the house? We realize you may not have a crystal ball. We also know life can certainly throw an unexpected curveball your way. Nonetheless, you still need to ask yourself this question. Is your answer five years or more? Most people average seven. The reason this question is important has to do with the expected resale[3] value of a property. A typical borrower relies on the appreciation (the profit) from the sale of the property to cover the *down payment* and *settlement costs*[4] on the *next* home purchase. If you sell too soon, you take the chance your home might not have appreciated enough in value to cover what you need to get into your next home. While there are circumstances that allow you to sell soon after you've purchased a home and still make a profit – often referred to as "flipping" – it is not the norm. Buying a home when you expect to move out in less than five years is a risk in most markets.

What are the local newspapers, your local Multiple Listing Service (MLS) reports and your area's real estate professionals all saying about job growth, market trends and the economy? If prospective home buyers do their homework by studying the ebb and flow of residential real estate trends and reports, they can reduce costly mistakes because they approach the home buying process in a proactive and intelligent manner. For example, you should look at:

> **Current job trends** - Are jobs being created or lost? Sources such as the U.S. Bureau of Labor Statistics can give you insightful information as to whether job growth is on the rise or fall for the city where you want to purchase. As a result of

---

[3] A *resale* is when the current owner, who once purchased the property, sells it.
[4] *Settlement costs* are the fees and charges associated with transferring ownership of a piece of real estate from the seller to the buyer. Either or both parties incur settlement costs.

job gains (or loss) are people and businesses moving into or out of the area? Or are people moving in and out at a fairly equal rate? Is this because some industries are growing and others are declining? How will this affect the neighborhood you wish to buy in? Check out http://www.bls.gov.

Market Trends - Market trends are usually detailed or summarized by your local MLS and the real estate section of your local newspaper. They assist us in understanding housing affordability as well as housing supply and demand. "Housing affordability" is also known as the median home price for a given area or neighborhood during a specific period of time. Some areas are obviously more affordable than others. Every month, your local MLS provides a report on the number of homes sold, the homes listed in comparison to previous year(s) and/or month(s), and how long homes were on the market before they sold. Use this report to see if the trends show an increase or decrease in sales over the last year or two. Decide what's driving this increase or decrease. It is often tied to job growth or job loss. This information is easily accessible via the internet, or by calling several top-producing real estate agents in your area.

What determines a good buy or bad buy?   Before we begin to answer this question, it's important to note that, no matter how much research you do, you can always exceed or fall short of your anticipated results. Think about it. Almost everything we do has a risk associated with it. Does that stop you from raising a child, going to college or getting married? Probably not. You just hope you've done enough research and made enough of the right moves to bring the results you want. What determines whether a real estate purchase is a good buy or a bad one is relative, and completely personal. You may want to base this "good or bad" decision on whether or not you'll make a profit of $75,000, for example, on the home you're purchasing now and will sell in three years. If the trends and indicators you reviewed all show this is possible, then it's probably a good buy! For a different homeowner, a "good" purchase may mean choosing to live in an older community so the children can go to school in a certain district, even though the family could afford to live elsewhere. You are the only one who can set the "good or bad buy" expectations, and put a plan in action to achieve your goal. Check out the *Home Search Criteria Checklist*, which will help you define your goals.

Mistake # 6: *Not putting forth effort to conduct your own research*

There are two important things to remember:

- See for yourself – with your own research – what's happening in your area
- Don't depend on just one source, because it may tell you *only what you want to hear*

The information you need *is* out there. Here are a few national websites with local information you may want to check out to help you with your research:

- **www.Realtor.org** – The National Association of Realtors website – They analyze the economic, policy and structural effects of changes in the real estate industry.
- **www.Metrostudy.com** – Metrostudy - Maintains the country's largest database of primary housing market information combined with sources on future developments, demographics, job growth, and the economy.
- **www.stats.bls.gov** –The Bureau of Labor Statistics (BLS) produces Economy at a Glance pages at the national, regional, state, and metropolitan area levels.

Get a Comparative Market Analysis (CMA)

Knowing the average cost of a house in the city or subdivision where you might purchase is certainly a good start. You can find these averages on a form known as a Comparative Market Analysis,[5] also referred to as "comps" (see Chapter 16 for more discussion on this subject). *The CMA is the most useful tool to make sure you do not pay too much for any property.* Obtain this document from your real estate professional.

A CMA's comparative numbers are defined by your search criteria, which can be broad or specific. For example, the number of bedrooms and baths, the square footage range, the year the house was built, if there is a pool, or if you want comps from a specific subdivision. Specifying the time period is an important search criterion as well. A CMA gives you the ability to track the pricing trend – if prices are rising or falling – for that neighborhood.

CMAs are valuable tools because they're so comprehensive and flexible. Be sure to get one for the house you're interested in purchasing. *Using a CMA puts financial facts in your hands, which helps set aside any emotions that may be clouding your judgment.* Most real estate agents can easily gather this information for you through their MLS service – at no cost to you!

In Houston, our MLS is located at www.har.com. Here you can find statistics reaching as far back as ten years, along with a variety of charts and tables. If you are unable to find your local MLS, go to www.realtor.org, which is the website for the National Association of Realtors. Once there, click on *Directories*, then click on *State and Local Realtor™ Associations*, and finally click on *List of Regional MLS's only*. MLS's provide some information to prospective home buyers, but it's the organization's members, usually realtors, who have full access to the site. Don't be surprised if you need a real estate agent's help in accessing all the information you want.

Below is an example of what a Comparative Market Analysis will look like, although MLS's often differ as to *how* they portray the CMA information:

---

[5] A *Comparative Market Analysis* is a document used by professionals who are members of the MLS (Multiple Listing Service). Real estate agents have access to this information and they use it to gather historical information and trends for specific subdivisions and properties.

CRITERIA: *STATUS* ACTIVE AND SOLD, *BEDROOMS* 4 OR LESS, *BLDG. SQ FT* 2500 OR LESS, *SUBDIVISON NAME* "LAKES", *CLOSED* BEFORE 12/31/08

	_A_	Property Type:	Single Family							_B_	Status: ACTIVE		
	MLS # _C_	Address _D_	Subdiv. Name _E_	BR _F_	Bths _G_	# Gar _H_	Pool _I_	Lot SqFt _J_	Bldg SqFt _K_	Yr _L_	List Price _M_	LP/ SF _N_	DOM _O_
1	52852	8714 CADWELL	THE LAKES	4	2/1	1	N	9540	2,387	1960	$ 135,000	$ 56.56	274
2	969639	9602 LUCY LN	THE LAKES	3	3/	2	N	8025	2,319	1954	$ 136,999	$ 59.08	54
3	741741	8910 CADWELL	THE LAKES	3	3/	2	N	9540	2,329	1962	$ 140,000	$ 60.11	60
	AVERAGES			3	3	2		9035	2,345		$ 137,333	$ 58.58	38

*For your convenience, this CMA is also located on the website at www.MakeNoMistakes.com. Go to **forms** and then enter your pass code.*

			Property Type:	Single Family				Status: SOLD						
	MLS #	Closed Date _P_	Address	Subdiv. Name	BR	Bths	# Gar	Pool	Lot SqFt	Bldg SqFt	Yr	List Price	Sold Price _Q_	SP/ SF _R_	DOM
1	123456	5/08/98	8814 CADWELL	THE LAKES	4	2/1	1	N	9540	2,387	1960	$ 79,500	$ 77,900	$ 32.64	274
2	234567	4/29/02	9302 LUCY LANE	THE LAKES	3	3/	2	N	8025	2,319	1954	$ 79,900	$ 73,500	$ 31.69	106
3	3456978	7/28/02	8914 CADWELL	THE LAKES	3	3/	2	N	9540	2,329	1962	$ 94,700	$ 87,500	$ 37.57	27
4	456789	12/30/01	8814 BONOM	THE LAKES	4	2/1	2	N	35490	2,332	1966	$ 135,000	$ 130,000	$ 55.75	7
5	569874	10/30/02	8814 CADWELL	THE LAKES	4	2/1	2	N	9540	2,450	1960	$ 149,900	$ 147,000	$ 60.00	24
6	698745	6/7/02	9115 CADWELL	THE LAKES	4	2/0	0	N	16450	2,244	1962	$ 160,000	$ 159,100	$ 70.90	20*
7	741258	5/12/02	8822 BONOM	THE LAKES	3	2/1	2	Y	9000	2,526	1961	$ 120,000	$ 120,000	$ 47.51	43
8	369852	7/24/01	8822 BONOM	THE LAKES	4	2/1	2	Y	9000	2,526	1961	$ 125,000	$ 123,500	$ 48.89	88
	AVERAGES				4		2		13,323	2,389		$ 118,000	$ 114,813	$ 48.12	64

See below for an explanation of each section of this Comparative Market Analysis:

A	**Property Type**	Type of property you're comparing: single family, townhomes, multi-unit, etc.
B	**Status**	Status of the property: active (available), pending (an offer is pending), option pending (buyer has a contract pending inspections) or sold
C	**MLS#**	Multiple Listing Service identification number
D	**Address**	Address of the Property
E	**Subdivision Name**	Name of the subdivision or development where the property is located
F	**Bedrooms**	Number of bedrooms
G	**Baths**	Number of bathrooms
H	**# Gar**	Number of cars the garage will hold
I	**Pool**	Whether or not the property has a private pool
J	**Lot Sq. Ft**	Size (in square feet) of the land where the house sits
K	**Bldg Sq. Ft.**	Total size (in square feet) of the structure's living space
L	**Year**	Year the home was built
M	**List Price**	Price the seller is asking
N	**LP/SF**	List price per square foot of the building
O	**DOM**	Number of days the property has been on the market
P	**Closed Date**	Date the sale of the property closed
Q	**Sold Price**	Price at which the home sold
R	**SP/SF**	Sold price per square foot of the structure

In this example, we set the criteria for all Active and Sold properties with four or less bedrooms and 2,500 square feet or less, in the subdivision known as The Lakes, and that closed before December 31, 2002.

Historical information on past sales gives strong trend information for the geographic area you searched. Look closely at the numbers in your CMA. How do last year's numbers compare *to previous years*? Are the average numbers declining or increasing? We'll discuss how these numbers affect your purchasing decision in Chapter 16.

It's absolutely okay to ask questions, so if you're confused or curious, call your local MLS, a real estate agent or an economics student. Tell them what you are looking at and what you are trying to determine. Oftentimes a MLS service will give you a written summary of how the numbers break down in comparison to the year before, especially if you ask. Take the time to learn and understand how the numbers work and what they mean. Most importantly, see how your prospective home figures into the mix. If too many of your home's dollar amounts listed in columns M through R are higher than its peers', yet the data in columns F through L are similar, it may be time to rethink your purchase or at least work on negotiating a lower price.

> **Tip:**
> *Never buy the biggest home in a neighborhood because it is always the hardest to sell.*

Mistake # 7: *Failing to conduct various CMA scenarios on all properties of interest*

There are always benefits to owning real estate in any market; however, the key is to keep your risk low by not offering too much. Remember, in the end, you are the one responsible for the property and the mortgage on it. Therefore, you're the best person to review and understand this research. Most agents are more interested in your purchase or sale of a home than they are in contributing time to educate you on real estate. Therefore, you may have to ***take an extra step and ask to see CMA results using various criteria.*** Your criteria is based on similar features and attributes to the property you're interested in purchasing, i.e., similar square footage, pools, lot size, golf course, waterfront, renovated, year built, garage size, homes with the same number of stories. For example, here are just two ways to research information relevant to a prospective home:

- Look at all properties sold within the last 6 months, regardless of size, in order to determine what the average size of a home is in that neighborhood.
- What common criteria make this property comparable to the other homes in the neighborhood? Perhaps the neighborhood you're interested in offers both one- and two-story homes, and the one-story homes are in greater demand. It would be wise to pay close attention to the sales price per square foot (SP/SQ). If you're considering a two-story house, and don't exclude the pricier single-story residences in your search criteria, you'll probably pay too much.

> **Tip:**
> *Be sure to look at the numbers over a one-to-five-year period to see the trend for the specific location where you want to purchase.*

This is why looking at various scenarios are important. In this example, the more expensive one-story homes skew the average sales price for two-story homes in that neighborhood.

In Chapter 16, we'll discuss more about analyzing the comparative information in your CMA.

Reasons *Not* To Own

Throughout our years of conducting seminars, participants have shared many reasons why they should own their own homes and buy real estate. It wasn't until much later that someone finally asked, *"Why would someone not want to own now?"* What a great question! And here are some reasons why you might not want to own a home:

- **Too much responsibility**: The cost of care and maintenance to a house. For example, fixing a leaky faucet, painting the interior and exterior, mowing the lawn, replacing the broken water heater – the list goes on. If you are not the handyman type, you will have to call in a professional and that costs money. When you rent, you seldom have to worry about this. A quick call to the landlord and the problem is fixed.

- **Not being able to easily walk away from the property.** As a renter, all you typically need to do is give your 30-day notice to the landlord. When you own your home, you are the landlord. Just walking away from it would have significant financial and credit ramifications. If you want out, you'd have to sell it or rent it or figure out some other way to hold on to it without turning your finances and your credit into a living nightmare.
- **Possible job transfer.** Moving to a new city or job location in the next couple of years is another good reason to put your home buying on hold.
- **Having low credit scores.** Low scores might cause the loan's interest rate to be so high you couldn't really afford the loan. You might choose to wait, and work on improving your credit scores in the meantime. We'll cover this more in Chapter 6.
- **Owning a home is simply not a priority in your life right now.**
- **New to the area.** You might be unsure of which neighborhood would best meet your needs.
- **Heard too many horror stories.** Too many tales of woe might keep you renting.
- **Unfamiliar with the process of purchasing real estate.** You don't want to take the time to learn it right now.

One way to avoid some of these responsibilities is to purchase a condominium or townhome. They've become more popular because of the low-maintenance lifestyles they offer. However, they typically come with a monthly maintenance fee which you must add in to the true cost of home ownership.

In Summary, despite its many advantages, home ownership is not for everybody. Along with the monthly mortgage payment are additional, sometimes unwelcome, responsibilities. New home buyers don't always take these facts into consideration. However, allowing fear to stop you from at least investigating your options causes you to miss out on a wealth-building opportunity when done correctly. With this opportunity comes research, which allows you to determine when the time is right for you. To reduce financial risk, you should consistently review updated CMAs for any property that interests you.

Pass The Knowledge On!

CHAPTER 3

BE S.M.A.R.T.

You've decided you'd like to purchase a home in the near future. What do you do *now* to be able to buy *later*? Our advice: Be S.M.A.R.T: Rent only as long as it takes to save the money for a down payment, reduce your debts and improve your credit score. Prepare, plan and execute!

Mistake # 8: *Not being S.M.A.R.T. before you buy*

Purchasing *S.M.A.R.T.* means you took all of these wealth-building factors into consideration:

- **S**avings
- **M**ake Your Deal Upfront
- **A**ppreciation
- **R**esale Value
- **T**ax Advantages

<u>S</u>avings

Making payments on your property's mortgage can sometimes be referred to as a "forced savings" or equity[6] account. A portion of your monthly mortgage payment goes toward the amount you still owe on the principal[7] amount you originally borrowed. Each month, your principal balance declines, and you're building your home's equity. From the amortization table below, notice how a monthly payment of just the principal and interest of $1,011.31 is broken out each month (the original loan amount was $160,000 at 6.5% for a 30-year term). As a *principal payment* is made the Equity Accrued column increases by that amount and the Ending Balance decreases by the same. Note: When you order the Make No Mistakes™ System, you will receive a workbook which includes *all the excel spreadsheet* tools and checklists in excel format so you can download and save your own information, and return to it at your leisure.

Total Principal & Interest Payment	Principal	Interest	Taxes	Insurance	PMI	Ending Balance	Equity Accrued
$ 1,011.31	$ 144.64	$ 866.67	$ 400.00	$ 122.02	$ 66.67	$ 159,855.36	$ 144.64
1,011.31	145.43	865.88	$ 400.00	$ 122.02	$ 66.67	159,709.93	$ 290.07
1,011.31	146.21	865.10	$ 400.00	$ 122.02	$ 66.67	159,563.72	$ 436.28
1,011.31	147.01	864.30	$ 400.00	$ 122.02	$ 66.67	159,416.71	$ 583.29
1,011.31	147.80	863.51	$ 400.00	$ 122.02	$ 66.67	159,268.91	$ 731.09
1,011.31	148.60	862.71	$ 400.00	$ 122.02	$ 66.67	159,120.31	$ 879.69
1,011.31	149.41	861.90	$ 400.00	$ 122.02	$ 66.67	158,970.90	$ 1,029.10
1,011.31	150.22	861.09	$ 400.00	$ 122.02	$ 66.67	158,820.69	$ 1,179.31
1,011.31	151.03	860.28	$ 400.00	$ 122.02	$ 66.67	158,669.66	$ 1,330.34
1,011.31	151.85	859.46	$ 400.00	$ 122.02	$ 66.67	158,517.81	$ 1,482.19
1,011.31	152.67	858.64	$ 400.00	$ 122.02	$ 66.67	158,365.14	$ 1,634.86
1,011.31	153.50	857.81	$ 400.00	$ 122.02	$ 66.67	158,211.64	$ 1,788.36
Federal Tax Deductions	$ 10,347.35	$ 4,800.00			$ 800.04		

---

[6] *Equity* is the difference between what was borrowed to purchase the property and what is still owed on it.

[7] The *principal* is the remaining amount owed from the original mortgage loan amount. It doesn't include the interest you're paying each month on the loan.

Many refer to the building of equity as a forced savings tool because at the time of the sale you would recoup this savings if you sold the house for more than you originally paid, minus your expenses. ***Unlike a real savings account, the equity in your home is not very accessible.*** The only way to access this money is to:

- Borrow against your home using some other kind of loan:

  - Cash Out[8]
  - Home Equity[9]
  - Reverse Mortgage[10]

- Sell your home

The financial institution holding your mortgage loan controls access to your home's equity. ***To borrow against your own property, you'll have to re-qualify for a loan.*** Lenders frequently use a different set of qualifying guidelines for these types of equity loans than they use for first mortgages, so that money is not very easy to access. Worst case scenario, if you don't qualify, you will need to sell your home in order to access that money! Also, if your home failed to appreciate in value over the years, you might not see the return you hoped for. Again, it's important to do your homework and ask the right questions before making such a big decision.

---

[8] A *Cash Out Loan* is when you refinance your mortgage for more than you currently owe, then pocket the difference and do whatever you want with it, i.e. pay off bills or travel. It may sound good at first, but keep in mind it's like buying your home all over again. There are closing costs to pay, and you're back to square one in terms of how long it takes you to pay off your home.

[9] A *Home Equity Loan* is a separate loan on top of your first mortgage. Generally, it's used for a home improvement project. It comes with a higher interest rate than a Cash Out Loan because you usually don't pay closing costs.

[10] A *Reverse Mortgage Loan* is a home loan that offers a homeowner over the age of 62 an opportunity to convert a portion of the home's equity into cash. But, unlike a traditional Home Equity or Cash Out Loan, no repayment is required until the borrower no longer uses the home as the principal residence.

If you're hit by a financial crisis, it will take a lot longer to get the money out of your home than it would to withdraw it from a savings account. **This distinction is often referred to as *liquid* vs. *non-liquid* funds.** Funds are liquid if you can rapidly access them without any loss in their value. Non-liquid funds are the opposite. They usually take well over a day to access, and there may be a cost to withdraw the funds, which constitutes a loss in value. Real estate is considered non-liquid: it takes a minimum of several weeks to access the equity – no matter if you're doing it through a loan or the sale of the house – and there's likely to be a cost involved. Consider this situation:

> *Rick and Gail Hudson owned their home for eight years and had built quite a bit of equity in the property. They managed a down payment of 20% when they bought it. When Rick lost his job, they got behind on their bills and applied for a home equity loan to hold them over until Rick got on his feet again. Despite having great credit scores for 10 years, they didn't qualify for the loan. The bank would not consider them because the late payments dropped their credit scores below the set requirements. The Hudsons had to sell their house in order to avoid foreclosure.*

Here's another scenario:

> *You're 49 years old and for years you counted on the equity in your home to pay for your child's college education. Just as high school graduation approaches, the stock market crashes, and gas prices double or triple. Interest rates soar and reach 18 to 22 percent. Sound familiar?*

All of this actually happened in the 1980s. Let's say it happens again. At that high interest rate, it would certainly not make sense to borrow money against your home. So what do you do if you need the equity? Your choices are to take out a home equity loan, a cash-out loan with a high interest rate, or to sell your home.

But there's another way to maintain access to your money: it's called diversification, i.e., spreading your money around a number of investment vehicles. A simple way to follow this concept is to *plan to pay yourself* first each pay period by putting a percentage of money into an easily-accessible s*avings* account. A portion of your savings and invested money should always be in a liquid account. We included this concept of a liquid savings account in the Budget Spreadsheet, which we'll cover more later.

Make Your Deal Upfront

It is a good idea to get a Comparative Market Analysis, or CMA, on the house. It will serve as one of the tools you'll use to help you determine what purchase price to offer and to *make your deal up front*. This phrase means that, upon signing the closing documents, you have instantly created wealth for yourself because the home is worth more than you paid for it. For example, if another home in similar condition, size and location sells for an average of a $100 a square foot, purchasing your home at $90 a square foot may be considered making your deal up front. Using the above example of $100 vs. $90 per square foot, and the house is 2500 square feet, you have just earned $25,000! You created your deal upfront ($100 - $90 = $10, and $10 x 2,500 = $25,000). The contrast to this is paying $100 a square foot now, and hoping you make your money later, when you sell the home.

Appreciation

Can you see how, by tracking the trends, this property will be worth even more in two, five, or ten years? Appreciation is the increase in value of your property over and above what you originally paid for it.

The amount which property appreciates in two adjacent communities, for example, can vary greatly for a variety of reasons. These factors are usually tied to:

- Schools – Quality of the education
- Jobs – Access to opportunities to earn an income

- Lifestyle – Amenities in the area, including access to main transportation routes
- Improvements – Features that a property offers such as an updated kitchen, master bath or large yard with lush landscaping.

There are no guarantees that your property will appreciate in value over time. However, you can certainly reduce the risk it will depreciate by understanding the local area, how long you plan to own the property, and any costs associated with making the property comfortable for you and your family's needs.

Resale Value

When you decide to purchase a home, it's important to consider the potential resale value. A high resale value means a house will appeal to a large number of potential *future* homebuyers. ***This means you will have a greater chance of selling it quicker and for a profit when you're ready.***

Also, homeowners in different geographic areas value different things. For example, in Houston, having the master bedroom situated on the first floor is more desirable than it being on the second floor.

However, location, location, location is still the most common appeal to buyers, regardless of most other factors, including the house's purchase price.

Tax Deduction Advantages

There are numerous tax advantages and benefits to buying, owning and selling real estate. The laws are constantly changing, so it's important to check with reliable sources before you count on a particular tax advantage. We'll explain some of these benefits below, but if you don't understand all of them, there are plenty of good online sources that can help. Here are today's tax benefits:

- Tax deductions
  - Mortgage interest
  - Mortgage insurance
  - Property taxes
  - Closing costs[11]
- Tax credits
- Capital gains exemptions
- Depreciation
  - Rental property expenses
  - Capitalization
  - Home business expenses
- Cash flow on rental property

Mortgage Interest - In many cases, *these tax benefits make owning a home more affordable than renting.* For example, in the *early years* of paying your mortgage, most of your mortgage payment is actually applied to taxes and interest on the loan. This can feel depressing, because you're not reducing the principal amount owed as quickly as you may like. However, paying so much in interest makes *most* of the mortgage payment tax deductible.

Let's assume you borrowed $160,000 to purchase a home. The interest rate was 6.5% and it was fixed over the 30-year life of the loan. Your very first month's payment on the loan would break down like this:

Rent vs. Own			
Monthly Rent Payment	$ 1,540.00	Principal Payment	$ 144.64
Interest		Interest	$ 866.67
Renter's Insurance	$ 60.00	Homeowners Insurance	$ 122.02
Property Taxes	$ -	Property Taxes	$ 400.00
Mortgage Insurance	$ -	Mortgage Insurance	$ 66.67
Total Monthly Payment	$ 1,600.00	Total Monthly Payment	$ 1,600.00

---

[11] *Closing costs* are part of the total settlement costs associated with moving ownership of real estate from the seller to the buyer.

Mortgage Insurance - As you can see from the *Loan Calculation Table* below, most of this mortgage payment is tax deductible. Find a copy of this table on the website at www.MakeNoMistakes.com. The pass code is 550. Play with it in order to determine your monthly mortgage payment and how the monthly payments change over the term of your loan.

You can deduct the mortgage interest, the property taxes and private mortgage insurance (PMI). Private Mortgage Insurance (PMI), or just "mortgage insurance," protects lenders against loss in the event a borrower defaults on a mortgage. As of 2007, PMI also became tax deductible. Borrowers with adjusted gross incomes below $100,000 may deduct 100% of their PMI premiums. Deductions are phased out at 10% increments for borrowers with adjusted gross incomes between $100,000 and $109,000.

Property Taxes - Property taxes vary from state to state and subdivision to subdivision. Be sure to calculate your own tax rate. For example, here in Texas our average tax rate is around 3.0% of the appraised market value.[12] This means $15,947.39 of your total mortgage payment for the first year *is tax deductible.* Meanwhile, the amount you pay toward the principal each month reduces the amount you owe the lender and is your accrued *equity* when you sell the house. See the Loan Amortization Table on page 39.

Here's another way of looking at the federal tax deductions for the interest and tax benefits of owning a home vs. renting:

Federal Tax Deductions Rent vs. Own					
Monthly Rent Payment	$	1,540.00	Monthly Mortgage Payment	$	862.28
Renter's Insurance	$	60.00	Homeowners Insurance	$	122.02
Property Taxes	$	-	Property Taxes	$	400.00
Mortgage Insurance	$	-	Mortgage Insurance	$	66.67
Total Monthly Deduction	$	-	Total Monthly Deduction	$	1,450.97
Federal Tax Bracket (25%)				$	362.74
Annual Tax Savings				$	4,352.91

---

[12] *Appraised Market Value* is the opinion of the county tax district as to how much they believe the property is worth.

In this example, we assume you are paying $1600 a month, whether you rent or own. If we calculated only the estimated first year of interest and property tax deductions, you would be able to deduct $1,450.97 of your monthly mortgage payment, whereas you would be entitled to $0 if you rent. After this first calculation you can take the tax deduction a step further and determine the *true* tax advantage based on your federal tax bracket. If you are in the 25% tax bracket, for example, you would realize approximately $362.74 in monthly federal tax savings[13] for homeownership, compared to $0 for renting, or $4,352.91 for your first year of ownership.

We strongly suggest you talk with your tax consultant for a clearer understanding of your personal benefits. For complete information on the home mortgage interest deduction, see IRS Publication 936, Home Mortgage Interest Deduction, which is available online at www.irs.gov or at your local IRS office.

Tax Credit

As of this writing, the Senate approved an $8,000 home buyer tax credit in order to stimulate sales and soak up the excess inventory of unsold houses. The amendment expands an existing $7,500 home buyer tax credit to $8,000. Similar to the $7,500 tax credit of 2008, the 2009 tax credit is available to all first-time homebuyers and those who have not owned a primary home[14] within the past three years. However, the 2009 modification stipulates homeowners must own the house for at least three years, or they will be obligated to pay back the credit. This tax credit is a true tax credit and not a loan like the 2008 tax credit. As long as the home buyers do not sell the property within the first three years of homeownership, NO payback of the credit is required. When a home buyer files his 2008 or 2009 taxes, he can then apply the total $8,000 towards his total tax liability and, if there

---

[13] The *Federal Tax Rate* tax liability is not calculated on a straight line basis, as deductions and withholdings apply and can affect which tax bracket you're in.

[14] A *primary home, primary residence* or principal residence is the home in which a person lives most of the time.

are any funds unused, he would receive a refund check of up to $8,000. Applying for the credit is easy; simply claim it on your 2008 or 2009 tax return.

Additionally, there are income restrictions; buyers must earn less than $75,000 for singles or $150,000 for couples. It then phases out at $95,000 for singles and $170,000 for couples. This also leads to the loan limits being raised to $727,000 in high-cost areas. The purchase of the property must be made between Jan. 1, 2009 and December 1, 2009. Check out our blog at www.MakeNoMistakes.com and click on *Tax Credit* to keep updated, or go to our website and click on *Real Estate Forms*, then go to *First-Time Home Buyer Tax Credit Chart 2009*. You'll also see the difference between the 2008 and 2009 tax credits. It is our goal to always have the most current and helpful information available to you.

What's the difference between a *tax deduction* and a *tax credit*?

A tax deduction reduces the amount of your *income* that is taxable. Whereas, a tax credit reduces the amount of the *tax* you must pay. For example, tax deductions can put you down into a lower tax bracket, and that means that you will owe less in terms of taxes. So if you are currently in the 25% tax bracket, you could end up in the next lower bracket of 15% because of all of your deductions. Visit http://www.irs.gov for a look at the tax rate schedules by year.

A tax credit, on the other hand, works like this: If at the end of the year you owe $10,000 in taxes and your tax credit was worth $7,500, you would then be liable for only $2,500 in owed taxes to the federal government. Contact your accountant for more details on your specific situation.

Capital Gains Exemptions

For many people, homeownership is the single-largest deduction available. However, the real benefit comes from *not* having to pay capital gains taxes[15] on the appreciation of the property.

A 1997 change in a tax law allows for the exemption of capital gains taxes on the sale of a primary[16] residence. It works like this: If you lived in your primary home for at least two years within the past five, you qualify to take gains (profits) when you sell your house. "Taking gains" means you don't have to pay taxes on that particular chunk of money you've made; you can take the profit without paying taxes on it. This tax-free money maxes out at $250,000 if you file your taxes as a single person and at $500,000 if file a joint return.

In fact, this tax break can be taken every two years! We'll repeat that. This tax break can be taken every two years if the house was your primary residence, also known as your homestead. This is pure profit with no tax consequences! It's one of the moves the wise real estate investor uses to gain wealth! *That is, purchasing a home at or below market value and intending to sell it after two years, in order to make a profit without having to pay taxes on the gains.*

Here is one example that conveys how monumental this advantage is:

> *The Roberts lived on Long Island, New York. More than twenty years ago they paid $80,000 to move into an affluent neighborhood known for its great schools. Back then, they thought the home was a slight stretch for them, but as time went on it became very comfortable. So comfortable, in fact, they lived there for 23 years before they decided to move out of state to be closer to their grandchildren.*

---

[15] A *capital gain* is the difference between what you paid for the property and what you received when you sold that property. Taxes are then paid on this capital gain, often referred to as the *profit*.

[16] *Homestead*, also known as your *primary residence is* the permanent place where you reside and call home. How often you can take a homestead tax credit or rebate depends on which state you live in.

They paid $80,000 for the house in 1984 and then sold it for more than $700,000 in 2004. Because they file joint tax returns, the maximum amount they can exempt from capital gains taxes is $500,000. So of the $620,000 they realized from the sale of the house, they used the full tax-free amount of $500,000! They paid capital gains tax only on the $120,000 ($620,000 - $500,000 = $120,000), and even then, not until they filed their income taxes the following year. So the Roberts had use of all $620,000 prior to even having to pay a nickel of capital gain taxes.

With their tax-free $500,000, they moved to a new state, purchased a smaller house with cash for only $160,000, and still had $340,000 left for enjoying their retirement.

They also made the equity in their first home work for them while they lived there. During those 23 years, the Roberts' pulled out $120,000 from their home using a home equity loan.

With the cash, they updated their home, installed a swimming pool, paid for college tuition and paid off several bills. They wisely chose to take out a home equity loan instead of using credit cards to pay for these things, because the interest on the $120,000 home equity loan was 100% deductible, whereas the interest paid on credit card balances isn't. Over time, they paid off the home equity loans while they still lived in the house.

Thanks to home mortgage interest deductions and the capital gains tax deduction, owning real estate can be a wise investment. And if you purchase in an area where homes are appreciating, this tax break could become quite advantageous.

Closing Costs - When most people buy a home, they generally obtain a mortgage. With this mortgage comes closing costs. One of the costs associated with the mortgage is the loan origination fee. This fee is usually a percentage of the loan amount, and it's generally expressed as "points," which are equal to 1% of the loan amount. For example, one "point" on a $160,000 loan would be $1,600. Points are often broken down into two categories: the loan origination fee, and discount points.

The loan origination fee must be expressed as points in order for it to be tax deductible. When buying a home, points are deductible in the year they are paid, providing they meet certain conditions. The main conditions are that the mortgage is secured by your homestead property, that it's the home you live in most of the time and that you used this mortgage to either purchase or build your home, as opposed to refinancing the home.

> **Tip:**
> *Since your interest and property taxes are deductible expenses on your federal taxes, so are the prepaid interest and property taxes you make at the time your loan closes.*

There are also other key conditions that aren't as well-known:

- Your lender cannot inflate the points to include other fees you'll be charged. Home buyers can expect to pay a variety of fees, including those for an appraisal,[17] fee, a survey,[18], title insurance and so on. If you are not charged these fees but your points are higher than normal, your lender might have rolled several of your fees into your points. If this happens, you can't deduct the points.
- The cash you put into the deal must also exceed the amount charged in points. In other words, if your points were $3,000, but you only had to put in $2,000 to close on the loan, you wouldn't be allowed to deduct the points.
- Also, if the seller pays the buyer's points, the IRS allows the buyer to deduct this as an expense on his or her federal tax returns. However, the seller cannot deduct them, too.

---

17 *An appraisal* is the professional opinion of estimating the value of a property.

18 *A survey* is like a blueprint of the land. It shows the boundary lines for the land, any improvements (buildings, pools, patio, fence, etc.), easements and building setback lines. It will also show neighboring encroachments.

- Points paid to finance the purchase of a second home must be deducted over the life of the loan, not in the year in which they are paid.
- The points must be clearly stated on the HUD-1 Settlement Statement.
- There are income restrictions for how much you can deduct. For a list of specific requirements see a Certified Public Accountant.

Depreciation

In addition to the many deductions that real estate provides it also gives you the ability to depreciate it over time if and when it becomes a rental property, and to treat it as an expense on an income statement. Such reasons to depreciate the property could be a decline in the value of a house due to wear and tear, obsolescence, adverse changes in the neighborhood, to name a few.

Depreciation can only be applied to the building itself and not to the land, since land does not wear out over time. Residential income property must be depreciated over a 27.5-year period using straight line depreciation. Straight line depreciation stipulates that an asset must be depreciated by equal amounts each year over its useful life.

Rental Property Expenses - There may come a time when you decide to turn your home into a rental, which is often called an *investment property*. From that point on, all expenses can usually be deducted, capitalized and depreciated over a period of time. So as a landlord, you *still* get the benefits of writing off (reducing your taxable income by the amount of) your interest, expenses, taxes and repairs. Go to the Internal Revenue Service, www.irs.gov/publications, for more information on rental income and expenses.

Capitalization - Something that is capitalized is an asset or an item purchased to increase or maintain the value of the home often referred to as an improvement to the property. For example, room additions, heating and air conditioning, plumbing, interior improvements are considered improvements. In the eyes of the IRS an improvement differs from a repair. A repair keeps your property in good operating condition. Whereas, the improvement adds value of your property or substantially prolongs the life of the property. The capitalized cost can generally be depreciated as if the improvement were separate property. Please take note of this benefit and discuss it with your tax accountant.

Home Business Expenses - If you operate a business out of part of your home, you can take even more tax deductions. Not only does this tax benefit allow you to deduct portions of certain bills you already pay, you also have the ability to deduct part of the mortgage insurance, the cost of any computers you may have, and other expenses related to running your home (i.e., utilities). Talk to your account about which deductions apply during any given year. Or visit www.irs.gov/publications to get more information on how to write off home business expenses.

Cash Flow

The rental income can also provide you with additional *cash flow* each month if you charge more in rent than your actual mortgage payment and expenses. Can you imagine having enough cash flow on your properties to bankroll the vehicles you drive, vacations you take and even the mortgage on your own homestead property? All of this is possible! Even when money is tight, most renters will pay their rent first, before paying a car loan or making a credit card payment. No one wants to be evicted. You can reap the benefits of someone else essentially paying your mortgage payments. When you purchase and sell real estate correctly, it almost always remains a good investment.

Now, let's look at the flip side again: You're the renter. Let's say you pay $1,000 a month for rent. Each year, your rent goes up by 5%, which is the national average. At the end of five years you would have paid your landlord more than $66,000. You also wouldn't have had any tax advantages nor would you have built equity in the property. *You* would have been bankrolling the landlord's vehicles, vacations or even the owner's homestead mortgage! At the very least, you were investing in the landlord's future, and not in your own.

Learning from Past Mistakes

There are never any guarantees in real estate; however, if you ask questions throughout the process, use the tools and checklists in this reference guide, and aim to understand what you're signing, you significantly reduce your risk of failure.

Some of you have tried and failed to make profitable real estate purchases in the past. If you feel you failed, it's most likely because you ended up with a financial loss. Don't quit! If you are honest with yourself, you probably know you made some mistakes. Based on our experience, we can guess what went wrong:

- You may have decided to not use a real estate agent's help with the transaction because you believed the seller would pass the savings on to you – in the form of a lower sales price – because the seller wouldn't have to pay your real estate agent's commission.
- You may have had the wrong plan, approach or attitude. Perhaps you approached the process thinking you knew more than the professionals. And the professionals let you make your own mistakes.
- You purchased a new home without selling the one you lived in and now you're stuck with *two* mortgage payments. You chose not to listen to or hire a professional, and tried to sell the old home on your own at the price you thought it merited. Selling it on your own, For Sale By Owner (FSBO)[19] might have turned out okay, but you started off with an incorrect price. The extra time it took to sell the home cost you a lot of money in additional house payments!
- You tried purchasing real estate with the help of a professional but, unfortunately, that person was more focused on the commission than on helping you. Or, that professional tossed around confusing words and complex explanations that were difficult to understand, and you were embarrassed or too

---

[19] *FSBO*, or "For Sale By Owner," is when a seller chooses to sell a property on his or her own without the assistance of a real estate agent.

frustrated to ask for clarification. This is an intimidation tactic and it's occasionally done on purpose.

- The professional didn't bother to educate you during the process. You were uncertain about the questions to ask or what to look for. Through no real fault of your own, you were in the dark during much of the process. In the end, you own your home, but you might also have *financial, tax or legal issues, or problems with the house's structure that were overlooked.*

In Summary, owning real estate can be worthwhile when you're doing it for reasons that are right for you. Making a *S.M.A.R.T.* purchase will provide you with the security of owning your own home, and the ability to build wealth too! The real estate purchasing process is one of life's most exciting events. Be open to the opportunities by being prepared!

Pass The Knowledge On!

CHAPTER 4

WORK YOUR BUDGET BEFORE IT WORKS YOU

In this chapter we will show you how to make your budget work *with* you, instead of *against* you, as is so often the case.

For many of us, the word "budget" is uncomfortable. It often conjures visions of scrimping and doing without. But it doesn't have to be that way, since *a budget is simply a projected and actual financial plan on which we base decisions and fulfill our financial dreams.*

With our country's financial markets in disarray, most of us are trying to do more with less. But what many people aren't doing is taking the time to *look at the "what if" scenarios* as they make some of their financial decisions. When it comes to purchasing a home, making a bad decision can compound to more debt! Worse, it not only can cost you thousands, your retirement money but good relations with your family. To help you work through these "what if" scenarios, we have prepared a *Budget Spreadsheet* located on our website, www.MakeNoMistakes.com.

Mistake # 9: *Not taking time out to analyze your personal budget*

Your *Budget Spreadsheet* is designed to help you clearly see where you spend your income. We know the spreadsheet will help you be more aware of your financial health. In Chapter 2, we stated that there are reasons why owning a home is not right for everyone. This is a crucial point, because we want you to be honest with yourself as you determine if owning a home is the right move for you. Though home ownership offers many benefits, it can be a huge weight on your shoulders if you are strapped every month to keep up with your monthly payments. Don't be overwhelmed or afraid to work through the *Budget Spreadsheet*. Realities is sometimes harsh, but believe us when we say the reality of making a wrong decision on a home purchase is more than harsh – it's a nightmare. We're here to make sure your home-buying experience, whether you do it today or sometime in the future, is not a nightmare, but a dream come true.

Monthly Revolving Debt

Before we get started on the checklist, let's define a few terms. *Revolving debt* is an important one. This is debt a borrower has *applied for* and which carries *an outstanding balance*. You make payments on your revolving debt at *regular intervals*. Examples of revolving debt are credit cards, a car loan, and a mortgage note. *When you talk with a loan officer for the first time and he or she looks at your credit report, your revolving debt is primarily what the loan officer will use to determine if and how much house you can afford.* Even though you probably make other monthly payments for such things as utilities and medical bills, they will not appear on your credit report (unless you don't pay them at all, in which case they'll show up as collections) and they won't be factored into the loan officer's decision because they're not considered revolving debt.

Let's get started on your *Budget Spreadsheet*. You'll see excerpts of the spreadsheet in this chapter and that may be all you need for now, but you'll want to open up a copy of the spreadsheet and have it displayed on your computer screen while we explain how easy it is to get started. It's an Excel spreadsheet that uses several of the software's unique features, so you'll get more benefit from working with it onscreen than you will from a printed copy. **Note:** When you order the Make No Mistakes™ System, you will receive a workbook which includes *all the excel spreadsheet* tools and checklists in excel format so you can download and save your own information, and return to it at your leisure.

Using our sample numbers, the first section of the checklist looks like this:

INCOME			
Income	**Borrower**	**Co-Borrower**	**Comments**
Gross Monthly Income	$6,000.00	$3,000.00	
Total Combined Income	*$9,000.00*		

Before you begin to work on your budget, you'll see the spreadsheet is designed for a borrower and a co-borrower. The first question you must ask yourself is how will you take ownership? Chapter 7 discusses ways to take ownership of a property. If you live in a community property state, the lender *may* require that any debt your spouse has be added to the loan application, even if the spouse is not on the mortgage loan. Also, if one of the borrowers has great income but a low credit score, this could affect how you qualify for the loan. See Chapters 10 for more information on how you can positively and negatively affect your loan's interest rate, and how you can improve your credit score.

FICO scores are discussed in Chapter 6. In a nutshell, your FICO score is the middle credit score obtained from the three credit bureaus. It's important to know your FICO score and how it's used.

Let's begin with your *gross monthly income. This* is your income before taxes, 401k contributions or other deductions like federal and city taxes which are taken out of your paycheck. (What you take home with you each pay period is your *net income*.) The difference between gross monthly income and net income will be entered into this checklist later. Your gross monthly income is important because your loan officer will use it to formulate such ratios as your debt-to-income ratio, which is a number every lender requires.

Lenders use your *debt-to-income ratio,* or DTI, to determine what percentage of your income goes towards your debt, and ultimately the maximum loan amount you qualify for. This number is derived by taking your gross monthly income and dividing it *into* your monthly revolving debt. A high debt ratio might indicate that your monthly expenses are becoming unmanageable, and might discourage lenders from approving you for a mortgage loan.

As you enter each debtor's information in the *average monthly revolving expenses* section of the *Budget Spreadsheet,* be sure to notice what happens in the "Debt to Income" column, which shows the percentage of your income going toward that specific debt.

Using these sample numbers, we've determined that 18% of the income is dedicated to paying the average monthly revolving expenses. However, the proposed mortgage payment amount also has to be added since it will become part of the revolving debt. Another way of saying this is the borrowers' DTI ratio is 18% before the proposed monthly mortgage payment is determined and added.

AVERAGE MONTHLY REVOLVING EXPENSES				
Creditors	**Borrower**	**Co-Borrower**	**DTI Ratio**	**Comments**
Car Note	$780.00	$358.00	13%	
Bankcard A	$75.00	$230.00	3%	
Bankcard B	$50.00	$ -	1%	
Store Card A	$50.00	$60.00	1%	
TOTALS	**$955.00**	**$648.00**	**18%**	
Total Monthly Revolving Expenses	*$1,603.00*		*18%*	

When a loan officer looks at your loan application, he or she knows which loan programs are available to you, and the maximum DTI ratio each product carries. We have seen mortgage lenders accept DTI's as high as 55%, which means that 55% of the borrower's total income is going towards paying the monthly revolving debt. *Often, it's the lender's maximum DTI that will determine a monthly payment amount a borrower can afford, and thus the maximum amount a borrower can spend on a house.*

In the chart below you will see that a 55% ratio can garner a monthly (PITI)[20] mortgage payment of $3347.00 a month. The property taxes vary depending on the county, city or state you live in, so a monthly mortgage payment of $3347.00 might equate to a $380,000 to $450,000 home. Before you get excited, however, about calculating how much house you can afford based on a DTI ratio, first understand what each of these ratios means to you and the lender:

40% - Your expenses are *reasonable* compared to your income level.

45% - Your expenses are *high* compared to your income.

50% - Your expenses are *very high* relative to your income.

55% - Your expenses are *dangerously high* relative to your income.

As previously stated, these DTI ratios are based on *revolving debt only*, meaning the debt that shows up on your credit report. R*easonable* is where you want to be, though anything above a 45% DTI should certainly warrant you to look for areas to reduce debt or to decide to purchase less house. Once you have entered your own personal information into the spreadsheet; it will automatically calculate the maximum monthly mortgage payment based on the varying DTI levels and your revolving debt. So you would simply need to choose the maximum amount of affordable monthly house payment you believe makes sense for you and your family. In this example, if you would like to stay below a 40% DTI ratio your monthly mortgage payment should be no more than $1997.00 a month.

---

[20] *PITI* is the acronym used to define the components of a mortgage payment, that principal + interest + taxes + insurance.

DTI RATIOS				
Maximum DTI Ratio	40%	45%	50%	55%
Affordable Monthly Mortgage Payment	*$1,997.00*	*$2,447.00*	*$2,897.00*	*$3,347.00*

Here's where most buyers problems lie. Making a financial decision on the debt that shows up on your credit report only is a lie because it fails to take into consideration your *lifestyle* expenses.

Mistake # 10: *Failing to take into account your lifestyle expenses*

These expenses are based on choices you make because of a lifestyle you choose to lead. For example, it's fair to state that the larger your home, the higher the utility bills. Traveling on vacation is a choice and if it's something you enjoy doing, you need to plan for the cost associated with it.

Again, it is important to understand that the mortgage lender *does not look* at whether or not you like to party and buy drinks for everyone on the weekends. Or that you spend $200 a month in gas as you commute to work. A major mistake many home buyers make is failing to understand that when they purchase too much house it impacts the way they are accustomed to living. Imagine living only to pay on a house and not being able to do much else because you failed to consider your lifestyle expenses. You, and only you, are responsible for looking at your financial health. Here is a sample of our client's lifestyle expenses:

AVERAGE MONTHLY LIFESTYLE EXPENSES				
LIFESTYLE EXPENSES	Borrower	Co-Borrower	DTI Ratio	Comments
Alimony	$ -	$ -	1%	
Charity	$ -	$ 50.00	6%	
Child Support	$ 350.00	$ -	5%	
Clothing	$ 50.00	$ 300.00	3%	
Entertainment	$ 350.00	$ 250.00	1%	
Home Maintenance	$ 180.00	$ 150.00	3%	
Insurance	$ -	$ 100.00	0%	
Medical	$ 35.00	$ -	0%	
Savings	$ 50.00	$ 50.00	1%	
School Related	$ -	$ -	0%	
Taxes	$ 1,300.00	$ 750.00	25%	
Transportation	$ 200.00	$ 125.00	4%	
Travel	$ 75.00	$ -	1%	
Utilities	$ 230.00	$ -	3%	
Other	$ 50.00	$ -	1%	
Other	$ -	$ -	0%	
TOTALS	*$ 2,870.00*	*$ 1,775.00*	52%	
Total Lifestyle Expenses	**$4,645.00**		**52%**	
Total Monthly Expenses (Revolving + Lifestyle)	**$6,248.00**		**69%**	

In case you didn't notice, rent is not included in your lifestyle expenses since it will be replaced by your mortgage note. *Failing to review your lifestyle expenses and making sure they're in line with your income is what costs people thousands of dollars when life throws them an expected event and they're unprepared to deal with its financial consequences.* This brings us to the next section of the *Budget Spreadsheet.*

Monthly Planned Expenses

Very few loan officers will take time to ask about your future goals and plans. For example, if you are married and plan to raise children, this might cause you to lose one income stream or increase debt due to child care. So you would want to keep this in mind when you're determining how much house (*payment*) you can afford. Or, if you currently have 150,000 miles on your car and you know a new one is on the horizon, you need to add this to your planned expenses. It's up to you to take financial responsibility for the amount of debt you and your family can reasonably take on *now* and *in the future.* Below is an example of the planned expenses these borrowers intend to incur:

AVERAGE MONTHLY PLANNED EXPENSES				
PLANNED EXPENSES	Borrower	Co-Borrower	DTI Ratio	Comments
Student Loans	$500.00	$ -	6%	
Day Care	$600.00	$ -	7%	
Home Owners Association Fee		$ -	0%	
Increased Utilities	$200.00	$ -	2%	
Proposed Monthly Mortgage Payment	$1,997.00		22%	
Total Planned Expenses	$3,297.00		37%	

Keep in mind that your loan officer doesn't take into consideration your lifestyle expenses or your planned expenses either. He or she simply reviews your application, income and revolving debt in order to determine if you can afford this property now. But in reality, this isn't a very accurate way to determine if you can afford home ownership, is it? Sure, you may be able to afford the home now, but what about two or three years from now?

In the example above, the most important questions to ask are:

Do you see your income increasing or decreasing in the near future? If so, when and by how much? If not, the next section is relevant to you. (**Note:** *The Proposed Monthly Mortgage Payment number changes as you enter your values in the Loan Calculation Table discussed on page 68.* When you order the Make No Mistakes™ System, you will receive a workbook which includes *all the excel spreadsheet* tools and checklists in excel format so you can download and save your own information.)

What Does My Financial Picture Look Like?

In the example we show here, the couple is certainly living above and beyond their means when their total monthly expenses are considered.

TOTAL MONTHLY EXPENSES			
Totals	**Borrowers**	**DTI Ratio**	**Comments**
Total Monthly Expenses (*Revolving + Lifestyle + Planned*)	$ 9,545.00	106%	
If the DTI is (-) Reduce Your Total Expenses By:	$ (545.00)	-6%	

In fact, the borrowers are living above it by an average of 6% or $545 a month (total monthly expenses minus income) *if* they want to stay below a DTI of 40%. So even though the DTI, based on revolving debt, states you can afford to spend $1997.00 or even $2447 of your income on housing, your expenses should be telling you another thing, namely, *rethink your finances!*

Now, let's look at the −6%. This is the amount – at minimum – by which you will need to *reduce your expenses* in order to afford to buy a home with that monthly payment, if you're being realistic, and without living from paycheck to paycheck.

Unless this couple dramatically changes their lifestyle or they postpone their planned expenses, they have just set themselves up for a financial disaster.

If you're in a similar situation, here are eight feasible ways to avoid the financial disaster that's brewing:

1. Increase income by increasing the number of tax withholdings on your W-4[21]. By doing this you pay less in taxes and thus receive more of your income in your paycheck (rather than getting it back in a tax refund). Be sure to talk to your accountant about this tip.
2. Reduce current debt by not creating more debt.
3. Pay off current debt.
4. Reconsider your planned expenses.
5. Take on a tenant for additional income.
6. Take on another job, or change jobs in the same field to a higher-paying job.
7. Continue to rent until you are able to reduce debt and increase your savings.
8. Decrease the amount of house you're willing to purchase.

(**Note**: *A positive number in that column simply means that you are living at or below your means in order to afford to buy a home. And that would be a good thing.*)

You can see how easily many homeowners got into financial trouble and lost their homes to foreclosure in recent years. In this case, the loan officer considered only the couple's monthly revolving debt – as is customary – and didn't consider the couple's lifestyle or planned monthly expenses. Unfortunately, neither did they. Consequently, they applied and were approved for a mortgage with $2,700 monthly payments. Yet within the first few months of living in their new home and making that $2,700 monthly mortgage payment, the couple realized they'd made a serious mistake – and a very expensive one. They were in financial hot water, and disaster was imminent.

---

[21] *W-4* is an Employee's Withholding Allowance Certificate IRS form that determines how much Federal Withholding Taxes will be deducted from an employee's paycheck.

Clearly, you can see why a budget is so important and why YOU must be prepared to tell the loan officer how much house you can afford, including PITI!

Note: When you meet with loan officers, they'll review your initial application, and calculate your income and revolving liabilities. They do this to come up with a number that indicates how much house you can afford. In other words, how much house you qualify to buy. That number is your *MAXIMUM* limit. *We strongly suggest that, on reviewing and analyzing your Budget Spreadsheet, you should be prepared to tell the loan officer the monthly mortgage payment that you're comfortable with! It's dangerous to borrow at your maximum limit because it can force you to live from paycheck to paycheck or, worse yet, cause you to get behind on your bills.* Should something unexpected happen in your financial life and you can't make your house payment, you'll be in a very bad position. When you buy property, it's always best to prepare for the unexpected: Have a back-up plan and a little nest egg set aside for emergencies, and do not borrow at your maximum limit! Hopefully, you're not in the same predicament as our example couple.

Lay out everything on this or a similar spreadsheet so you'll understand how your income arrives and leaves your household. Once you have accounted for everything, take the time to discuss what expenses you can look to *reduce* or *just do without* in order to own your home. The spreadsheet is set up for you to do as many *what if* scenarios as you like. Taking a serious and realistic look at this information will motivate you to improve your financial well-being.

Calculating the Proposed Mortgage Payment

Let's discuss the various components of a mortgage payment. A mistake many borrowers make is focusing on just the principal and interest parts of the payment. For budgeting purposes, please note there is much more to your mortgage payment and failing to include all of it can cost you thousands!

Mistake # 11: *Budgeting for the principal and interest payments only*

Unfortunately, when borrowers ask about the dollar amount of their new mortgage payments, they are often told only the principal and interest sections of the payment. This is the portion of each payment that goes toward repaying the money they borrowed from the lender, which is the principal, and the interest on the loan. This figure *may not* include, for example, the real estate taxes, homeowner's insurance or private mortgage insurance (PMI). This is why it's so important to understand the components of a mortgage payment.

There are really four parts to your complete monthly mortgage payment. A payment that includes all four components is often referred to as PITI:

Principal – Part of your monthly payment goes toward paying back what you originally borrowed, or the principal. As you make payments, the amount you owe on the original loan shrinks. This is referred to as paying down the principal.

Interest – Your lender loaned you the money to purchase the house in exchange for your agreement to pay interest on the loan. As you repay the loan, less of each month's payment is devoted to interest and more of it is devoted to paying your principal. Most loans are structured so that the majority of the interest is paid in the loan's early years.

Taxes – This portion of your payment goes to pay your property taxes, which could be imposed by such taxing authorities as the city, county, state or local school district.

Insurance – There are two types of insurance that may apply here:

- *Hazard insurance,* often referred to as homeowner's insurance. It is used to protect the value of your home, and thus the lender's investment, from fire, wind and storm damage. Flood and earthquake coverage usually require *separate* policies.

- ***Mortgage Insurance*** is additional insurance protection that you must pay on behalf of the lender to protect them against you defaulting on the loan. This payment is made to an independent mortgage insurance company, which issues a mortgage insurance policy. The amount that is usually guaranteed to the lender is the 20% of the loan amount less your down payment. The remaining 80% of the value of the property is assumed to be recouped when the property is foreclosed[22].

There are two types of mortgage insurance as it pertains to lenders coverage, private mortgage insurance (PMI) and mortgage insurance premium (MIP). PMI only applies to conventional loans, whereas MIP applies to FHA loans[23]. MIP is mandatory on all FHA loans. PMI, on the other hand, is only required *if* you make a down payment of *less than 20%,* and it can be eliminated up front or eventually.

Get Realistic About How Much House You Can You Really Afford

Now that you understand the components of your total mortgage payment its time to calculate the proposed mortgage payment that makes sense for you! We have created a tool known as the *loan calculation table* located on the same sheet as the *Budget Spreadsheet.* This table will allow you to run various *what if* scenarios as it pertains to your *proposed mortgage payment.* Simply enter the variables, such as offer amount, down payment, interest rate being offered to you and the term of loan. Be sure to also enter such variable information as your tax rate, monthly insurance and PMI amount, which you can get from your realtor, insurance agent and loan officer, respectively.

---

[22] *Foreclosing* is the legal process the lender takes to sell the property when a borrower defaults on the loan.

[23] *FHA loans* are federal assistance mortgage loans insured by the Federal Housing Administration. The loan may be issued by any federally qualified lender.

Loan Calculation Table	
Offer Amount	$193,600.00
Down Payment	5%
Down Payment Amount	$9,680.00
Loan Amount	$183,920.00
Annual Interest Rate	6.50%
Loan Period in Years	30
Start Date of Loan	1/1/2009
Optional Extra Payments	$0.00

Total Monthly Mortgage Payment		
Monthly Principal & Interest Payment		$1,162.50
Monthly Property Taxes	3.00%	$484.00
Homeowner Insurance	0.75%	$121.00
PMI or MIP	1.50%	$229.90
Monthly Mortgage Payment		$1,997.40

Once you finish entering these variables into the spreadsheet, you can then play with the offer amount to determine how much house you can afford, being careful to take into account your down payment, the interest rate currently offered and the number of years you plan to borrow. The results will show you a proposed monthly mortgage payment. Your goal here is to focus on the *monthly mortgage payment* amount to determine the maximum offer amount or sales price of your affordable home. (**Note:** As you run your *what if* scenarios these numbers will automatically populate the monthly mortgage payment both in your loan calculation table and in the monthly planned expenses table.)

Paying into an Escrow Account

When the borrower makes a mortgage payment to the lender, the principal and interest go directly to the lender to pay off the note and *the taxes and insurance segments go into an account known as an "escrow" or "reserve account" until the property tax and insurance bills are due.* These bills are typically due annually or semi-annually. At that time, the escrow agency simply deducts the appropriate amount of money from the escrow account and pays the bill. This way, the borrower doesn't have to come up with a large sum of money to pay real estate taxes and the insurance bill. Mortgage escrow accounts are a good idea for most borrowers. Fortunately, in many cases, they're mandatory. These escrow accounts decrease the number of foreclosures due to unpaid taxes and insurance. Homeowners who choose not to escrow often *get into trouble – if they are not honest with themselves, and do not save aside the money for the taxes and insurance.*

To assure that there will always be enough money in the account, lenders ask for more than they actually need as a cushion, or "reserve." If the taxing authority or the insurance provider raises the rates, the lender doesn't have to come to the borrower for the difference. The lender simply dips into the reserves, which is the extra money sitting in the account to pay your taxes and insurance bill for the year. At closing, lenders typically require two to four months' equivalent of taxes and insurance to set up this escrow account. They are collected from the borrower at closing in the form of *prepaids*.

Can You Avoid Paying into Escrow?

Yes. Here's how:

- Contribute 20% as your down payment
- Find a second lender who will take on a second note to reduce the risk for the primary lender
- Take out a subprime mortgage

It's important to consider, however, all the ramifications of *not* paying into escrow. For one thing, borrowers usually pay ¼ to ¾ points higher interest rates if they don't pay into this monthly escrow account.

There are two big advantages we see to *not* escrowing:

- You pay less at closing because you don't have to pay the required prepaids, i.e., the two to four months of taxes and insurance premiums
- You pay less every month because you only pay the principle and interest to your lender

Borrowers who choose not to escrow now have one or two big tax payments during the year that they must pay on their own. This usually means saving money each month to make these big payments when they're due. For some people, that's not a problem. A borrower can also make separate arrangements to pay his or her insurance premiums directly to the insurance carrier, often on a monthly basis once the first year has been paid in advance. If you're an expert saver, choosing to *not* escrow might work for you.

The downside to all of this is we've seen too many people with good intentions not have the money to pay their taxes on time. The annual or semi-annual tax payment is usually due toward the end of the year, often during the holidays, which is an expensive time of year anyway. Not paying a tax bill is serious business. Interest and fines accrue on unpaid tax bills, and eventually a tax lien could be placed on the property. Everyday, borrowers lose their property in auction sales for as little as the back taxes due. A mortgage escrow account is an easy, worry free way to manage your tax payments and insurance premiums.

Now let's take a look at our sample couple's savings situation.

Savings

Today's lenders are looking at how much a borrower has in savings after the down payment and closing costs have been paid. This helps lenders determine how risky you are as a borrower if you lose your income for a short period of time or have an unexpected event that sets you back financially.

Many lenders look for borrowers to have a minimum of six months of total (principal, interest, taxes and insurance) mortgage payments on hand in liquid savings for just these reasons. So if your mortgage payment is $1,997, you should have at least $11,982 in a liquid account, such as a savings account, after all costs associated with purchasing your property.

There are a wide range of guidelines out there stating how much people should have in liquid savings accounts. Some experts say two to three months' worth of take home salary, while others believe it should be six months' worth of living expenses. The point is you need something to fall back on in the event of an emergency – and emergencies *do* happen.

401K

Borrowers often tell us they have much more in their retirement accounts, such as their 401Ks. This is great, but this type of savings is not liquid. It carries a penalty if you use it prior to retirement unless you use it as a "hardship withdrawal." One acceptable hardship is making a down payment in connection with the purchase of your primary residence. However, keep in mind that this type of withdrawal is very costly. The cost is the earnings you forgo on the money withdrawn, plus you have to pay taxes and penalties on the amount withdrawn, which must be paid in the year of withdrawal.

Sometimes you can borrow against your 401K. *The major risk in this, however, is if you lose your job or change employers, you must pay back the loan in full within a short period, often 60 days.* If you don't, it is treated as a withdrawal and subject to the same taxes and penalties. While your 401K account can usually be rolled over into your new employer's 401K or into an IRA, without penalties or tax payments, a loan on the other hand from a 401K cannot.

In Summary, your loan officer will look at only a portion of your financial portfolio. He or she focuses on your income and the revolving debt that appears on your credit report to determine your debt-to-income (DTI) ratio. The rest is left up to you to figure out! The loan officer's concern is whether or not the DTI falls within the guidelines of the loan program in which he is trying to place you. But *you* are the one who is ultimately responsible for your financial well-being. To do that, you must take the steps necessary to understand how funds come in and go out of your household. You must be prepared to tell the loan officer what size monthly mortgage payment you are comfortable paying each month. To do that, you must take into account your revolving, lifestyle and planned monthly expenses, as well as any unforeseen expenses that will affect your savings.

Your monthly mortgage payment consists of PITI: principal, interest, taxes and insurance. Be sure to take into account your mortgage insurance situation. Most lenders prefer you to escrow, and they'll compensate you for this by offering a lower interest rate on your loan. Using escrow services is an extremely easy, safe and affordable way to make sure your property taxes and homeowner's insurance premiums are paid in full and on time.

Live within your means and you'll be able to enjoy your new home for years!

Pass The Knowledge On!

CHAPTER 5

PROFESSIONALS REDUCE MISTAKES

Everybody has an opinion on how to purchase real estate and, once they know you're considering this big purchase, they'll all offer advice. You'll be inundated with tips, referrals and a surplus of information. While many people have good intentions, the reality of it is – everyone has enough knowledge about real estate to be dangerous!

Mistake # 12: *Not hiring the right professionals*

In this chapter, you will learn about one of the first things you should do as you start your quest for your ideal piece of real estate: Put together the right team of people. These professionals will use their experience to advise you throughout the process, helping you to save time and energy, and decreasing your chances of a costly mistake.

The first person to choose as part of your team is a coach. Coaches use their expertise earned over many years to help you through the process. CEOs, presidents, executives and world-class athletes have coaches, and there's no reason you can't too. This does not mean you give up control. You're the boss. It's not hard to find a good coach *if* you know what to ask and what signs to look for when interviewing your candidates.

So, just who is this coach? Well, a good real estate agent would make an ideal coach. Not just any real estate agent, but a *good* one. ***The beauty of using a top-notch real estate agent as your coach is there's NO cost to you for this person's expert time and services.*** Your coach/real estate agent gets paid by the seller when you purchase the property! You may think we want to push the use of a real estate agent because that's our profession, but let us explain. We'll illustrate our point with a story:

> *Years ago I contracted to have work done on my patio. I was very unhappy with the work and the craftsmanship. Unfortunately, I put down a substantial deposit. After several discussions with the contractor, I realized my only recourse for restitution was to go to small claims court. Eventually, months later, we went before the small claims court mediator.*

> *I was well-prepared when it was my turn to present my side of the story. I had contacted and received advice from several law firms. I spoke with friends who were attorneys and believed I had enough ammunition to go into the courtroom and win this battle. Several attorneys were willing to represent me that day, but I thought their fee of 40% was much too steep for what I perceived they had to do: simply show up.*

> *During my presentation to the mediator, he asked if I had a certain piece of evidence in my possession, which I did not. Suddenly, I remembered one of the attorneys asking me the same question. I chose not to get the evidence when the attorney first brought it up because, in my mind, it was inconsequential. So within minutes, and after I had prepared for months and lived with an ugly patio, the mediator rendered his decision. I lost $5,000.*

> *I thought I could do this process on my own and save the $2,000 attorney's fee. Hindsight, of course, says if I had not tried to be such a know-it-all, and if I had valued the experience of an attorney, I could have walked away with*

$3,000; instead I got nothing. Except an ugly patio and of course, a lot of wasted time and energy.

The moral of this story: Use a professional! If I am not someone who is in the courtroom dealing with civil litigations on a daily basis, why would I attempt it on my own, without a professional? A coach, in this case, would not only have represented me and spoken the language of the legal system, but he would have advised me. Most importantly, the coach would have anticipated various scenarios and requests from the defendant and mediator.

The same applies to real estate! If you are not dealing with real estate on a daily basis, why would you chance it on your own? My excuse was I didn't want to share with the attorney any of the $5,000 I expected to win. But in real estate, the buyer doesn't have to spend a penny to get the skilled, experienced services of a good real estate agent.

Some of you might still say this has nothing to do with real estate. Maybe not, but it has everything to do with the importance of teaming up with a professional. Throughout this reference guide you will read many stories which show real estate buyers choosing to do it their own way -- and losing thousands of dollars. A few may win, but many more will lose. And loss can come in many forms, including financial issues, legal problems, wasted time and emotional stress. *As much as you think you know, there will probably be a point during the transaction when there is something you won't know – and it could cost you greatly!*

What Makes a "Good" Real Estate Agent?

A "good" real estate agent does more than just unlock a house so you can see the inside. Good agents bring training, guidance, knowledge and practical experience to buyers and sellers during real estate transactions. In other words, they assist you in reducing mistakes.

All real estate agents are licensed by the states in which they do business. Similar to attorneys, real estate agents have strictly defined legal relationships with their buyers. They are obligated to deal with you honestly and fairly. They also have a fiduciary responsibility since they may handle money on your behalf. By law, a real estate agent has to perform the duties of an O.L.D. C.A.R:

- **O**bedience – The agent is obligated to act in good faith and obey your legal instructions.
- **L**oyalty – The agent should place your interest above his or her own.
- **D**isclosure – The agent must keep you informed at all times of all facts which could affect your decisions.
- **C**onfidentiality – The agent is obligated to keep confidential anything about you which might harm your negotiations.
- **A**ccounting – The agent must report the status of all funds and give you accurate copies of all documents affecting your transaction.
- **R**easonable Care – The agent has to help you find a suitable property and keep your best interest in mind at all times.

However, just because an agent is licensed does not qualify that person to be a "good" real estate agent.

How do you decide if you can trust your real estate agent?

Only a small percentage of people in any profession will ever strive to perfect their skills. The rest are happy just learning enough to get by. Please understand this: It does not take much to get licensed. For example, in Florida if you are a high school graduate or have your GED and want to earn your real estate license, you are required to take only 63 hours of classes. You can easily accomplish this by going to class for *only one week*, from 8:00 a.m. to 6:00 p.m., Monday through Sunday. Most real estate students' goals are to simply get through the boring class, pass the state test, and earn their licenses. Consequently, newly-licensed real estate agents don't have any practical experience until they find clients to be guinea pigs. All the class training in the world doesn't compare to actually going through a hundred *real* transactions with *real* experiences.

You may ask, "What about the national real estate companies touting how great and knowledgeable their agents are?" The answer is they're not all great and knowledgeable. As often as these large real estate offices apparently offer training, it is usually an individual agent's choice to participate in any of the training classes or programs the real estate brokers offer. *No matter what size company your agent is affiliated with, ask him or her about her recent continuing-education classes.*

Most agents are contracted, not employed. A real estate broker typically owns the agency and holds the active licenses of the real estate agents in that office.

The goals and objectives of a real estate broker and a real estate agent are different. The *broker's goal* is to bring on board as many *agents* as possible to help grow the company's business. A *real estate agent's goal* is to bring in as many *buyers and sellers* as possible to grow his or her individual business.

Although it is in the best interest of the broker to place well-trained agents in the field, the broker's No. 1 objective is to attract as many agents as possible. Brokers charge monthly fees to their agents; brokers also expect to receive a portion of each agent's commissions.

Consequently, there are many real estate agents who are just winging it. They're trying to run their businesses with virtually no business experience. Little of this is taught in real estate schools. This lack of experience is difficult to overcome. Most busy real estate agents don't make time to help each other. Many view it as helping their competition so they're not interested in sharing trade secrets. As a result, agents often learn by trial and error – by making mistakes that cost you money.

Also, real estate is a straight commission business: no sales, no income! As a result, many real estate agents start trying to work the business part-time on the weekends. They're not committed to working the business full-time. This increases the risk of making mistakes because real estate is so detail oriented. There are countless small pieces which need to come together in the right order and in a timely fashion. This can be very difficult to do if you're working only part-time. Years of practice makes perfect, and you need a lot of practice to become good – let alone perfect.

Here is a list of mistakes and characteristics which should immediately disqualify a real estate agent from being your coach or representative:

- **Unprofessional** – You should be able to see this at the first meeting. One way to tell: Is the agent taking notes? If not, walk away.
- **Incapable of Asking the Right Questions** – You should get a sense of this from your first meeting, based on the questions he or she asks you.
- **Inability to Articulate** – An agent who is unable to communicate well with you will have a hard time doing the same when it's time to negotiate. This could impact your deal.
- **Unable to Complete the Forms** - Are the forms you received on your first visit filled out completely? Can the agent explain the documents he or she is presenting to you?
- **No Business System in Place to Handle Multiple Clients** - Ask them to show you their client-management systems and how they work during your first meeting with the candidates. A system could be a database management program like Top Producer, Act or even a detailed day planner.
- **Inadequate Negotiating Skills** - Real estate agents work extremely hard and deserve all of their commissions. However, to test their negotiating skills ask them to reduce their commissions. See how they respond. This will definitively tell you how they may negotiate on your behalf. Keep in mind you're not really asking them to lower their commissions on your purchase - you're just testing their skills. Later, tell them why you asked this question and see how they handle these revelations.
- **Inability to Understand the Financial Aspect of the Business** - Ask each agent to explain a Settlement Statement to you. After reading this book you should have a good sense of whether or not the agents feel comfortable in explaining Settlement Statements – because you will.
- **Poor Follow-Up Skills** - This may be difficult to determine until you get farther into the process. However, if they don't

return your initial calls within two hours, this may be a sign. If they don't use some type of planner to keep track of their tasks, this is another sign. How and when do they follow-up with you after your initial meeting with them?

- **Unconcerned With Your Deal as Long as They Get Paid -** You may sense this if they don't take time to fully explain things to you or if they appear uninterested in helping you learn more about the home-buying process. And what kind of questions do they ask you? Do they appear to care about getting to know you better?

Finding a "Good" Real Estate Agent

How do you find the right real estate agent or coach? How do you find someone who takes his or her business, education and training seriously? Start by asking your family, associates and friends. Drive into a community where you may want to buy and see which agencies' – and agents – yard signs are prominent. Also, keep in mind that we can help, too, by introducing you to real estate agents who are familiar with our **Make No Mistakes System**. Simply go to our website and click on *Find a Good Real Estate Agent*, then contact the ones in your area whom you may want to interview. But no matter how you locate your pool of real estate agents, take time to interview them. You'll find the right person.

On the other hand, one of the worst mistakes you can make is entrusting thousands or millions of dollars to someone because you owe that person a favor, or because the agent is a family member or friend. This is one of the quickest ways of not only ruining that relationship, but also costing yourself thousands of dollars and having to live with it for years.

Mistake # 13: *Trusting your real estate agent completely you that don't ask questions*

Trusting your real estate agent to always have your best interest in mind, which then stops you from asking questions throughout the process, is a common mistake. Become knowledgeable enough to know what questions to ask. Visit our website, www.MakeNoMistakes.com, for a copy of the checklist, *Identifying a Good Real Estate Agent.* Click on **"Real Estate Forms,"** enter book code 550 and select your checklists to download.

Using this checklist will help you decide if you can rely on this person's advice and if this is who will best represent you. If you are not sold on this person's recommendations and suggestions, always ask more questions. Not understanding a real estate agent's advice can cost you money.

A good real estate agent meets all your realty needs. In fact, we based our company's name on it: One Call – One Team. In other words, *you should be able to make one call to your real estate agent, who should have the network, the resources or a team of people who can properly address all your realty needs.* A "good" agent should have access to attorneys, title companies, inspectors, specialty inspectors, repairmen, insurance companies, banks, anything and anyone related to fixing or renovating a home and closing your real estate transaction.

The process of buying the right home or property encompasses an enormous amount of details. Occasionally a buyer will feel a real estate agent did not do much. When that happens, you can bet the buyer must not have noticed many of the agent's day-to-day activities, especially if the agent found the buyer's perfect home quickly. What that buyer failed to realize is the agent's experience – gained over many years – shielded the buyer from many of the details occurring in the background. A good agent does not become good by just reading books. *Agents become "good" through experience, education, trials, tribulations, understanding their roles, and knowing when it's time to make the moves which best serve their clients.*

Years ago, a reputable friend referred a client to us. As a result of our established relationship with this friend, we made several exceptions when we took this referral. One exception was failing to discuss the new client's financial position in detail. In fact, when we brought up the subject, he told us we didn't need to concern ourselves with his finances because he worked for the financial institution funding the loan. Under normal circumstances, this type of attitude and conduct would not have been acceptable to us, but because of his association with our friend, we made the exception. Nonetheless, we continued to search for the right property.

As our client got off work one evening, he came across a property that interested him. The price was more than he wanted to spend, but he insisted this was the one. As his real estate agents, we reviewed the criteria he initially set, and tried to make sure he would be comfortable at this price. He assured us he could handle it. We proceeded to put together the offer and negotiate the terms.

He called one evening and said because he had found the house, he felt we weren't entitled to our full commission. In fact, he wanted to use part of our commission toward his closing costs. His actions indicated he didn't value what we did for a living, and his words were condescending.

Our immediate reaction, of course, was "the nerve of this guy!" However, we remained calm and reminded him it was our efforts of showing him properties for more than six weeks which helped him fine tune his criteria. Finding the actual house is just one part of the broad scope of work a real estate agent handles. In other words, he was not entitled to any portion of our commissionable dollars. He became upset, ignored our advice and recommendations, and moved forward anyway.

On closing day, we kept our part of the agreement to represent him by showing up at the signing. When we got there, we found that his deal, which he chose to handle himself near the end, cost him dearly. The cost included unresolved repair items and an additional outlay of cash at closing due to his inability to rewrite the contract to cover his costs. He paid a *high price for being a know-it-all and having the wrong attitude.*

There are times when a good real estate agent can often make a transaction seem so easy that you may question what the agent has done on your behalf. Take a look at the list of *Buyer Services* located in the appendix to get an idea of what steps a good agent takes on your behalf to serve your buying needs.

When you draft an offer[24] to a seller, the specific legal and business language used defines the requirements the seller and buyer must each fulfill. For example, a seller asks $360,000 for his home. The buyer offers to pay $350,000. The buyer also wants to take possession of the home within 30 days and wants the seller to replace the carpet. The seller agrees to the 30 days, but wants $352,000 and is only willing to professionally clean the carpet.

> **Tip:**
> *Trust is earned, not given.*

This is typical. There is often a lot of dialogue between the parties until the buyer and seller at last agree on the terms. The real estate agents facilitate this dialogue. Once an offer is accepted and executed[25] it becomes a contract. Your real estate agent's role at this point is to provide experience and guidance, and to ensure everyone is doing their part to comply with the terms and to complete them within the specified time periods.

We will never forget a certain real estate deal we worked on with a contract stating we had to close and fund[26] on a specific day. That day turned out to be the Monday after Hurricane Katrina ravaged the Gulf Coast in 2005. Our fellow Houstonians left the city in droves, anticipating disaster in our city. Instead, New Orleans was the center of the disaster. Our Houston mayor, nonetheless, asked all businesses to close that

---

[24] An *offer* is the negotiable price and terms you present to the seller of the property *before* it is accepted by the sellers as a binding contract.

[25] *Executed* means both parties, buyer and seller, agree on the price and terms of the contract, then sign it to make it binding.

[26] To *fund* is when the seller receives his or her monies, in the form of a check, from the buyer and/or the buyer's lender.

Monday so citizens would have time to return to their homes and resume to their normal lives.

Following the mayor's instructions, both the title company and bank closed that day. The seller of the property, however, said because the buyers didn't follow the terms of the contract, they were in default. Needless to say, our clients were in an uproar because they couldn't believe the seller would use such a tactic under the circumstances. It turned out the seller had a more lucrative offer waiting in the wings, so he used the language in the contract to his advantage to wring more money out of our clients, who still wanted the house.

To make this long story short, our clients paid an additional $14,000 because of not meeting the terms in the contract, plus more than $2,000 in legal fees to deal with the buyer.

You're probably asking, how could we, as their agents, have allowed our clients to be so vulnerable? This was a classic case of one side, in this case, the buyers, trusting the other side to act honorably. The buyers believed the situation did not warrant drafting an amendment[27] to extend the close date. As their representatives and coaches, we offered our guidance and experience, but we can never force buyers to do anything they don't want to do.

> **Tip:**
> *Put everything in writing.*

The moral of this story? Buying and selling real estate is like a game and if you don't play it often, find someone to be on your team who does. And most importantly, heed your agent's advice! "Good" real estate agents understand the rules. They know how to maneuver around the nuances, pitfalls and inherent dangers of legal and financial issues. Determining your next move on your own could be the decision that costs you dearly if you make the wrong choice.

---

[27] An *amendment* to a contract is simply an additional document that changes the terms or price of the original contract.

How Your Real Estate Agent's Commission Works

So how does the buyer's real estate agent get paid? Most often, it's by the seller. When the sellers contract with their listing agent,[28] they agree on a commission, generally about 6% of the sales price. That commission is often split between the two agents – the listing agent, and the selling agent, who is also known as the buyer's agent.[29]

When one agent agrees to represent both sides, there is an exception to this standard practice. Such an agent is often described as an intermediary.[30]

In most cases, the seller pays the commissions from the *equity*, or *appreciation*, the home accrued; the equity is easily accessible when the home sells.

After splitting the 6% commission, the two agents then have to split their 3% commissions with their brokers; that is, with the owner of the agency each agent represents. Some of these fees can be as high as 50%, depending on the brokerage. Your real estate agent may also be entitled to other compensation, known as a *"Bonus to the Selling Agent,"* or *BTSA*, from the seller. Remember, your agent is referred to as *the buyer's agent* or *the selling agent*, so don't get confused as to which agent receives the BTSA. Sellers and their agents use this bonus as an incentive for garnering the support of the buyer's agent. A seller hopes the buyer's agent will use his or her influence to sway the buyer toward that particular seller's property. Don't hesitate to ask your agent if there is a BTSA offered for the sale of a property you're considering. In fact, you *should* ask, because you need to know what is motivating your agent – hopefully, it is your best interests! Unfortunately, we've seen agents search for properties with these bonuses, and then try to influence their clients to purchase those properties.

---

[28] The *listing agent* is the licensed representative who sells the house on behalf of the seller.

[29] The *selling agent* is also described as the agent who represents the buyer.

[30] An *intermediary* is an agent who is employed to handle both sides, selling and buying, of the transaction.

In Summary, we wish you success in finding a coach. A professional real estate agent who's committed to the process and committed to you is well worth your time and energy to locate. Take your time to interview several prospects. Use your *Find a Good Real Estate Agent Checklist* and be prepared to ask questions. These professionals have a responsibility to serve you. Once you find a person with whom you work well, hang on to that agent, as he or she will only get better as time goes on.

Remember, there are a relatively small number of agents who take their real estate businesses seriously. Your coach should be someone who does more than just unlock doors to homes you want to see. A "good" real estate agent possesses specialized skills, principles, concepts, practices and – most importantly – *experience*, which will help you successfully reach your goal.

It's important to value your agent's role throughout the process. Your agent should be encouraging, provide timely help and offer a safety net to protect you from mistakes. It's your agent's job to make it easy for you. If it looks and feels easy, be assured your agent is working hard and doing a good job.

Pass The Knowledge On!

Section II:
Understand Your Home Loan Before You Start House-Hunting

CHAPTER 6

CREDIT – IS IT IMPORTANT?

In this chapter, you will learn the importance of your credit report and how you can lose thousands of dollars with a difference as small as just one point on your credit score. Also, we will explain how it impacts the type of loan you get and how you can improve your credit score.

When you're in the process of buying a house, there's one number that is more important than all the others. You probably think it's the price of the house, or your income or maybe how much money you have in your bank account. While these numbers are important, it's your middle credit score we're referring to that is your make-or-break number.

Mistake # 14: *Failure to know what's on your credit report before you start the loan process*

Lenders retrieve your information from all three credit bureaus but only the middle of the three credit scores is used for the loan decision. This score will determine your interest rate, and if you will be dealing with a prime lender who offers some of the lowest interest rates, or a sub-prime lender who offers some of the highest.

Your middle credit score is determined by dropping the lowest and the highest of the three credit bureaus' scores. These scores are also known as your FICO scores. FICO stands for "Fair Isaac Corporation." It is a mathematical calculation measuring your capacity to repay a loan. The FICO is very important because the middle score will tell lenders what they need to know about how reliable and financially responsible you are as a borrower.

Most lenders will look at more than your credit score to determine if they will give you a loan, but your credit score is the biggest factor affecting the interest rate you're offered. Your credit report shows information on credit accounts you've applied for, their credit limits and whether or not you pay on time. It will also show outstanding balances, when you opened the account, your scheduled monthly payments and any final payments due. It might also surprise you to find your report contains personal information, such as your current and past employers and residences.

Inquiries on Your Credit Report

If you have recently applied for credit it will show up as an *inquiry* on your report. This could raise a red flag with your mortgage company. The lender may interpret the inquiry as additional debt *forthcoming.*

FICO credit scores range from 300 - 850. You will often see ads based on good credit, bad credit or no credit. This is usually a reflection of your credit score. Good credit means a relatively high score, bad credit means a relatively low score and no credit means you have not yet established credit (the three credit bureaus don't have any information on you).

Having good credit certainly offers more opportunities and more choices. Bad credit, on the other hand, makes things more challenging for you – but not necessarily impossible.

Knowing your credit score and understanding what is on the report are key to determining how much leverage you have when borrowing money.

But first, you should determine if all the debt listed is truly yours. Mistakes happen frequently on reports, particularly if you have a common first and last name, for example, Maria Martinez, Robert

Smith or Michael Jones. So prepare yourself to address this with your loan officer.

Obviously, paying your bills on time is THE best way of improving your credit score. Nothing messes up your credit score quicker than late payments. Defaulting on loans or filing bankruptcy will also send your score in the tank. In this time of computer technology, late payments and forgetting to place the envelope in the mail is old school. Today many banking institutions offer online banking systems that allow you to program when certain payments need to be paid and for how much. You can easily set up automatic transactions with your bank for bills that are typically the same each month. Having your bill-paying tasks on auto pilot reduces forgetfulness and increases your credit scores.

Keep all bills in a folder in a special place. Make it a point to pay your bills twice a month, before the fifteenth and the end of the month, or immediately after each paycheck. This is a simple yet effective step toward preserving your good credit.

If you find that you're unable to pay all of your bills, your first priorities should be your mortgage payment, if you currently own a home, and any student loans you may have. Foreclosure and late mortgage payments are the only things that mortgage lenders are very reluctant to forgive.

Loan programs exist for people who have had foreclosures, but those borrowers often pay higher interest rates and make significant down payments. It's important to pay student loans because it's a loan backed by the government. FHA, VA and now Fannie Mae[31] and Freddie Mac[32] loans are government entities (more on this

---

[31] The Federal National Mortgage Association (FNMA), commonly known as *Fannie Mae*, is a U.S. publicly-traded stockholder-owned corporation authorized to make loans and loan guarantees. *Fannie Mae* is the leading participant in the U.S. secondary mortgage market, which exists to provide liquidity to the primary mortgage market. The secondary mortgage market's role is to safeguard the available funds that mortgage companies, savings and loans, commercial banks, credit unions, and state and local housing finance agencies have to lend to home buyers.

[32] The Federal Home Loan Mortgage Corporation (FHLMC), commonly known as *Freddie Mac*, does the same thing as Fannie Mae. Our government established these two companies so there would be competition between them, and thus do away with a monopoly in the mortgage financing industry.

subject later) and frown upon late pays and defaults on government loans. Also, a derogatory (late-pay or no pay) comment on your credit report has a bigger impact when you're young and don't have as much positive credit data to balance a negative comment.

Remember, anyone who has access to your social security number has access to place derogatory information about lack of payment on your credit report. However, late payments on monthly medical and utility bills, for example, don't show up on credit reports unless the bill ends up in collections.

You should get a copy of your own credit report before you start applying for a mortgage. Check your credit from 90 to 120 days before beginning the house-hunting process. This will give you time to allow unused accounts to close, and to correct any errors. Know what's on your credit report before the lender sees it because you don't want any surprises. You are allowed at least one free copy of your credit report each year. You can get a copy from each of the three credit bureaus:

Trans Union   (800) 888-4213

Experian   (888) 397-3742

Equifax   (800) 685-1111

The credit *report,* which lists your creditors and how you pay them, is free. However, a copy of your credit *score* is approximately $7.95 for each credit bureau. Congress mandated this access in 2004 by the Fair and Accurate Credit Transactions Act. Or simply go to www.FreeCreditReportguide.org.

What's an Acceptable Credit Score?

An acceptable credit score depends on the loan program. Remember, credit scores *don't* approve or decline anyone, *lenders do!* Lenders base their decisions on varying criteria and requirements, also referred to as guidelines. There is more to an "approval" than a credit score.

If your credit score is low, it doesn't mean you can't get approved. It just means your loan officer has to shop for someone who will approve the loan. It's more difficult today, but there are programs available to assist you. Typically, it's not *if* you'll get approved for a mortgage, but at what "term*" and at what "cost."*

There are programs to help you buy a house if you have credit issues. The Federal Housing Administration (FHA) is now operating like a sub-prime lender with lower minimum credit score requirements. See the programs they offer at www.fha.gov. Don't worry about the myths; the FHA is not as restrictive as you may have heard.

Here's what happened in 2008 to change the nature of FHA loans. One of the benefits of an FHA loan had been that credit scores were not a factor in determining a borrower's eligibility, but in 2008, several lenders implemented credit score requirements for FHA loans. Initially, the requirement demanded a minimum credit score of 500, which changed to 550, and soon 580 became the norm. This happened because the lenders were in self-defense mode at a time when they were blamed for our country's volatile economic situation. FHA underwriters and lenders are held responsible for defaults on the loans they approve, so they quickly tightened their requirements. The good news is the FHA program is far more attractive to low-score borrowers than the old subprime loans were. And at the same time, the FHA is a top solution for high-score borrowers too, which is one result of the government's 2008 Economic Stimulus Package. *Now, FHA loans are available to a wide range of borrowers, even those who may think they cannot be approved – so don't decline yourself without trying.*

We work with borrowers who have been declining *themselves* for years for a variety of reasons. For example, a borrower may have been declined for a credit card and for whatever reason, didn't try again. Or maybe a borrower didn't understand credit scores, or perhaps that borrower listened to someone who gave bad advice. For whatever reason, people put off buying houses and didn't apply for loans. They could have been in their new homes years ago, but they gave up, with little to no effort.

If you take time to investigate your options before you start, you will know what you need to do to qualify for a mortgage loan, either now or in the future.

Credit scores mean different things to different lenders, yet there is some consensus. Here's an example showing how lenders may rate credit scores:

740 and higher   Considered the best credit.

700 to 739   Considered excellent credit.

631 to 699   Considered good credit. The borrower will have access to good interest rates, but may not qualify for the very best interest rates and terms.

500 to 630   Considered risky credit. The borrower may need to pay a higher interest rate plus a higher down payment to get the loan. Certain loans will be off limits.

499 to 300   Considered very risky credit. The borrower may not be eligible for a loan. The borrower more than likely has a foreclosure, liens, and/or credit judgments showing on his or her report.

The Importance of Improving Your Credit

First, let me say you are not alone!!! We live in a country where millions of people have bad credit due to loss of work, income and sickness. Unfortunately, if you have low credit scores, you pose a high credit risk to lenders. If they offer you the loan, it will be at a higher interest rate and/or require you to put down a larger down payment amount. Here's an example of what a low credit score costs you on a loan amount of $200,000:

Type of Credit	30-Year Fixed Interest Rate	Monthly Principal and Interest Amount	Total of 360 Months (30 Years) of Payments
Good Credit	6%	$1,199.10	$431,677.04
Bad Credit	11%	$1,904.65	$685,655.03
What It Costs You		**$705.55**	**$253,977.99**

It would cost you $253,977.99 more over 30 years, or $705.55 a month, because you had bad credit when you took out the loan. Our example above shows two extremes – a good credit score garnering a loan at 6%, and a bad credit score earning a loan at 11%. What about everyone in between? How would their monthly payments be affected by the interest rates they received? Based on the same $200,000 loan:

30-Year Fixed Interest Rate	Monthly Principal and Interest Amount	Total of 360 Months (30 Years) of Payments
7%	$1,330.60	$479,016.00
8%	$1,467.53	$528,310.80
9%	$1,609.25	$579,330.00
10%	$1,755.14	$631,850.40

So just imagine if you stay in this home for all 30 years and keep the same interest rate. The difference between the 7% and 10% interest rates is $152,834. That's a lot of money you could have done something else with.

So how do you stop from giving all that money away? As stated earlier – and it's worth repeating – you have to know what your credit scores are, understand what they mean and know how to protect them. Your credit score plays a major role in our society and how creditors view you when you want to borrow money or purchase items on credit. *In fact, today, insurance companies and even employers look at your credit reports to see how you spend money, to determine your credit worthiness and to verify your employment. There are even creditors who use scoring models based on where you spend your money as a way to determine their risk. For example, in a recent article written by Money magazine, credit card holders who frequent certain types of establishments pose a higher risk. To our surprise, one of these was marriage counselors.*

Most borrowers don't review their credit reports until the lender orders it from the credit bureaus, reviews it and gives the borrowers the bad news. Then you have to make a decision. Is it worth giving up the idea of finding the house that you worked so hard to save up for, or do you start working on your credit so you can get a better interest rate? Or worse yet, you found the house first, before trying to get a pre-qualification[33] letter, and now your options are limited. Having to walk away from the house at this point costs you emotionally and financially.

It's a more painful situation when you have mentally committed yourself to a house. You may have shown the property to friends and family, driven by it several times, or even signed the contract, put money down or window-shopped for furniture. Knowing your credit situation before you start looking for a home will save embarrassment and give you an opportunity to work on improving your scores. *You will also negotiate from a position of strength, and you won't feel compelled to take the first option the lender offers you.*

Using a Different Identity on Your Application

Applying for a mortgage using another identity is known as mortgage fraud. In fact, the mortgage application asks if you've ever been known by any other name. If you say "yes," they'll want to know the name(s). Rest assured, these aliases' credit reports will be checked, and the mortgage lender will look for connections between the alias and any possible fraud. Mortgage fraud is at an all-time high and all

---

[33] A *pre-qualification* letter is from your loan officer, stating that, based on review of the information in the credit report and on the loan application, and assuming all the information is true and correct, the borrower qualifies for a mortgage loan.

lenders are on high alert. We have to be careful to watch for and avoid people who want to involve us in fraud.

A brand new real estate agent referred his first client to us. "I have a client who needs pre-approving. She already found a house and is ready to buy NOW!!!" We agreed to meet with the buyer right away so she could fill out the loan application and we could pull her credit report. The first warning bell went off when we looked at her credit report: it said this person is known to use an alias. It advised us to check her social security card and other forms of identification.

On the application she stated she was an attorney and had been in practice for 10 years. We called the state bar association, which had no attorney listed with that name, nor was there anyone with that name licensed to practice law in Texas. We turned down the application because there were too many inconsistencies. We later found out she was going to jail for hot checks and forgery.

Mistake # 15: *Lying on your loan application*

As you can see, people lie on their loan applications. It does not pay to do so, not even a little bit. Keep in mind it's not a good idea to erase your old credit report by creating a new identity, unless you are interested in going to jail. Your unique identity is the same as your social security number. There are credit repair companies that offer this type of service, but you will be asking for nothing but trouble and it could land you in jail.

It's the loan officer's job to look for red flags and, if they don't catch them, you can be sure the underwriters will. Take our advice: Don't lie on your application. You'll be asked to prove and support your answers with documentation. And don't leave things off the application.

Mistake # 16: *Not knowing what has immediate impact on your credit scores*

Follow this good advice when you apply for a mortgage loan, since any of these actions could negatively impact your credit score:

- *Do not use your credit cards unless absolutely necessary.* The lender will most likely pull your credit again, just before the loan closes, and if you have charged up your credit cards, it will have a negative impact on your credit scores. It may also change your debt-to-income ratio (see below). Either one could mean you won't get the loan at all, or the terms will be changed so the loan costs you more.

  We had a borrower who did not follow this advice and the loan was turned down. The lender sent us an email stating that the loan was denied because of low credit scores. We thought that was impossible since we had just pulled the credit ourselves, and the borrower had a 661 middle credit score. But after we reviewed the lender's credit report, we saw where the borrower had charged up her credit cards. Her scores dropped 36 points, which made it impossible to get the loan she wanted.

- *Do not overstate your income.* Be able to document how much income you earn. It is best to *round down*, as opposed to up. If you don't have proof, you can't use it. Being paid in cash is not proof.
- *Do not make any large purchases*, e.g. furniture or an automobile. Lenders check to see if you have made any sudden purchases that may impact your ability to repay your mortgage loan.
- *Do not apply for any credit*, including credit cards. Lenders and the credit bureaus believe if you apply for credit, it's your intention to use the credit. This impacts your score, because you're theoretically planning to increase your debt.

- *Do not co-sign for ANYONE!* Co-signing for someone basically means you are prepared to take over the payments. We can't begin to share with you how many times we hear from people how their grown children or friends ruined the considerate gesture of the co-signor. So unless you are going to check that the payments are being made on time every month, or you're in a position to pay the debt yourself, don't do it.

Mistake # 17: *Quitting your job before you close on your loan*

- *Do not change your employment status.* DO NOT, and I mean, absolutely DO NOT, quit your job before you close. Home buyers sometimes think that if they have already been approved for a home loan, they will be fine quitting or changing jobs. Lenders get a little fidgety when they see you job hop even if there's more money in it for you, unless it's within the same industry. Lenders often verify employment before closing.
- *Do not have your credit pulled unnecessarily.* This act is defined as an *inquiry*. Lenders view an inquiry on your credit history as a potential for more debt. Too many inquiries will negatively affect your credit score.
- *Pay ALL bills on time.* Need we say more?
- *Do not cancel or close credit accounts that show excellent payment histories.* Accounts with excellent payment histories, even if you don't use the account any longer, are positive and helpful to building your scores. So keep all good trades and don't close them out.
- *Do not spend any of the money you have set aside for closing or down payment.*
- *Provide all paperwork requested by the loan provider immediately.*
- *If you're refinancing, continue to make your mortgage payments until it is time to close on your new loan.* And even then, verify with the closer that the first lender is not expecting any more payments. Do not miss a payment because you think

you will soon be signing off on the new loan's paperwork. Keep in mind, when you make a payment, you are actually paying your mortgage in arrears. That is, making a payment in August pays for your ownership of the property in July.

Mr. and Mrs. Rodriquez were first-time homebuyers and our clients. We sat down together and took them through the home-buying process. We specifically discussed not only the process but all the things they should NOT do while applying for a home loan. Everything went well; they initialed and signed our forms, stating they understood what we explained to them.

During the meeting to sign and close the loan, the escrow officer (the title company's representative who handles the paperwork on behalf of the lenders), handed me the phone. It was the lender calling. We could not imagine what he wanted to discuss at this late date. Both the sellers and the buyers were in the conference room, preparing to sign all documents.

We'll never forget this conversation.

"Are you aware that your clients recently purchased a truck?" the lender asked.

"Oh no," I said, "not my clients! My clients received very strict instructions not to purchase anything."

"Well, Ms. Walters, I am afraid your clients did not listen to you, and because we pulled the credit report and noticed this additional debt, we will not be able to provide funding for this loan."

We knew this was a mistake so I asked the lender to give me a few minutes to talk with our clients. We stepped out of the room and asked Mr. and Mrs. Rodriquez if they recently purchased a new truck. They looked at us like children who were caught stealing from the cookie jar. How could this be? We were very clear about not making any purchases.

Mr. Rodriquez said, "Well, yes, but the truck salesman told us the truck payment would not show up on our credit for at least 30 days so we had nothing to worry about."

Well, the truck salesperson was right. The loan would not show up on the credit report for 30 days, but the *inquiry* showed up the day the credit was pulled. The underwriter got wind the borrower was either contemplating or making the purchase. To make a long story short, my clients walked out of the title company not owning a new home. They had a new truck, but no place to park it.

Lenders will often pull credit reports a second time, in addition to the one the loan officer initially pulled. They are searching for recent inquires and changes to the credit report which could prevent the borrower from paying the mortgage. Even if the borrower thinks he'll have no trouble making an additional payment each month, the mortgage lender structured and offered the loan believing there would be no other new debt.

The moral of the story is anything can happen right up to the last hour, so follow your loan officer's guidance. If you are uncertain about purchasing anything before you've completely signed all the paperwork and taken possession of your new home, the safest answer is NO!

Writing a Letter of Explanation

Prior to 2008, almost all lenders accepted written letters of explanation for negative credit issues. Because of today's higher foreclosure rates, and with stricter guidelines in place, many lenders refuse to look at written explanations.

This is where a good loan officer can help you locate a lender who will accept a letter of explanation. Lenders are human too, and in most cases they will work with you if their guidelines allow it. They understand people lose jobs, get sick, or have other unavoidable problems.

After you find a lender who will accept a letter, write an explanation showing you at least tried to solve the problem. More importantly, show the problem was isolated and point out it happened some time ago. It helps if you have at least two years of good credit history since the incident, which makes it less likely to happen again. If the lender asks you to write a letter, do it! If they accept your explanation, they may approve your loan.

Questions and Answers About Credit

Q: Is it smart to close all of my credit cards before I apply for a mortgage loan?
A: Your credit score will not be harmed by open credit cards and, in most cases, if they're in good standing, they will help. *An outstanding balance of more than 50% of the credit limit hurts your score.*

Q: Will one late payment hurt a good FICO Score?
A: Late payments will hurt you; even one late payment can drop your score from 50 – 100 points. Being late on your mortgage payment can stop you from getting a new mortgage for a new home.

Q: Will it take seven years to improve my credit score once I've had problems?
A: You can improve your credit in a short period of time. Most mortgage lenders look at a two-year history when making a mortgage loan decision. The most recent entries carry more weight than older ones. However, it does take seven years for a derogatory (negative) entry to be removed.

Q: If I pay my bad debt, will it be taken off my credit report?
A: Sorry to tell you this, but most bad debt, charge-offs and late payments will stay on your credit for seven years. But the credit bureaus will allow you to give an explanation on your credit report, or to dispute the debt.

Q: Will checking my credit score drop my score?

A: This is a tricky one. *You* can check your score as many times as *you* want within a 30-day period and your score will not be affected, if you do this through www.freecreditreportguide.org. When you're shopping for a mortgage, however, it is not a good idea to have multiple mortgage companies or businesses in other industries pull your credit, e.g., a mortgage company and a car dealership. Your score can drop as much as 10-20 points even if they tell you it won't be affected. Try not to do it. Sometimes one point can make a big difference between being able to go prime vs. sub-prime.

Q: Will it cost money to fix the mistakes on my credit report?

A: There are people and companies who will charge a fee to fix errors on your credit report, but you can do the same thing yourself by contacting the three credit bureaus. By law, a bureau has to correct any mistakes found on your credit report. You simply need to contact them in writing and work with them to correct the errors.

Tips on How to Improve Your Credit Scores

Here are a few tips to improve your credit scores before you start looking for that new house:

- Pay your bills on time, and pay at least the minimum amount due.
- Contact your creditors immediately if you miss a payment, and work out a payment plan before they report you to the credit bureaus.
- Do not close credit card accounts in good standing. These accounts show you have a record of managing your debt responsibly. Someone with no history of credit is seen as a higher risk.
- Avoid charging to the limit on your credit cards. It is better to spread out your charges on two or more cards than to max out one card.
- Ask creditors to raise your credit limit so you do not appear over-extended.

- Do not open new accounts, which imply you're acquiring new debt. This will lower your score.
- Aim for a rich mix of credit; for example, revolving credit (credit cards, department store credit cards) and installment debt (car loans, student loans).
- Correct errors on your credit report.
- If you suspect your creditor should be reporting positive information to the bureaus but isn't, contact the creditor or the bureaus directly to set the record straight.

Do not assume that a high salary guarantees a good credit score. Find out the key factors dragging down your score so you can fix them. Once you are comfortable with where you stand in regards to your credit report the next phase will be to fill out the loan application.

The Application Process

The Fannie Mae/Freddie Mac standardized *Form 1003* is the most commonly-used application for home mortgage loans. This form is also used for FHA and VA loans. You can find a copy of the Form 1003 on our website at www.MakeNoMistakes.com. The purpose of the loan application is obviously to apply for a mortgage loan but it's also used to prepare for the seller's request of a pre-qualification or pre-approval letter and to address any potential qualifying obstacles the borrower may have. For example, any one of the items listed below can pose difficulties for a borrower:

- **Low credit scores** – At the time of this writing, a score below 620 is considered low.
- **Collections** – Creditors, such as utility and medical companies, tax liens, bankruptcy status and judgments against you, fall under this category. These creditors sometimes are overlooked by sub-prime lenders, but never by prime lenders.
- **Limited trade lines** – A term used to describe that you currently have no creditors or less than three to which you are making monthly payments.

- **No open trade lines** – This is similar to limited trade lines except you may have had some creditors who extended credit to you in the past, but do not report to the credit bureaus.
- **No rental history** – You have not established yourself as a renter with a landlord.
- **Short employment** – You have been in your place of employment less than two years or have not been in the same profession for more than two years.
- **Source of cash for down payment and settlement costs** – Funds have to come from sources that are acceptable to your lender. A loan from a friend may not be acceptable, however, a gift from a friend or family member may.
- **Income and expenses** – The underwriter may not accept the borrower's entire income, which will increase the debt-to-income ratio. Common examples of income that's not acceptable to an underwriter are:

  - Income that is not proven by a W-2
  - Income not proven by a 1099 Tax Information Statement
  - Income from child support and alimony that are not paid and documented through the court system

Sometimes it's not only about finding the lender who is willing to loan you the money at a reasonable rate, but finding one who is willing to overcome qualification problems. Most lenders are on guard now because of the worsening economy. As a result they have tightened their lending guidelines. Having a loan officer who will go to bat for you becomes valuable in these situations.

Pre-Qualification vs. Pre-Approval

In today's real estate market few agents will waste time showing you homes if you are not *pre-qualified* or *pre-approved* first. Though neither designation truly guarantees you'll get the loan, there are always additional steps required. And whenever there are additional steps, anything can go awry.

Mistake # 18: *Getting pre-qualified and not pre-approved*

A pre-qualification is not highly regarded since all that is required is for the borrower to fill out a loan application and a credit report review. Based on what the borrower *states* in the loan application and the credit report, *the loan officer* will determine the borrower's eligibility for a loan and the dollar amount. At this stage, no employment, rental history or income *verification* has been done on the borrower.

The pre-approval indicates that the loan officer has reviewed your credit report, financial history, rental history, pay stubs, W-2's, tax returns, etc., and verified your employment. ***Preapproval indicates to sellers that you are a serious home buyer who has taken the additional steps to qualify.***

Mistake # 19: *Believing you are approved when there are conditions*

If you look closely at your pre-approval letter you may see that it actually states that you are "pre-approved *with conditions*." But what does "pre-approved with conditions" mean? Each completed phase of the mortgage process leads to an "approval." The word "approval" in the mortgage business means many things. It's used loosely and is often interpreted as getting the money to purchase your home. That's not always the case. Typically, this is when buyers' stress and tension levels go up. Most people only hear "you're approved," and they don't understand what "with conditions" mean. Loan conditions mean your loan is approved conditionally. There's a big "if" involved. Below are typical examples of conditions under which loans may be approved. In fact, as you review each one, repeat this sentence before each example and you'll clearly understand what conditions are. "We, the lender, will loan you your requested amount if you…"

- Provide copies of your children's birth certificates
- Explain why you filed for bankruptcy four years ago
- Prove that your child support payments are current
- Provide a copy of your tax returns

- Provide a letter from your lender showing your student loans are deferred, and for how long

Some conditions are easy to meet, while others are a lot more difficult and challenging. This is when working with an experienced loan officer pays off! Sometimes the conditions seem outlandish, ridiculous and crazy. Trust us when we tell you the loan officer and his processor know asking for documentation is going to frustrate you. This is often the least favorite part of their jobs. *You should view this process, however, as if you were lending someone $200,000. Wouldn't you want to know and see everything?* We know your answer is *yes*! The key is to remain calm and don't get frustrated with the process. Get the underwriters what they need. Delaying or debating simply delays your loan and causes your stress level to go up! Remember, the loan officer's job is to put together a compelling loan package. The goal is to show the lender and underwriter you are worth the risk, based on the information provided. Therefore, do your part and provide all the information that is requested of you. There will be more discussion on the loan process in Chapter 19.

In Summary, your credit is important. Heed your loan officer's advice in regards to what you should **not** do when applying for a mortgage and during the purchasing process. Your credit does not have to be perfect to own a home. It does have to be decent. The higher the credit score, however, the better the interest rate and terms on the loan – if you know how to look for the right deal and ask for it.

If you have bad credit or worry about your rating, you're not alone. Millions of Americans face or will face problems with their credit. Start making necessary credit repairs 90 to 120 days before you start shopping for a house. You'll benefit for the rest of your life, every time you need to borrow money to make a purchase, because you decided to repair your credit.

If you would like more information on credit reports, refer to www.freecreditreportguide.org. At this site, you'll find information on:

- How credit reporting actually works

- How to get your free credit report
- Ways to avoid identity theft
- Ways to improve your credit score

Your goal when you initially fill out an application is to receive a pre-qualification or a pre-approval letter, so you can begin the search process. However, note that there are always conditions associated with your pre-approval so prepare yourself to be responsive when that time comes.

Pass The Knowledge On!

CHAPTER 7

TAKING OWNERSHIP CORRECTLY

In this chapter you will learn about several forms of *legal ownership*, which is – for the purpose of ownership – how your name is listed on the title of the property or the mortgage loan. Choosing incorrectly could cost you thousands!

Mistake # 20: *Not knowing which form of ownership you should use*

The way you take ownership is a very important factor because it affects who:

1. Has the right to sell the property
2. Will own the property upon the current owner's death
3. Is responsible for the mortgage loan
4. Gets to take advantage of the tax benefits

These factors are important to know – and discuss – before two or more people buy property together. If you're a single person, your decisions should be based only on your desires. As a married couple, or as business partners, you should discuss how divorce, death and other significant changes impact home ownership.

In the next few pages, we'll provide several examples of when to use different forms of ownership. But first, let's define them. Here are the three main forms of ownership:

- **Severalty** - The title is held by *one* owner.
- **Co-Ownership** - The title is held by *two or more* persons.
- **In Trust** - Often referred to as simply "a trust," this is a tool a *third-party* person uses to hold the property's title for the benefit of one or more other people.

Forms of ownership are state-specific. Some states, for example, allow married couples to own real estate under community property laws. This simply means *what's yours, is mine*, if it was acquired by one spouse (as opposed to both spouses jointly buying the property) during the marriage. ***Make sure you know if your state is a community property state, especially if only one spouse is purchasing the property.*** We suggest you talk with your real estate agent or seek legal advice about the various options.

When there is more than one person involved in the purchase of property there are *two* aspects to consider:

1. Who is going to pay for it
2. Who has rights of ownership in the property

Mistake # 21: *Buying property based on "I Love You"*

Let's talk about these two important points now. This topic, difficult though it may be, needs to be covered. We have seen many unmarried couples who, based on their plans to get married or move in together, purchase real estate together. This can sometimes be a huge mistake! People in love and planning to get married don't like to think about what seems impossible – that they won't actually get married. Yet so many things can get in the way of a couple actually walking down the aisle. This is just too big of a problem to sort out if the wedding doesn't happen. The real problem is when the marriage doesn't happen and only *one person* has signed his or her name on the mortgage loan, yet *both* people have legal ownership in the property.

Henry and Sharon were in love and were planning their wedding. Neither of them could imagine one without the other. They found the perfect home, and because Henry had the stronger income and better credit score, they took out the mortgage loan in his name. Sharon wasn't working at the time and couldn't contribute financially. Henry paid the down payment and all closing costs, yet the ownership title was in both their names.

Before they married, Henry decided he preferred life as a bachelor. He broke up with Sharon, who was – naturally – upset. Henry wanted to sell the house. Sharon was upset about the break up and told him he could sell it only if he agreed to pay her $20,000 from the profits and equity of the property. Henry needed her signature in order to sell it, so he agreed.

Consequently, Henry has spent $20,000 (the amount he paid Sharon), the down payment, and the closing costs on the loan when he purchased the property. We can only hope that the property gained value while he owned it, and he was able to sell it at a price high enough to recoup the money he put into it. Sharon, on the other hand, has a broken heart – and $20,000 in cash.

Real estate is a serious commitment and investment. You should view it in terms of a business arrangement. Do not allow emotions to interfere with your decisions unless you have money to lose. Better yet, decide upfront how you will handle the sale of the property if the marriage does not take place. Let's discuss the various forms of ownership you should consider:

Severalty

If you purchase the property in severalty, you are the only party: a party of one. Let's return to our original four points to help determine which type of ownership is best for you:

1. *Who has the right to sell the property?* You are the sole owner, so you have the right to sell it.
2. *Who will own the property upon death?* You will have to will[34] the property to your heir(s).
3. *Who is responsible for the note?* If there is a mortgage note on the property you are responsible for paying it.
4. *Who is affected – positively or negatively – by the tax implications?* You are solely responsible for any taxes owed. You can also take the tax benefits.

Co-Ownership

If you decide to own the property with someone else, then the agreement must state the percent interest each party owns in the property, unless it's owned equally. Forms of co-ownership are:

- Joint tenancy
- Tenancy in common
- Community property

Joint Tenancy – The interest in the property is owned by two or more people with the *right of survivorship.*[35] This means the interest in the property transfers from one owner tenant to the other on death, as you'd expect it to between a husband and wife. Unlike tenancy in common, where one person can transfer ownership upon death, in joint tenancy the last survivor takes the title in severalty, as an individual.

1. *Who has the right to sell the property?* If the joint owners must mutually agree to sell the property, they must equally divide the proceeds of the sale.

---

[34] A *will* is a legal document that dictates your wishes your death.

[35] *Right of survivorship* means the last owner living owns all the property, and on his or her death, the property will become part of that person's estate. An owner who died earlier cannot leave it behind for his or her heirs.

2. *Who will own the property upon my death?* Interest passes from one owner to the other surviving owner, like in husband and wife.

3. *Who pays the mortgage loan, and does the creditor have any rights to the property?* Who pays the mortgage is determined by the owner. All parties have equal ownership in the property. However, it is possible to have just one of the party members liable to the lender for a mortgage note while all parties enjoy the benefits equally. On the other hand, if the mortgage note is not paid the lender has the right to foreclose the property. The options are to continue making payments, have the mortgage paid off by a life insurance policy or mortgage protection insurance, refinance it or pay it off from the proceeds of the estate.

4. *Who has the tax implications?* The owners share them equally.

Joint tenancy works well when both spouses are still alive. When the first spouse dies, ownership transfers to the second spouse. It can become a problem if the second spouse dies and there is no provision as to how the property is transferred. This could leave the ownership question up to the probate court to decide. See Chapter 23 for more information on probate.

Furthermore, if you later decide to add your children or other heirs to the title to your home, you may have created a taxable event. Gift taxes are owed in the year you add people's names to any of your assets that have a value of over $10,000. This also makes that person named a co-owner of your property and if he is sued, files for bankruptcy or gets divorced, *then your assets would be listed as part of his holdings. Which means his creditors would have access to your possession as a result of his actions.*

Tenancy in Common – An agreement in which each owner holds his or her fractional interest in the property in severalty. This means they can sell, convey,[36] mortgage or transfer interest *without* the consent of the other owners or "right of survivorship." It's more and more

---

[36] To *convey* interest in a property means to transfer ownership from one person to another via a written form, such as a deed.

common to see residential property purchases structured this way. As property prices rise, a tenancy in common ownership allows buyers to pool their resources and buy more real estate than they could or would on their own. This type of co-ownership allows each co-owner to choose who will inherit his or her ownership interest on death.

How does tenancy in common stand up against our four points for choosing the form of ownership?

1. *Who has the right to sell the property?* You have the right to sell *your interest* in the property, though we are seeing more written language giving the other owner(s) the "rights of first refusal," as well as buyer approval to make sure the prospective owner is qualified.
2. *Who will own the property upon your death?* Each owner has the right to leave his or her share of the property to any beneficiary on the owner's death. If there is no will, the interest will pass to the deceased's heir(s).
3. *Who pays the mortgage loan?* All names on the mortgage note are equally responsible, in the eyes of the lender, to pay the note. The terms of how it is paid – and who pays how much – should be done in a separate agreement among the owners. The lender is not interested in how the property is divided or who is paying how much, but only that the mortgage loan is paid. If the loan defaults, everyone listed on the mortgage note will suffer the consequences equally.
4. *Who has the tax implications?* The owners will decide the fractional tax interests.

The two most common mistakes in creating a tenancy in common or a co-ownership agreement are:

1. Deciding "we'll just work out the details later" to avoid confrontation.
2. Assuming everything will work out exactly as planned.

The reality is life happens and so do disputes. For these reasons we strongly suggest you work with an attorney, who will ask you a series of "what if" questions before moving forward. Your answers to these questions will point you toward the best form of ownership for you.

Community Property – Nine states (Arizona, California, Idaho, Louisiana, Nevada, New Mexico, Texas, Washington and Wisconsin) adopted community property laws. The laws are based on the theory that both husband and wife are equal partners rather than one entity. Thus, any property acquired during the marriage is considered mutually owned, with a 50-50 partnership.

1. *Who has the right to sell the property?* Both signatures are required in order to sell, convey, mortgage or transfer interest.
2. *Who will own the property upon one person's death?* The surviving spouse inherits the property, if the surviving children are common to both spouses. If the person who died didn't have a will, the surviving spouse still gets to keep his or her own share, but the other half is given to the children of the deceased spouse.
3. *Who pays the mortgage loan, and does the creditor have any rights to the property?* Because one spouse died, only the second spouse's name remains on the mortgage loan. That person is completely responsible for the debt, at least in the eyes of the lender. If the loan defaults, only the remaining spouse will suffer the consequences; the decedent's credit is not tarnished.
4. *What are the tax implications?* The owners will equally share the tax interests.

Of course, when a married couple divorces in a community property state, nearly anything can happen in terms of how the real estate is divided. If this happens to you, be sure to change the ownership names on both the property's title *and* on the mortgage loan. It's usually easier to change the ownership names on the title than it is on the loan. You need to do both, however, because if both spouses' names are left on the mortgage note, they're both still responsible for paying it, in the eyes of the lender. And remember, if the spouse who receives the property pays more than 30 days late on a mortgage payment, the lender will send negative reports to the credit agencies for *both* spouses because both names remain on the loan.

This happens all too often, and it can be a real pain to go back and fix. It can also be a very unpleasant surprise. Get outside help or advice if you need it to accomplish these two changes.

Separate Property – Property owned prior to the marriage or acquired through an inheritance or by gift. It also includes any property acquired with separate funds, perhaps as a result of an insurance settlement or a contractual agreement with the other spouse. Separate property can be sold, conveyed, mortgaged or transferred *without the consent* of the non-owning spouse. What makes this law interesting is if there is an improvement made to the property and if any part of that improvement debt was paid from community funds. If that happens, the non-owning spouse may be entitled to an interest in the property. Also, income earned from this separate property can be considered community property. Talk to your accountant or attorney if you'd like more information on keeping income earned from a separate property *out of* community property. Remember, this is only a concern in the nine community property states listed above.

1. *Who has the right to sell the property?* Separate property can be sold, conveyed, mortgaged or transferred *without the consent* of the non-owning spouse.
2. *Who will own the property upon my death?* When the owner of the separate property dies and leaves no will, the surviving spouse may acquire the property, but unlike joint tenancy, either spouse may will his half-interest to others if he or she so chooses.
3. *Who pays the mortgage loan, and does the creditor have any rights to the property?* The separate person listed on the mortgage note. The creditor only has rights to the property if the mortgage note is not paid.
4. *Who has the tax implications – both good and bad?* The separate owner has the tax implications.

However, mistakes that often occur with separate property include commingling and transmutation. Commingling occurs when separate and marital assets are combined and there is no distinction between separate and marital property. To prevent a finding from a divorce court, spouses need to keep separate, clear and accurate accounts for each item of property.

Transmutation involves separate property that the spouses have treated as marital property, making it impossible to tell what type of property the spouses had intended it to be, even though, in reality, only one of the spouses paid for the property.

Another problem in the case of divorce relates to the property valuation date. The valuation date is sometimes used to determine an amount or a fraction of the property's value the spouse receives. Some examples of valuation dates are the date of trial, the date of separation, the divorce date, or the hearing date. Based on this it could serve as either an advantage or disadvantage depending on which side you're on. Again, it is best to have ownership discussions with a licensed attorney.

Trust

This is an entity developed to transfer ownership of property to a third party who will manage or hold it for the benefit of one or more other people. There are various forms of trusts and we strongly suggest you contact your attorney for the best option. See Chapter 23 for more information on how wills and trusts can affect ownership status of real estate.

In Summary, failing to investigate your ownership options can cost you or your loved ones thousands! Take these four factors into consideration:

1. Who has the right to sell the property
2. Who will own the property upon the current owner's death
3. Who's responsible for the mortgage loan
4. Who gets to take advantage of the tax benefits

Decide early on which form of ownership you're interested in and keep your emotions out of the decision. Simply making a decision because you are in love today could prove to be costly if you fall out of love tomorrow. Consult an attorney if you have questions.

Pass The Knowledge On!

CHAPTER 8

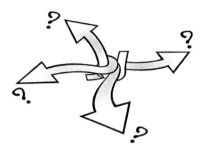

WHERE DO YOU GO FOR FINANCING?

In this chapter you will learn the mistakes to avoid while you find financing for your real estate purchase. Choosing the wrong loan product can cost you thousands. We will discuss various financing sources and how you can use this information to choose for yourself the best product, without having to completely rely on whatever your loan officer offers you.

If borrowers are ever intimidated, it's during the financing stage, so they tend to not ask questions. *Financing* your home is important, maybe even as important as *finding* your dream home. You may think you are buying a house, but what you're truly buying is a *mortgage note*. In actuality, not finding the right mortgage will most likely turn a dream home into a nightmare. The wrong mortgage product can mean the difference between enjoying your home for years to come and facing foreclosure. Just ask the thousands who have lost their homes. To prevent foreclosure from happening, borrowers should understand their own budgets, decide the mortgage products that best fit their situation and be prepared to ask questions when they don't understand something.

Before we begin, let's first be clear on several words which are often used interchangeably in the mortgage lending business. One of them is *lender*. Depending on whom you are talking with, a lender's role can mean a variety of things. The actual definition of a lender is someone who lends money. There are a number of sources who can provide financing, but they are not all lenders. The most common institutions that specialize in mortgage lending are banks, credit unions and mortgage bankers, all of which are known as the primary market.[37] Also, you will find that these lending institutions often categorize themselves into prime lenders or subprime lenders depending on the types of products they offer and the guidelines they use. The same financial institution can certainly wear both hats. Let's look at defining both prime and subprime lenders.

Prime Lenders

Prime lenders usually offer the lowest rates with the lowest fees, but only to those with excellent credit. This means no late mortgage payments or any other late payments within the last 24 months. Prime borrowers should also have a debt-to-income ratio (see Chapter 4 for more information) of 40% or less, meaning your monthly debt payments should equal 40% or less of your monthly income. For example, if your income is $5,000 a month, your monthly revolving debt[38] should be no more than $2,000 a month.

With a few late payments on your credit report you may still get approved with a prime lender, but your rates will probably be higher. You may be able to offset this with a down payment of 5% or more, or by showing large cash assets in your account. In today's credit market, those who have some credit problems should consider a FHA or VA loan. There is more information on this subject in Chapter 12.

---

[37] The *primary markets* are those lenders who *provide* mortgages to consumers. Primary market lenders sell consumers' home loans to the secondary market for a profit, which frees up primary lenders' money so they can offer even more loans to the public.

[38] Monthly *revolving debt* is the monthly debt reported to the credit bureau each month as paid or late. Therefore, your cellular, light and water bills would not show up unless you choose not to pay them at all or not for very long stretches of time, which would then be reported as collections.

Sub-Prime Lenders

Sub-prime lenders seldom, if ever, identify themselves as such. In fact, many of them went out of business due to the high rate of foreclosures. Some were independent, but many were affiliates of prime lenders operating under different names. The only clear giveaways were that the interest rates the sub-prime loans offered were typically higher than those quoted by prime lenders, and they came with a two- or three-year prepayment penalty.[39]

Sub-prime lenders take a higher risk when they lend, so they must cover the costs associated with this. Their loans go into default far more often than prime loans. You'll want to avoid sub-prime lenders if you qualify for prime financing. However, not everyone can do this.

Most borrowers seek financing from sub-prime lenders for the following reasons:

- Their credit scores range from low to average
- They have a smaller down payment amount
- Their debt-to-income ratios are greater than 40% (some prime lenders have ceilings at 38%), whereas some subprime lenders go as high as 55%
- The borrowers don't have an ability to document income and other assets
- They lack knowledge about various loan products
- They fear their local banks' rejection

As of 2009, many subprime lenders are back and as strong as ever. *Be Alert! They have rebranded themselves with the help of the Federal Housing Administration by shifting their business to FHA loans.* For a person who lost hope of owning a home when the sub-prime market collapsed, FHA-backed loans have become the other

---

[39] A *prepayment penalty* is a charge the borrower pays when a mortgage is paid off before a certain period of time elapses, which allows the lender to avoid significant losses (of anticipated earnings) due to the borrower refinancing with a different lender or even selling the house.

option. Though FHA is a government entity who sets guidelines and rules for your FHA-backed home mortgage loan, it doesn't stop loan officers from working the system to charge unnecessary fees. *Always start with a prime lender first before exploring options with a subprime lender.* There's more discussion on this subject in Chapter 12. Let's now take a look at the difference between various financial institutions.

Banks

A bank is a financial institution that provides financial services, usually for profit. Banks accept deposits from customers and, in turn, make loans based on those deposits. Traditional banking services involve lending money and processing simple to complex transactions, including mortgage loans. Banks loan money from their depositors, and banks profit from interest they earn on loans. Lending helps banks make money, so never be afraid to approach a bank. They need *you* to increase their profits.

Banks are typically prime lenders. If you're considering a bank as your lender, keep in mind banks are limited by their own guidelines and regulations, which are usually very strict. To be more competitive most banks have expanded their product lines to include FHA–backed loans.

Credit Unions

A credit union is owned and controlled by its members. The membership is restricted to a defined group of people. An example may be employees of specific companies, or people who live, work, worship, or attend school in a certain area, or are part of a particular occupational group, like teachers. Only members are entitled to borrow money from credit unions. As a lender, credit unions are not subject to the same kind of regulations as a traditional bank.

Since you are a partial owner of the credit union at which you do business, it is a great place for you to apply for a loan. It's always to your advantage if your lender knows you, and this is more likely the case if you're with a credit union. Even if your credit score is poor, sometimes credit unions can rely on other factors to determine if you are credit worthy.

What is a Mortgage *Banker*?

A mortgage banker is a state-licensed banking entity which makes mortgage loans directly to borrowers. Mortgage bankers do not offer commercial banking services, which mean they do not receive income from checking or savings account deposits. They simply offer mortgages. Mortgage bank lenders fund loans with their own money, and then sell the mortgages to such secondary lenders as Fannie Mae or Freddie Mac. This sale returns to the mortgage bank most of the money it loaned to the borrower. The mortgage banker, however, still has a small interest in the mortgage, so the bank continues to receive a small percentage of the interest paid each month by the borrower.

Mortgage banks also have strict guidelines and regulations. A typical mortgage banker's business model is structured so that, in the event a loan he or she funded defaults, the mortgage banker may be required to buy back the loan from the secondary market[40] and even pay penalties. This business model forces mortgage bankers to have higher lending standards. Mortgage banks generally operate under the banking laws of the states in which they do business. For a complete list of mortgage bankers, check with your state banking or financial department.

What Is a Mortgage *Broker*?

Many people use mortgage brokers, especially if they were turned down or had bad experiences with their local banks. Mortgage brokers

---

[40] The *secondary mortgage market* is where primary market lenders sell mortgages, which gives them new funds to offer more mortgages to new borrowers. Keeping mortgages the full 15 or 30 years would quickly use up primary lenders' funds. If this happened, homebuyers would have a more difficult time finding mortgage lenders.

are not banks, so they do not lend money and cannot be referred to as lenders. They represent many lenders, both prime and sub-prime. Mortgage brokers are the salespeople for banks, mortgage bankers and others who offer mortgages but don't want to deal directly with the public. Mortgage brokers sometimes specialize in different types of loans, such as FHA loans, bad credit loans, no down payment or no credit loans. These loans offer more flexibility for consumers who may not have excellent credit scores. Mortgage brokers should be well-versed in providing credit advice to consumers who have problems qualifying for loans. Mortgage brokers can do this, however, only after they take a borrower's application and review the credit report. After that, they shop[41] the loan and perhaps even lock the rate with the chosen lender.

Mortgage brokers earn fees for providing services to borrowers which include taking the application, assembling all the documentation, finding the best lender and working out any problems after the borrower accepts and signs off on the loan. They don't receive a fee from the lender unless the borrower actually closes on the mortgage, thus brokers are motivated to produce complete and timely loan packages.

Sometimes borrowers try to go directly to the bank the mortgage broker is dealing with, thinking they can save on the mortgage broker fee. This is usually not successful. A bank would not take the chance of losing many loans a mortgage broker can bring, in exchange for one borrower -- you. Don't do this unless you want to take a chance of destroying the relationship you have with your mortgage broker.

What is a Branching Company?

One of the unique things about branching companies is that they can be either a broker, banker or both. They sign up brokers and loan officers to work as a net branch of their company. They handle all back office needs, such as accounting, payroll, state compliance and licensing for

---

[41] *Shop* is terminology describing the act of the loan officer searching for appropriate rates and terms among various lenders.

the net branch, or the branch can, in some cases, choose to do this for themselves. The loan officers in the branch don't have to be licensed by the state if the branching company is a bank. They work under the license of the bank. Most have a unique broker/banker/branch strategy that gives them the power of working like a broker and using the leverage of a bank. When working with a branching company, watch out for the fees. Some fees are obvious while others tend to be hidden, and depending on the specifics of the mortgage package and the company itself, there can be even more fees added to the standard amount.

Online Lenders

Online lenders offer loans via their websites to borrowers. Generally speaking, online lenders provide loan information, application forms, mortgage rates and mortgage calculators right on their websites. The online applications are transmitted over an *encrypted* web page for security. Ideally an online lender will provide a prominent telephone number offering assistance to borrowers as well. Also, many online companies take applications and then forward them to various lenders who actually make the loans. These lenders then contact the borrowers for details and inquire about which loan products the borrowers want.

People are so busy today they like everything to be just a click away. To accommodate the needs of busy borrowers, most mortgage companies have created online websites. If you go this route, your application will be reviewed and then you will need to provide other details such as your income level, amount of savings and credit report information, for example. Then, in most cases, you will wait for a quotation, which can take anywhere from a few minutes to a couple of days. Beware if it comes back too quickly. This could indicate the online lender is just giving teaser rates to try to lock you in as a borrower. Companies use teaser rates, often times a "start rate" to keep you interested, stop you from shopping elsewhere, and capture your contact information. Teaser rates usually come with other stipulations, such as higher fees to make up for their low teaser rates. Unfortunately, you may not be aware of these fees until you have fully committed to the loan – meaning, you have provided documentation they requested and maybe even paid an application fee. Teaser rates with higher loan fees are an indication you should run in the other direction!

You will also see many lenders quoting very low interest rates on their websites, which do not take into consideration your complete financial picture. Many factors influence a lender's decision.

Lenders have a "start" rate for each of their various types of mortgages. The lender typically advertises this rate. A par or a "start" rate is aptly named because it's where the lender starts when determining your rate. You will have "adds" and "deducts" from the start rate to determine what rate you end up with. This is where most borrowers get into trouble because all they hear or see is the start rate. Once that rate is fixed in their minds they do not want to listen to facts or what their real rate will be. This is why quoting the start rate works so well to get the borrowers' business. Be aware few borrowers end up with the advertised start rate.

Mistake # 22: *Shopping for your loan on the internet only*

Shopping for a mortgage over the internet has advantages and disadvantages. The first *advantage* is you don't have to go through the tiring process of meeting different lenders; you can shop and compare many loans on your own. Obtaining a mortgage loan quote does not cost you anything but a small amount of time. You can also shop 24/7, so if you work all day, you can do your mortgage shopping at night when traditional mortgage offices are closed.

A *disadvantage* of shopping online is simply the anonymous nature of the internet. You don't know who you're dealing with, yet you give this person access to all of your *personal information*, such as your social security number, date of birth and bank account numbers. If you wish to use the internet to shop for a loan, we highly recommend you stay local and find a person whose office you can visit and whose hand you can shake.

We are not proponents of purchasing a mortgage loan over the internet, unless you live and do business in a very remote area where there are very few choices. If you choose a local lender who directs you to the company's website to continue the process, by all means do so. Just make sure the website is secure before you enter in your personal information. You can verify this when you see the "s" following the "http" in the browser when you type their website address, that *https:// www.* But, we recommend you not make a buying decision based solely on information you found on the internet. Every city has mortgage brokers, banks, and credit unions willing to loan money. So the question becomes, why would you want to deal with someone whom you can't find if there is a problem?

A married couple – who had just become new clients of ours -- attended one of our seminars where we typically discuss our opinions and thoughts about using the internet to shop for a mortgage loan. The clients, JD and Teresa, chose not to listen to our advice and soon faced a rude awakening.

Using the internet, they found a company located in another part of the state to complete their loan application and find a mortgage rate. On the phone, the loan officer, John, was very pleasant, and systematically answered JD and Teresa's questions, as well as ours. Naturally, we asked about the fees John listed on the loan paperwork. John assured all of us that, while the numbers shown were estimates, the actual figures would not vary by more than a couple of hundred dollars.

Well, closing day arrived. We met at the title company with all the necessary documents. JD and his wife had certified checks in hand and were ready to close. When we began to review the final numbers, however, the difference between John's earlier, estimated fees and the fees listed on the final paperwork was about $1,900, and not in our client's favor. Keep in mind it's a Friday, and JD and Teresa planned to move into the new house that weekend. No one could reach John, the loan officer, on either his office phone or cell phone. JD sat there, trying to figure out what to do, and hoping we wouldn't say, "We told you so." (We didn't, of course!)

Considering all this, these were JD and Teresa's options. Option #1: Wait to hear from John no matter how long it took and how much it inconvenienced everyone. This included the seller who expected to get his money that day, the title company official who had another client waiting in the reception area, the movers who were in the process of loading all JD and Teresa's furniture into a moving van, and the landlord who expected the rental to be vacant later that day.

Option #2: Let everyone know JD and Teresa would not sign the documents until the situation was straightened out to their satisfaction. Then thank everyone and leave the closing meeting.

Option #3: Cancel the deal completely and lose the money they already invested in the purchase, including earnest money, the cost of inspection, the option fee and the cost of the appraisal.

Option #4: Just sign the papers, write a personal check for the difference and chalk it up as a learning experience.

JD and Teresa chose option #4.

As you read this, you may believe you would choose option #2. However, real estate is unlike any other purchase you will ever make. It's often an emotional purchase, which causes people to do almost anything to get in the home – even disregard professional advice. And the mortgage industry knows this! Sometimes this works in their favor and they get away with adding new or higher fees at the last minute. Having a good coach by your side pays off at a time like this, if you listen!

Had JD chosen #1 or # 2 and decided to wait it out, once they finally reached the loan officer, he might have made the appropriate changes. Obviously, #2 (adjourning the meeting and not signing until everything is resolved) is more dramatic and would have been stressful to all parties involved. However, both scenarios would have taken a while to address because all changes must be approved by the lender and all the paperwork must be reprinted. It's also possible John, the loan officer, would have insisted on reaching a compromise with JD and Teresa on the fees.

Option #3 was certainly JD and Teresa's last resort, to be used if and when neither side was willing to budge.

The moral of the story is if JD and Teresa had chosen a local loan officer, they still might have paid about the same amount of money. However, it would have been easy enough to drive to the loan officer's office and insist on talking with someone when the office is only across town, at most. Instead, they had to deal with a surprise and the stress tied to this news. The most frustrating part of this situation, however, is the inability to reach their non-local loan officer or speak with anyone else in his office that could have helped rectify the situation. That would not have happened if JD and Teresa worked with a local loan officer.

Remember, these unethical sales tactics happen less often when buyers show the loan officer they have a keen eye for detail. That's why asking plenty of questions and using your checklists throughout the process are extremely important. Walking away from a deal that sounds too good to be true is always a challenge. Once a loan officer offers a borrower a low interest rate and/or low closing costs, borrowers have a hard time hearing anything else. Thus, they make decisions based on bogus information. Even if a different, more honest loan officer were to bring this situation to the borrower's attention, the second loan officer is not likely to get the deal because of the unrealistic expectations the first loan officer set. This is why option #4 (just sign and chalk it up as a learning experience) is so popular among some loan officers: because it usually pays off. The loan officer sold the borrower exactly what the borrower *wanted to hear*.

Though the states' mortgage lending departments frown on this type of business activity, there is just not enough manpower to deter this bad business behavior. It's more prevalent over the internet because of the lack of face-to-face communication. The online companies who use these unethical practices feel they have less accountability to their customers because they're not meeting the customers in person. And, unfortunately, it works.

If you do choose to use the internet, be sure to check out what other online shoppers have to say about a particular company. Go to www.consumeraffairs.com and search for any company you're considering using. Select *Finance* at the top of the home page, and then select *Mortgages,* where you'll find a list of lenders. Also if you find that you are a victim of this bait and switch type tactic contact your state Department of Savings and Mortgage Lending.

In Summary, mortgage lending institutions have been around for a long, long time and many changes have taken place in the way they do business, from walking into a bank building to surfing the internet. Yet some choices still remain difficult, such as which institution to select, and knowing who you can trust to not take advantage of your inexperience.

Prime lenders still offer the best rates, but you must have top-notch credit *and meet all their criteria.* There are still sub-prime lenders, but be sure to know all your options before you make a decision. The bottom line is it's still important to research a lender and ask the right questions. Online mortgage shopping may be the way of the future and may seem like a great idea, but nothing compares to dealing with a person you can call and see in a moment's notice.

Pass The Knowledge On!

CHAPTER 9

FINDING A GOOD LOAN OFFICER

In this chapter you will learn how to find a good loan officer and determine the most effective questions to ask in order to determine who will give you the best deal and do the best job. Doing a good job holds just as much weight as a good deal since working with a bad loan officer can cost you thousands! These costs can vary, from paying too many fees, to using the wrong loan product, to a delayed closing date.

Most people believe you should shop for a mortgage, but we believe you need to shop for a loan officer first, *then* the mortgage product. A good loan officer will work to understand you and your personal financial concerns. It's the loan officer who will make or break your financing experience.

A mortgage is a product sold by a lender, and it's true that most lenders sell the same or very similar products. This means you need someone who can guide you through this complicated maze called a loan process and communicate it in terms you can understand. At the same time, however, it's important that you not approach this process unprepared. Doing so will only show that you lack knowledge about mortgage financing, which could cost you thousands too!

A good loan officer will understand the ramifications of all your risk factors, and know how to make the deal happen. When you work with a good loan officer the opportunities are in the details. Examples include discovering the borrower needs more secure income to qualify for a loan, or knowing in advance the lender won't accept child support payments not paid through the court system, or finding a lender who will accept a high loan-to-value ratio on the loan.

Loan officers should already know which lenders will do what type of loans based on borrowers' circumstances. If loan officers are not good at paying attention to details, they will not only waste your time, but they can cause loans to be denied or delayed. They must be able to ask questions and have checklists in place to avoid any mistakes on their part. In this profession, experience pays dividends.

Mistake # 23: *Working with an inexperienced loan officer*

So where do you start? Begin with your good real estate agent, who will function like a coach. Your agent will probably have several potential loan officers in mind for you. Most likely, he or she will not refer someone to you who will fail to get the loan done on time or cause problems. But don't forget to ask such questions as, *"how many loans has this loan officer closed for you?"* If the officer has only closed a few for the agent, that agent doesn't really have enough experience to make a good referral.

If your agent is one of the top agents in your town, then you can usually consider that agent has found some of the best loan officers to be part of his or her team. Understand that good real estate agents are very busy. If they have to spend too much time tracking down the status of their client's loan, it's a problem for them. More than likely, the referred loan officers have earned the right to be on this agent's referral list and they want to stay there.

This should be a starting point for compiling your list of loan officers to interview. If you are taking out a jumbo, subprime, investment or reverse mortgage (all types of loans we'll cover later), you may want to talk with a loan officer who specializes in that type of loan. Loan officers often specialize in niche products or types of loans, and a borrower can benefit from their expertise.

Last but not least, ask your friends who they used for their mortgages. Ask if they had any problems and if they closed on time. Keep in mind that just because a loan officer worked well for them doesn't mean that loan officer will work well for you. That's why it's so important to take time out to interview three loan officers.

Professionalism is extremely important in the mortgage business. If you have ever worked with an unethical person, you know what we're talking about. Here's why: Your loan officer has your personal information, including your credit report, social security number, banking information, credit card account numbers and a copy of your driver's license, for starters. For this reason, you have to have confidence in who you're working with.

You must put the loan officers you interview to the test. What's your first impression of how they conduct themselves? Do they appear organized? Are they suitable for further interaction? Sad to say, but some loan officers will take advantage of borrowers they know lack the knowledge to understand what the loan officer will present them. They give the mortgage business a black eye, since they're doing what's best for them and not what's best for the borrower.

Continue to assess the loan officer's working style. Ask if the loan officer takes your application or if a data entry clerk takes it over the phone. This is a sign the loan officer may not be the person who actually works your loan, or it could mean the officer is new to the business. We believe it takes at least two years of full time work to become a seasoned loan officer. *Look for longevity and stability. They're both very important in today's troubled financial market, especially with so many changes occurring each day.* Not even the good loan officers can keep up with every change, and so they don't find out about some changes until they contact the lender or, in some cases, actually submit loans. Your loan officer should be able to move quickly before the next change occurs and without making costly mistakes, and submit a complete file to the lender so no time is wasted.

As the borrower, you will also be an important part of the team. You must be able to supply the information in a timely manner (usually ASAP) so you don't lose a great interest rate or a good lender because you couldn't do your part before the criteria for the loan changed.

Here's a list of mistakes and poor character traits which will help you spot a loan officer who might not do the best job for you. Beware of a loan officer who:

- Doesn't know the mortgage products
- Doesn't return phone calls in a timely manner
- Is always in a rush to close your loan
- Doesn't take time to answer your questions
- Is not clear when answering your questions
- Doesn't take time to explain the loan process
- Doesn't take time to explain all the paperwork
- Doesn't follow-up
- Constantly says he or she is the best (no need to say it – demonstrate it!)
- Puts down the competition
- Adds unexplained fees at the last minute before closing
- Charges unjustified points (we'll cover these later)
- Doesn't have systems in place to handle multiple borrowers
- Lacks negotiating skills
- Doesn't ask the right questions to uncover your needs
- Doesn't explain how the company disposes of confidential or sensitive information

Most loan officers have training, but common sense is also important in this business. So is how they treat the borrower. Did they take time to answer all of your questions and educate you during your meeting? Or did they rush you, without answering your questions? You should not talk with a loan officer without your list of prepared questions, which we'll discuss more later. Visit our website at www.MakeNoMistakes.com for the *questions to ask* in order to *Identify a Good Loan Officer*. Click on **"Free Real Estate Forms,"** enter book code 550, and select your forms.

How Your Loan Officer Gets Paid

Loan officers work for a broker or a banker. They do not own the businesses they work for. Banks and credit unions typically offer one type of pay structure to their loan officers, while a broker offers a different type. Usually, the broker pays his or her loan officer a percentage of the commissions earned on the mortgages the loan officer completes. Mortgage banks can use the same or similar pay structure as a broker.

In general, the broker, bank and credit union earn their money in two ways: on the "front," which is paid by the borrower in the form of fees shown on the settlement statement, or on the "back," which is paid by the lender and known as the YSP (see below).

Some examples of fees paid on the "front" are the loan origination fee and broker fee. Though it is customary to charge a percentage of the loan amount, referred to as "paying points," a flat fee is possible too. A point is 1% of the loan amount.

The "back" is paid from the lending institution to the broker in the form of a yield spread premium (YSP). The YSP is a bit like a rebate or finder's fee the bank or credit union rewards the mortgage broker with for bringing a borrower's loan to that lending institution. The full definition of *YSP is compensation paid to a mortgage broker in exchange for providing a loan to a borrower at a certain interest rate above the posted "par interest rate.[42]"*

If today's par rate was 6.00%, this means the mortgage broker could offer you an interest rate of 6.00%; however, he would not receive any compensation (YSP) from the bank for bringing your loan to them. The mortgage broker would need to charge you directly for his fee, and he would do this in the form of charging origination points or broker fee(s) on the front.

However, let's say you accepted a rate of 6.50% from the mortgage broker, and today's par rate is 6.00%. In order to get your loan at a rate that's 0.5% above par, the bank will offer the mortgage broker an YSP of 1.5% of the loan amount if he locks in this 6.5% rate with you today. The YSP of 1.5% is the cash rebate which is given to the broker for selling the borrower the higher interest rate. Don't get confused: the YSP is usually more than the difference between the rate you accept (in this case, 6.5%) and the par rate (6.0%).

---

[42] *Par* is the starting point of an interest rate. If your loan officer offers you *par* on your loan, he or she is not making a commission on your loan.

If you have a $200,000 loan, as in our example, the mortgage broker will earn $3,000 in a YSP from the bank when your loan closes. This is an example of the mortgage broker earning his fee on the "back."

Today's Date:	10/22/2008	Lock Period			30-Day Lock
Loan Amount	Interest Rate	15- Day YSP	30- Day YSP	45- Day YSP	Commission
$200,000	6.00%	0	0	0	$0
$200,000	6.25%	0.75	0.75	0	$1,500
$200,000	6.50%	1.5	1.5	1.25	$3,000
$200,000	6.75%	1.65	1.65	1.5	$3,300
$200,000	7.00%	2.25	2.25	1.5	$4,500

There are a few things borrowers should know about a YSP. First, the YSP changes daily with the posted interest rates, so the 1.5% paid in our example could be 1.0% the following day. It's important to lock your loan rate, because not only does it lock in the interest rate but it also locks your broker's compensation from the lending institution. Also, *the broker receives less compensation the longer you lock an interest rate.* Rates are locked in durations of 15, 30, 45 and 60 days. The broker may offer you a higher interest rate on your loan, or give you the option to pay a fee directly to him or her to compensate for the lower YSP the broker will receive from the lender because you're opting for a longer lock-in period. *You need to examine your options – a higher interest rate, a direct fee, the length of your lock – and decide which route is best for you.*

If you want to know how much your mortgage broker is receiving in YSP, just ask. Then compare it to the YSP amount indicated on your Good Faith Estimate (see Chapter 13 for a thorough discussion of Good Faith Estimates, or GFE). If the YSP does not appear on your Good Faith Estimate, ask for it to be added immediately. Note: Mortgage bankers and banks are not required to show the YSP.

Look in the Good Faith Estimate column marked "POC" (Paid Outside of Closing) or under "Compensation to Broker" (do not get confused with "paid out of loan proceeds" – it won't appear there). Also, look closely at your HUD Settlement Statement (see Chapter 21) at closing to make sure the YSP is the same as what's listed on your GFE. Make sure you did not get charged "junk fees," which can legally creep in and are designed to help compensate a mortgage broker if the broker offered – and you accepted – a loan rate at or near par.

Keep in mind mortgage bankers do not have to disclose what they earn on the "back." Mortgage brokers, however, must disclose it. Don't assume mortgage brokers are more expensive because of the YSP. That's not usually the case. If you approach the subject of a YSP with bankers, they are likely to say they don't earn a YSP and that their compensation is based on volume.

Because it's important to understand *how* various types of loan officers get paid, we explained it in some detail. Letting a loan officer know you understand what a YSP is, basically, warns him or her that you are an informed borrower. You don't have to know the exact dollar amount (especially if you're working with a loan officer at a bank or credit union), just that it exists.

Asking the Loan Officer the Right Questions

If you can ask the right questions and show you're somewhat knowledgeable about mortgage financing and the loan officers' roles and responsibilities, you'll benefit throughout the home-buying process and for years to come. You don't need to ask 100 questions, just a few good ones over the phone to determine who makes the cut before you take time to visit them in their offices.

Before you call those you have chosen, have your list of questions handy, and pen and paper or a laptop for taking notes. Be sure you know your current criteria, that is, what a lender would consider to be your strengths and weaknesses. Refer to the *Lender's Loan Criteria* in Chapter 10. You'll also need your *Budget Spreadsheet*, which will help you draft your questions regarding a reasonable monthly mortgage payment based on all your expenses, not just the revolving accounts.

At the beginning of your call, state your purpose, which is to borrow money for the *purchase* of a property. Find out the best way to forward the application to them so they have time to review it. Then follow up with a phone call confirming that they have received your application and you are aware that your social security and date of birth are not on the form. Explain you are simply at the point of interviewing loan officers. Here is how a conversation might flow using questions from, the Lender's Loan Criteria in Chapter 10, as a guide.

Questions to Ask Loan Officers Over the Phone

After finishing the pleasantries and introductions, such as how you heard about this particular loan officer, you might begin your interviewing process like this:

1. **"I am looking for the best mortgage that will satisfy my current and future situation.** I have already sent you my application via email [or fax]. The balances and debt should be current since I have transferred the information from a credit report I was able to pull myself. There's also other information that wasn't on the application which I believe is pertinent criteria in determining your best offer:

   - My mid credit score is_____.
   - I have all documentation to support my application, so I am a "full doc" borrower.
   - I have the following collections that are over ____ months old and I (have/have no) intentions of paying them off.
   - I plan to use <u>5%</u> as my down payment amount.
   - I do/do not wish to escrow.
   - I have $__ cash on hand to cover closing costs.

2. Then ask, **"Do you have any other questions?"**

Here you are testing to see how the loan officers react to this approach. Did it make them nervous or did they come back with other questions that lead you to believe they were listening, and could handle objections as part of the negotiating process? One skill necessary to be a "good" loan officer is an ability to communicate effectively with the processor and underwriters. *A talented loan officer can think quickly and find multiple solutions to obstacles that invariably crop up as underwriters assess your loan request against standardized requirements and guidelines.*

Some underwriters believe it's their job to approach your loan package looking for what *doesn't meet* their guidelines, as opposed to how they can make this request work. More importantly, the question then becomes, can the loan officer find the right lender who will be attracted to your package and who will offer the best rates and terms based on your criteria?

3. Next, ask specific questions about the loan officer, such as, **"What type of loans do you specialize in and, on average, how many loans do you originate in any given month?"**

The answers can be very important if you have such specialized needs as:

- Investment loan
- Jumbo[43] loan
- Bankruptcy or collections on the credit report
- Low credit score
- First-time home buyer

---

[43] A *jumbo* loan is a mortgage with a loan amount above the industry-standard definition of conventional conforming loan limits, which is $417,000, or $625,500 in Alaska, Hawaii, Guam, and the U.S. Virgin Islands. They carry a higher interest rate and additional underwriting requirements. A loan in excess of $650,000 is referred to as a super jumbo mortgage.

Some loan officers have no experience working with specialized or non-conforming loans, so they might not be able to handle the problems which could arise during the loan process. A loan officer who lacks experience working with your specific needs will not be the best fit.

4. Another appropriate question is, **"Do you have any new loan products I might be interested in?"**

Unfortunately, some loan officers' lending decisions are based on their comfort level and familiarity with certain products, as opposed to what's best for the client. It's human nature to take the path of least resistance. Being a "good" loan officer, however, means answering all of the questions with the client's best interests in mind. Subsequent questions for these phone interviews can include:

5. **"Based on my current criteria, how many loan programs do you think I qualify for? And why do you believe these are best suited to me?"**

Listen to the answers they give you. Do they rattle off a quick number of lenders, believing they fully answered your questions? Or do they summarize your situation to make sure they understand it correctly, then give thoughtful answers specific to you?

6. **"What are your typical closing costs on this size and type of loan?"**

If you ask someone at a mortgage brokerage this question, make sure the quoted fees include those from the *wholesale lender* as well as the broker's own fees. In other words, when using anyone other than a bank there are two sets of fees: theirs and the wholesale lenders. If you don't specifically ask about them, the loan officer might quote just one set, which means you'll be unpleasantly surprised on the day of closing.

The door is open to mistakes when you ask vague questions, which easily result in vague answers. That's why it's so important to ask the *right* questions. If you feel uneasy about something, *ask for clarity* so you understand.

7. "What did you do before you became a loan officer?"

Their responses will tell you a great deal about these loan officers, including the type of business experience they have, and if their skills are transferable. If you don't see an obvious link between what the person used to do and today's career choice of loan officer, feel free to ask more about that.

Almost anyone can become a loan officer, so it's very important to learn more about the person who will be integral in structuring your loan request and obtaining it from the lender. *Former President Bush signed a new law on July 30, 2008, called "Title V – Secure & Fair Enforcement Mortgage Licensing Act" (SAFE), which requires all loan officers be licensed.* **Any loan officer can take an application, but only an experienced one can advise you on the best product for you, and then skillfully close your loan, especially if you have special circumstances.**

> **Tip:**
> *When a processor, or anyone else who is not licensed, gives advice on loan products associated with the brokerage, they've broken the law.*

8. "When you quote a rate to me, what can I expect your average 'yield spread' to be on the back?"

This question alerts loan officers that you know enough about the business to be dangerous. Chances are they won't try to pull a fast one on you.

Remember: A yield spread at "par" means the loan officer is personally not making any money from the lender, based on the rate quoted. This isn't necessarily a good thing; everyone should make some money. If the officer says Par + 2, or 2, this means he or she is earning 2% of the loan amount. Remember, if you are dealing with a banker their pay structure is different.

This yield spread question's purpose is to show loan officers your knowledge of the subject, and to remind them they should do their best to earn your business. NOTE: ***We do NOT share this information with you so you can squeeze all you can out of your loan officer, leaving the officer with nothing. Remember, this is a team effort.*** When you try to go cheap or take advantage of someone, you get what you pay for. The right loan officer equals the right loan.

Rick and his wife shopped for their loan over the internet. The day before closing, Rick called us, saying he was unhappy with his loan. He believed the loan officer was unfamiliar with the rules and so didn't account for certain price adjustments. Since this wasn't what he'd been quoted, apparently, Rick wanted the loan officer to pay for these adjustments. Also, Rick wanted the fees reduced by 50% because of this inconvenience. His career as an attorney didn't give Rick the expertise to pull this off, so he called us in at the last minute to be the bad guys.

We explained to Rick how it works: When he receives an estimate of the closing costs, that's what it is -- an estimate. The couple-hundred-dollar difference was to be expected. Rick did not accept this explanation, however. We talked with the loan officer and realized exactly what Rick was trying to do: squeeze every penny out of the loan officer's commission by making it sound as if the loan officer made a mistake. Rick threatened to pull out of the deal if he didn't get his way, and take the loan to someone else. We knew he meant it, so we explained this to the loan officer, who understood it was a matter of taking less or losing it all. He chose the former, which meant earning $900 less than he'd expected – and was entitled to earn.

Rick succeeded with his unfortunate tactics to save money. After he signed the loan papers, however, he went to his new home – only to discover all the appliances were stolen! Had Rick done a walk-thru of the house on the day of closing, as we always recommend, he would have known the appliances were missing before he signed the loan papers. However, he neglected to do the walk-thru because he was so focused on cutting the loan officer's fees. He lost sight of another detail which, in the end, cost him more money than he squeezed out of the loan officer.

Here's another story, which illustrates a similar point:

Vicky, our client, never seemed happy about anything. Even though she purchased a new town home in a very nice area of town, she gave everyone involved a hard time and constantly complained. We believe it was her way of coercing people to work extra hard to please her.

On the day of her closing, she said she brought a certified check covering only the amount which the loan officer quoted her on the first round of estimates. She claimed she saw the second round of estimates, noticed the difference in cost, and contacted him to ask if she needed to include the difference in the amount on the certified check. And, according to her explanation, she didn't get an answer so she didn't know to bring the larger dollar amount. But she did know, because we discussed it with her well before the day of closing meeting! That discussion was part of our coaching and preparation process. At the closing, however, she insisted the loan officer's manager get involved, and was adamant about creating an unpleasant situation. Vicky went to her new home smiling because she thought she profited by $1,300.

Given Vicky's penchant for complaining, we weren't surprised to hear from her less than three weeks later. Vicky said she felt she got a bad deal. Evidently a friend bought a larger unit in the same complex for $12,000 less.

A good attitude – one which is fair to both sides – produces favorable results in the long run. Neither Rick nor Vicky figured that out, and both paid the consequences. On the flip side, we have had clients who were such a pleasure to work with that people were willing to go above and beyond for our clients at the slightest opportunity. The moral of our stories: Just as with all things in life, you can attract more prosperity by using honey than by using lemons.

In Summary, you now have the questions and knowledge necessary to find a professional loan officer who's committed to the process and committed to you. Such a loan officer is well worth your time and energy to locate. Choosing a loan officer is no different than choosing a dentist or attorney: they all have a responsibility to serve you. The best ones will ask questions about your current and future plans so they can determine what will best meet your needs. And when you find someone who works well with you, keep in touch with that person for years to come. A good loan officer will only get better in time.

As a borrower, your only concern should be to get the best interest rates and terms available, given your criteria. If you focus on taking advantage of someone involved in your home-buying process by thwarting that person's ability to earn a standard, legitimate and reasonable fee, you're not using your time effectively. Chances are, it will come back to haunt you at some point. Nothing is done for free; everyone needs to earn a living. Have a positive attitude throughout the process and make it a win-win situation for all involved.

Take advantage of the information in this chapter to select a "good" loan officer. Learn what *not* to do. Ask questions, do your research and expect to receive answers in writing. If you approach this process as we suggest, you will not only gain knowledge and a carefully-selected, properly-financed new home, you'll Make No Mistakes About… Buying Real Estate, and save thousands!!!

Pass The Knowledge On!

CHAPTER 10

HOW YOU AFFECT YOUR INTEREST RATE

In this chapter we'll cover the information that affects your interest rate. One factor which directly impacts it has to do with the type of information you provide to your loan officer. While some of this required information may be personal or embarrassing to share, trying to hide or cover up the truth, however, can cost you thousands!

When you apply for a loan, the first form you will fill out is a mortgage application, known as the *Uniform Standard Loan Application*. You can get one of these forms, also known as a 1003 or a "ten-o-three," by going to the **"Real Estate Forms"** section on our website, www.MakeNoMistakes.com and entering 550 in the book code field, or by asking for one at most local banks. After the loan officer reviews your loan application, he would then need your social security number and date of birth in order to pull a credit report and determine:

- What's the maximum amount you can afford to spend on a property
- If there are any special circumstances which need to be addressed

- What interest rate and terms to offer you
- How to structure your loan

Remember to be upfront with your loan officer. Don't wait or try to hide something you know is a problem; it will likely come up. Most things can be handled if they're made clear in advance.

Being less than honest and trying to cover up a bad situation is a sure way to be denied a loan. Everything usually comes out in the wash. Anything negative will appear on your credit report or turn up during the verification process. Part of the verification process begins when you provide all the documents supporting what you have stated on your loan application. These documents are listed in the *Borrower's Paperwork Checklist,* which is also located on our website, www.MakeNoMistakes.com, under **"Real Estate Forms"** (enter 550 in the book code field and select this checklist).

No matter when it surfaces, negative information will come to the attention of the underwriter.[44] Remember, underwriters look for inconsistencies. They verify all the information you provide – *that's their job!* If you're caught lying about anything, your loan will be denied and your loan officer will have to start all over again with another lender, if that's an option. This always causes delays in closing. It's best to just be upfront with your loan officer, which will help him or her know how to best structure the loan package.

> *A borrower came into our office to apply for a home loan. She had completed our online loan application, which gave us time to review it before the appointment. When we first go over a loan application with a client, we always start and finish with this statement: "Is everything on your application correct and the truth?" We do this to give the borrower time to come clean if need be. We realize it's hard for some people to share personal information with a complete stranger, especially if that information reveals certain shortcomings. In*

---

[44]An *underwriter* is a professional who works on behalf of the bank and who determines how financially eligible a customer is, and how risky it is for the bank to loan money to that person. Underwriters' decisions are based on guidelines set by the bank and its investors.

this instance, we noticed the borrower was receiving child support, so we asked if it was court-ordered child support. She said yes, and that it would take her a week to get the necessary documents as proof. We submitted the loan package to a prime lender in order to receive the conditions for the approval of the loan. One of the conditions, as we had suspected, was proof of her court-ordered child support.

We were quite pleased because it appeared all of the lender's conditions would be easily met, and because of this, our client would receive a great interest rate on a 30-year fixed loan. We again requested the document from her, which she never provided. We later discovered she didn't have a court-ordered arrangement, only an agreement with the baby's father. Needless to say, the prime lender denied this loan because of this little white lie.

There is nothing little about a lie when it comes to getting approved for a mortgage loan. This lie not only cost her valuable time but a low interest rate. The prime lender would not calculate her child support as "Other Income" without proof from a court order. Since the court was not actually involved in determining child support payments from the father this additional income was considered risky. Also, the borrower did not disclose to anyone that she had never been married to the father; therefore there was no divorce decree. Since she and the father made their own arrangements for payment, she never filed for child support through the courts. Unfortunately, some kind of official statement from the court regarding child support was one of the loan's conditions. We had to start over – and lost valuable time – because her income alone was not high enough under the prime lender's guidelines. However, she was approved with a subprime lender because that lender was willing to accept a higher debt-to-income ratio (DTI).

Criteria Affecting Your Interest Rate

Your financial picture, along with certain aspects of how your loan will be structured, determines the interest rate the lender will offer you. Many factors influence a lender's decision, and it's important to recognize and understand them, especially those over which you have some control.

Lenders have a "start rate"[45] for each of their various types of mortgages. This is the rate that the lender typically advertises. A "start" rate is aptly named because it's where the lender starts when determining your rate. Figuring out a home loan rate and determining the value of a car, for example, are very similar: both use "adds" and "deducts" from the start rate (or starting price, in the case of the car) to determine a new, customized rate (or price) for you.

Below is a table, which shows examples of how one borrower's financial information impacts the loan's interest rate, either positively (a lower, better rate) or negatively (a higher, worse rate).

Before looking at the table, please take a moment to read the names of the columns, from left to right, and their definitions:

- **Criteria Questions** - Criteria or information the lender needs.
- **Info Requested on the App?** Is the criteria typically requested on the mortgage loan application?
- **Borrower's Answers to Criteria Questions** - Examples of a borrower's answers to the questions asked in the Criteria column.
- **Lender's Requirements and Guidelines** - Rules which most lenders use to determine rates.
- **Rate Adjustment** - How the "start rate" will be adjusted, based on the borrower's answers to the Criteria questions.

Please keep in mind this table's data is for reference only. The actual content and results vary among lenders.

---

[45] The *start rate* is the beginning rate, before adjustments pinpoint the final interest rate offered.

Lender's Rate Calculation Table:

	CRITERIA QUESTIONS	INFO REQUESTED ON THE APP?	BORROWER'S ANSWERS TO CRITERIA QUESTIONS	LENDER'S REQUIREMENTS AND GUIDELINES	RATE ADJUSTMENT (+/-)
1	Purpose of Loan	YES	Purchase	Purchase, Investment Refinance, or Cash Out	Investment & "Cash Out" loans start with higher interest rates. Refinance rates start lower.
2	Owner Occupancy	YES	Primary	Owner Occupancy vs. Non Owner Occupancy	Non Owner Occupancy start at a higher rate.
3	Credit Scores	NO	680	Determines whether to use Prime or FHA	Varies with lender – Prime Lenders usually want FICO scores of 620 or higher, but lower scores receive higher rate.
4	Loan Amount	YES	$200,000	Jumbo loans larger than $417,000, Conforming loans less than $417,000	Varies with lender, sometimes a low amount equals a higher rate.
5	Down Payment Amount (Determines Loan-To-Value Ratio)	NO	5%	Lender's guidelines for 3.5%, 5%, 10%, 20%	Less than 5% increases interest rate unless FHA or VA loan.
6	Term of the Loan	YES	30-year	15-year, 30-year	15-year note offers a lower interest rate.
7	Employment History	YES	4 years	More than 2 years at the same company	Less than 2 years increases interest rate or declines the loan.
8	Two consecutive years of Tax Returns or W-2s	NO	full doc	Tax returns or W-2's included means file is a "full doc" vs. "stated income" (non documented)	Stated income no longer available. Self employed must show tax returns and tax returns are ordered from the IRS.

	CRITERIA QUESTIONS	INFO REQUESTED ON THE APP?	BORROWER'S ANSWERS TO CRITERIA QUESTIONS	LENDER'S REQUIREMENTS AND GUIDELINES	RATE ADJUSTMENT (+/-)
9	**Monthly Income** (Round down as opposed to up)	YES	$4,000 a month	Used to determine debt-to-income ratio. Above 40% and less than 55% falls into a sub-prime or FHA category.	Sub-prime category means higher interest rate.
10	**Outstanding Collections** (federal liens, child support and student loans make this more challenging)	NO	2 medical collections which I do not intend to pay	Loan automatically goes to sub-prime lender with any unpaid collection. Rate determined by type of collections, time period and why they're unpaid.	Higher interest rate
11	**Do you plan to escrow your insurance and taxes?**	NO	Non-escrow	Only available with a 80/15/5 loan or a sub-prime lender or with 20% down payment	Not escrowing increases interest rate.
12	**Rate Lock**	NO	close within 15 days	Maximum of 30 days	Lock available only for Prime. Not offered for sub-prime loans.
13	**Amount of Cash on Hand to Cover Closing Costs**	YES	1%	Varies with 1%, 2%, 3%, 4%, 5% (of loan) amounts	Varies by the loan officer.

1. The *purpose of the loan* determines your start rate. The four most common purposes are:

   - Purchase
   - Investment
   - Refinance[46]

---

[46] A *refinance* can occur when a borrower already owns the property and has not yet paid off the current mortgage loan. For any of a variety of reasons, the borrower wants a new mortgage loan to pay off the original loan. The most common reason to do this is to reduce a monthly mortgage payment. Also, refinance "start rates" tend to be a little lower because the borrower already

- Cash Out

2. A loan on a property that is going to be *occupied by the borrower* is referred to as "owner occupied." ***An "investment property" often requires a down payment of 10% or more and comes with a higher interest rate because it's considered a non-owner occupied property; an investment.***

3. You will also need to know your *credit scores*. The higher your score, the better your interest rate.

4. The amount of the loan impacts the rate. A *loan amount* above $417,000 is considered a "jumbo" loan and is therefore subject to a higher interest rate. On the other hand, lenders will sometimes penalize you if the amount is lower than what they prefer to work with. For example, some lenders will not loan less than $50,000, or they'll charge a higher interest rate for loans less than $50,000.

5. The minimum preferred *down payment* amount for a conventional loan is 5% (3.5% for FHA). Anything above a 95% (96.5% with FHA) loan-to-value ratio (LTV) will increase the interest rate. For example, if the sales price of a home is $200,000 and you ask to borrow more than $190,000, you will be in a higher interest rate bracket because you are putting down less than 5%. Before you make a decision on this, however, look at the benefits of putting down more or less money. Here's one way to evaluate your options:

- 95% (LTV) equals a payment of $1,200.93 a month at 6.50%.
- 90% (LTV) equals a payment of $1,108.29 a month at 6.25%.
- The difference is $92.64 a month.

---

owns the home. Additionally, the new loan amount is typically smaller than the original amount because the borrower has paid down the principal and built equity. Last but not least, a borrower will often refinance when current rates are lower than the original loan's rate.

- In order to get the lower interest rate, you had to come up with an additional 5% on $200,000, which is $10,000.
- It will take you 9 years to make up the difference on $10,000. $10,000 divided by $92.64 = 107.94 months, or almost 9 years.
- Do you plan on staying in the home more than 9 years? The average homeowner stays eight years.
- Do you have *other* cash sources you can access in case of an emergency? Perhaps 6 months of living expenses.
- Can you earn more than 6.25% on the $10,000 in another investment vehicle? For example, is it possible for you to earn more than 6.25% in a mutual fund, CD or the stock market over a period of 9 years? If the answer is yes, then it may serve you better to take this cash and invest it in one of those investment products. If the answer is no, then you should know the additional $10,000 you put down on the home is saving you at least $92.64 a month.
- Would the additional down payment save you from paying PMI? If the additional down payment made the difference of putting down 20% or more, you would avoid having to pay mortgage insurance.

Mistake # 24: *Putting too much cash down and not leaving enough in savings*

Putting down too much cash on a house can become a problem. Real estate is not an investment vehicle from which you can easily get cash from unless you are an investor earning cash flow from leasing the property. Therefore, before you put down all the cash you have, be sure there are other sources of accessible cash for emergencies. Some buyers believe paying cash for a property impresses a seller and motivates the seller to take a lower offer since there is little or no financing involved, slowing down the closing process. Even a little financing, however, is still financing. To the seller, it doesn't matter if you finance 5% or 50% of the sales price. A cash deal where there is absolutely NO financing involved may hold some weight with the seller, if the offer is reasonable.

6. The most common *term of a mortgage loan* is 30 years, amortized[47] into 360 payments. A 15-year note offers a lower interest rate but since it is amortized over only 180 months, the monthly payment is higher.

7. Lenders examine several factors about a borrower's *employment history* because it indicates the borrower's ability to repay the loan. It's a very important factor. Lenders look for consistency, so even if you changed jobs within the last two years, as long as it was in the same field, it's usually acceptable. However, jobs that are commission-driven may pose some challenges. The lender may use only your W-2s for the previous two years as proof of your base income, and disregard your commission. This is typical for borrowers who've had a large commission payout in one year and a lower one in a subsequent or prior year.

8. Lenders expect you to provide *full disclosure* of everything on the application. That's full documentation; if you show you worked for the same company for the past two years, they will want to see two years of W-2s. There was a period when borrowers could simply "state" income they earned so long as they had high credit scores and the amount of income made sense based on their job title. This product came with a higher interest rate, but attracted the self employed and sales commission job holders.

   The rules have changed in that lenders are now requiring borrowers to sign 4506T documents which allow lenders to order tax returns submitted to the IRS. This is another quality control measure taken by lenders to stop any fraudulent loans from happening. If the tax returns are found to be different than what was submitted the lender will stop the mortgage process and deny the loan.

---

[47] *Amortized* means gradually reducing the loan, via monthly payments over a period of time, until it is completely paid.

9. Proof of monthly income and current liabilities (debts and other money you owe) is needed so the loan officer can determine your DTI. Remember, that's your monthly gross income divided *into* your monthly revolving debt. Monthly revolving debt shows up on your credit report. Whenever you apply for credit, agree to pay a portion of it back every month, and then use the credit (to buy a car, get a student loan, or buy something from a store), it's considered monthly revolving debt and is factored into your DTI. See Chapter 4 for more information on monthly revolving debt and DTI. Also if there are any taxes due the borrower must show proof that the liability has been paid to the IRS. If the borrower has a written payment plan executed by the IRS then the amount of the monthly liability will be counted as part of the borrower's debt.

> *Tip:*
> *Round **down** as opposed to up when you state your income on a loan application. Round **down** to the nearest $100 on monthly income; and **down** to the nearest $1,000 on annual income.*

- Prime lenders prefer DTI ratios of 40% or less but will accept higher ratios with credit mid scores greater than 720.
- Sub-prime lenders will work with DTI ratios which are less than 50%; although some will go as high as 55%.
- FHA ratios are 31% - 43% and for new construction, 33% - 45%.

10. The lender will review your credit report for any outstanding collections, which are creditors you have decided not to pay for whatever reason.

- Prime lenders do not allow any outstanding collection balances.
- Sub-prime lenders will make limited exceptions.
- FHA will require a letter of explanation for any adverse credit on your credit report. The VA will consider factors based on an individual's personal circumstances and look strongly at the overall payment pattern before making a final decision.

The lenders will also look to see how many "trades" you have and if you use them regularly. A trade is any creditor with whom you have an established line of credit. Not having any trades is not good because it doesn't allow you to establish credit and payment patterns. A few lenders will provide loans for borrowers with no credit scores because they understand that every business does not report customer information to the credit bureaus. Borrowers can establish alternate trade lines with their light bills, gas bills, and rent payments, or any account where they have an established credit history. The borrower's name must be on the account and the account must be at least two years old. On the other hand, having too much credit and too many outstanding balances is a detriment to your credit score.

11. A borrower needs to decide on the escrow vs. non-escrow option early in the loan process. Borrowers make this decision based on whether or not they want to pay their taxes and insurance payments on a monthly basis along with their principal and interest payments. This is choosing to escrow.

In this situation, the mortgage company rolls the principal, interest, taxes, insurance and (if applicable) PMI payments into one dollar amount. Then, the mortgage company deposits the taxes and insurance into an escrow or reserve account, typically a *non-bearing interest account*, which is managed by a company that pays the tax and insurance bills on your behalf.

The non-escrow option is only available to a borrower who wants to pay his or her own insurance and taxes (usually annually or semi-annually) instead of monthly. However, in most cases a prime lender will permit this *only* if the borrower chooses to spread the risk of default by taking a 80/15/5 loan. That is, one lender will loan 80% of the loan amount, a second lender will take on the other 15% and the borrower will put down the last 5%. An 80/10/10 loan is another option. Any of these options will satisfy the first lender's requirement of reducing the total amount owing him by 20%. Lenders view this as reducing their risk, and they're more inclined to believe you have the discipline to pay taxes and insurance debts on your own as they're due. Keep in mind, however, the interest rate on the second loan will be much higher and more difficult to find in today's market.

- Most prime lenders *will not allow* a borrower to choose to non-escrow unless the borrower opts for the 80/15/5 option or puts a down payment of 20%. And even then, the borrower will have to meet additional qualifications.
- Sub-prime lenders *will* allow borrowers to non-escrow upon request and if they can fulfill the additional requirements.

12. Interest rates change daily. Therefore a rate lock is sometimes an attractive option offered by prime lenders. If you choose to *lock* your rate, this means the interest rate will not change during the lock period regardless of how the market changes. Lock periods usually come in 15-, 30-, 45-, 60-, and 75-day locks. You will usually pay for locks longer than 30 days. We recommend borrowers take a 30-day lock to cover any unexpected events.

13. Unfortunately, letting some loan officers know you have a lot of easily accessible *cash on hand* is an invitation for them to charge you higher closing costs, especially if you have credit challenges. In other words, if they know you have saved up $10,000 for closing costs, you may find your closing costs are $10,000! This is a touchy subject because there are times when showing you have lots of cash can make the difference between being approved or not. In today's tight credit world, lenders look more favorably on cash in the bank that could cover up to six months of mortgage payments. Comparative shopping will help you with this problem. There's more discussion on this subject in Chapter 13.

You can see why it's so important to *not* skip the step of trying to understand the Lender's Rate Calculation. Rushing through this process produces results that cost you money!

In Summary, you'll find mortgage interest rates are similar among most lenders and banks. What differentiates one *lender* from another are the guidelines lenders follow to assess the criteria you provide, and the YSP the lenders offer loan officers. What differentiates one *loan officer* from another is how he or she addresses your needs and interprets your criteria. Much of the criteria you provide, along with your credit score, will determine what your final interest rate will be. And as we have seen, there are many factors which affect that rate. One of them is the *start rate* your lender will use. Be sure to always give complete information to the lender; it may be something you leave out that makes the difference between receiving a great rate and a decent rate.

Pass The Knowledge On!

CHAPTER 11

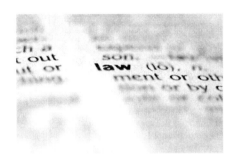

THE INSIDE STORY OF MORTGAGE LENDING LAW

In this chapter we'll cover which regulations govern real estate finance and how they protect borrowers. It's important to have a general idea about these safeguards so you are prepared for any unusual situation.

There are several pieces of federal legislation that impact financing in the real estate marketplace. They are:

- Equal Opportunity Credit Act (ECOA)
- Community Reinvestment Act (CRA)
- Home Mortgage Disclosure Act (HMDA)
- Truth in Lending Act (TILA)
- Home Ownership and Equity Protection Act (HOEPA)
- Fair Housing Act (FHA)
- Real Estate Settle Procedures Act (RESPA)

The Equal Credit Opportunity Act

The Equal Credit Opportunity Act (ECOA) ensures that all consumers are given an equal chance to obtain credit. This doesn't mean all consumers who apply for credit get it. Factors such as income, expenses, debt, and credit history are still considerations for creditworthiness.

This law protects consumers when they do business with any creditor who regularly extends credit, including banks, small loan and finance companies, retail and department stores, credit card companies, and credit unions. Anyone involved in granting credit, such as real estate brokers who arrange financing, is covered by the law. Businesses applying for credit also are protected by the law.

Under ECOA, creditors are *not* allowed to:

- Discourage an individual from applying due to gender, marital status, age, race, national origin, or because the individual receives public assistance income.
- Ask for the applicant's gender, race, national origin or religion as a basis of deciding credit. The creditor can ask real estate loan borrowers to provide this information on a voluntary basis, because federal agencies use this information to enforce anti-discrimination laws.
- Ask if an applicant is widowed or divorced.
- Ask about marital status if the applicant is applying for a separate, unsecured account. In community property states, however, a creditor can legally ask for this information.
- Request information about the applicant's spouse, unless the spouse is applying with the applicant, or the spouse is allowed to use the account, or the applicant relies on the spouse's income (or on alimony or child support from a former spouse), or if the applicant resides in a community property state.
- Ask the applicant about plans for having or raising children.
- Ask the applicant if he or she *receives* alimony, child support or separate maintenance payments, if the payments are not relied on to get credit. The creditor, however, can legally ask the applicant if he has to *make* such payments.

Creditors may *not* base credit decisions on:

- Gender, marital status, race, national origin or religion.
- Having a telephone listing in the applicant's name.
- The race of people in the neighborhood in which the applicant wants to buy, refinance or improve a home.
- Age, unless:
    - the applicant is a minor
    - the applicant is age 62 or over, in which case the creditor will favor the applicant due to that person's age
- Age is, however, used to determine other factors, such as whether income will change because the applicant is ready to retire.

Creditors may *not* evaluate income by:

- Refusing to consider public assistance income in the same way as other income.
- Discounting income based on gender or marital status.
- Discounting income because it comes from part-time employment or from pension, annuity or retirement benefit programs.
- Excluding regular alimony, child support or separate maintenance income.

Creditors must give notice to applicants stating if their application was approved or declined, within thirty days of the customer turning in the application. If the application was declined, the creditor must give the applicant a notice, within 60 days, that specifies the reasons for rejection or disclose the applicant's right to learn the reasons.

The Community Reinvestment Act

The Community Reinvestment Act (CRA) is a federal act that was enacted in 1977. Its purpose is to encourage banks to help meet the credit needs of their communities, including low and moderate-income neighborhoods. It also prohibits *"redlining."* Redlining is the practice of designating certain communities, areas or neighborhoods as those that will not be serviced by the lender (or insurer, or other financial entity) on a discriminatory basis. Lenders must treat all applicants equally, and not deny credit because of where an applicant lives.

The Home Mortgage Disclosure Act

The Home Mortgage Disclosure Act (HMDA) was enacted in 1975. Its provisions are carried out through the Federal Reserve Board's Regulation C. Financial institutions are required to report annual information concerning the size, type, purpose, etc., of home loans. In addition, lenders are now required to report all first mortgages with interest rates that exceed the Treasury rate by 3%, and subordinate loans (such as second mortgages) that exceed the Treasury rate by 5%. The collected data is used to help set public policy, determine whether financial institutions are serving the housing needs of their communities, and to identify possible discriminatory lending practices.

The Truth in Lending Act

In 1968, the Truth in Lending Act (TILA) was enacted. It requires lenders to disclose specific information about terms and costs, including the annual percentage rate (APR), of all the lender's loans. TILA also governs how lenders advertise and disclose their rates, and gives consumers the right to cancel certain real estate loans within three days. TILA requires mortgage advertisers, for example, once they begin advertising specific terms, to give further information on those loans. For example, if a mortgage company wants to show the interest rate or payment amount on the advertised loan, the company must also provide the annual percentage rate and state if that rate increases. The APR takes into account interest, points paid on the loan, any loan origination fee, and any required mortgage insurance premiums.

The Home Ownership and Equity Protection Act

The Home Ownership and Equity Protection Act (HOEPA) is an amendment to TILA that was passed in 1994. It covers certain loans considered to be high-rate or high-fee loans. Borrowers covered by this legislation must be provided with certain disclosures at least three days before their loans are finalized. These disclosures include:

- Notice from the lender that the loan does not have to be completed, even though the application has been signed
- Notice from the lender warning the borrower that the lender will have a mortgage on the home, and the borrower could lose the residence and any money the borrower has in equity if the borrower fails to make payments as required

The Fair Housing Act

The Fair Housing Act is another federal act affecting real estate transactions. It prohibits discrimination on the basis of race, color, religion, gender, handicap, familial status[48] or national origin. It applies to sales and leases of homes and to home loan decisions.

The Real Estate Settlement Procedures Act

The Real Estate Settlement Procedures Act (RESPA) was enacted by Congress in 1974. Your lender is required to follow certain rules and guidelines regardless of the state you live in. RESPA requires disclosure of estimated settlement costs and dictates the format that the information must be presented in. This form is best known as the *Good Faith Estimate* (GFE). You must receive it, along with the Truth in Lending form (TIL), within three days of filling out the loan application.

---

[48] *Familial status* is the state of the household, including the number of children under the age of 18 residing in the home, and if the adult(s) are married or single parents.

Under RESPA, lenders are regulated by the United States Department of Housing and Urban Development (HUD). RESPA incorporates a series of disclosure requirements as a way of controlling settlement costs and protecting consumers from unnecessarily high ones. In March 2008, HUD proposed reforms to RESPA to simplify and improve the disclosure requirements for mortgage settlement costs. One recommendation was to improve and standardize the Good Faith Estimate form, to make it easier for borrowers to use it for mortgage loan comparison shopping among loan originators.[49] However, even with this reform it is still difficult for borrowers to comparatively shop, especially if there are two or more GFEs to consider. This is why we designed the *Lender Comparative,* to make it easier for you to understand the GFE, regardless of what format it's given to you in. There will be more on this in the next chapter. The reform also provides for more accurate estimates of costs for settlement services shown on the GFE, and for better disclosure of the yield spread premiums (YSP) on the GFE. Visit the HUD website at www.hud.gov for a copy of the proposed reform.

Part of RESPA's education process requires the lender to give you a *Settlement Cost Guide* booklet, which describes the home-buying process. You can obtain a copy by visiting www.hud.gov. This booklet will help you understand home-buying settlement services and how to shop for them.

In Summary, there are a variety of federal laws designed to protect home buyers as they secure financing. Many of these laws prohibit discrimination, including race, gender, income sources and geographic location of the property.

The Community Reinvestment Act and the Home Mortgage Disclosure Act require lenders to receive and equitably assess applications from prospective borrowers across all segments and geographic areas of the lender's service area, and to document and report that they have done so.

---

[49] *Loan originators* are loan officers who originate loans, that is, who take the loan application and match it up with a loan product.

The Truth in Lending Act requires lenders to disclose how they calculated their advertised rates, specifically, as well as all the rates they have available.

The Real Estate Settlement Procedures Act (RESPA) requires your lender to follow certain rules and guidelines, especially with regards to disclosing fees and charges you'll be expected to pay. This law is there to protect you. Use it to stop any action before it happens by letting all parties know you are knowledgeable and will use the laws to protect yourself.

Pass The Knowledge On!

Section III:
The Best Home Loan For You

CHAPTER 12

TYPES OF LOAN PROGRAMS

While many people rely on their lender's recommendations to decide on a loan program, you should understand the basic differences. The standard loan programs are Federal Housing Administration (FHA), Veteran's Administration (VA) and Conventional (Fannie Mae or Freddie Mac). These loan programs all have guidelines to determine the level of risk associated with a wide variety of borrowers. All other loans without these standard guidelines are considered "non-conforming" loans.

FHA Loans

The Federal Housing Administration's (FHA) mission was designed to help low-income and disadvantaged persons buy a home. But with the recent problems suffered by the mortgage industry, it has become the *"new sub-prime"*. FHA loans are the new alternative to sub-prime loans for first-time home buyers and home buyers with less than perfect credit. FHA is not a lender, nor does it package and sell loans in the secondary market. ***The FHA insures loans against default.*** Because of this extra security, mortgage lenders can make loans to borrowers with less than perfect credit, which allows more risk than would otherwise be acceptable. As a result, FHA offers loans requiring borrowers to make down payments as small as 3.5%. In addition, a mortgage insurance premium must be paid up front or financed as part of the mortgage. The premium is around 1.5% of the loan amount. Another benefit of applying for a mortgage backed by FHA is that the chances are great that you'll receive a lower, more affordable interest rate than that offered by a sub-prime lender.

Borrowers with FHA loans have several *advantages*:

- No minimum credit score
- Non-traditional credit is acceptable
- Lower down payment requirement: 3.5% vs. 5% or more for a prime conventional mortgage
- Non-occupant, co-borrower is permitted
- No prepayment penalties
- The loan is assumable, which means it can be assumed or taken over by a qualified buyer
- Default assistance
- Non-credit qualifying refinances. If you already have an FHA loan you may qualify for a FHA Streamline loan which will adjust your loan terms only, and not require that your credit be reviewed or submitted in order to refinance the loan. Along with these benefits, the borrower will receive a lower interest rate than that of a sub-prime mortgage; in fact, interest rates for a FHA loan vs. a conventional mortgage are very close, if not identical
- Opportunity to use a gift as the total down payment
- Borrowers are allowed to include closing costs in the mortgage amount with limited fees
- Home improvement funds are allowed to be included in the purchase money mortgage amount

There are several *disadvantages* of an FHA loan:

- Maximum loan limits that vary geographically. Limits for each area are available on the FHA website, www.FHA.gov
- Up front mortgage insurance premiums are added to the loan amounts, which raise the loan amounts financed

- 1/12 of the annual mortgage insurance premium is included in the *monthly payment*
- The mortgage insurance premiums cannot be canceled for the first five years for loans with terms of more than 15 years, even if your loan balance reaches 78% of the original sales price. An exception to this rule is when the loan term is 15 years or less and 10% or more was put down. The MIP will then be cancelled when the loan balance is 78% of the original sales price
- The only way to eliminate the mortgage insurance premiums is to refinance into a conventional Freddie Mac or Fannie Mae mortgage, or payoff the FHA insured loan
- Strict qualifying guidelines
- More extensive, and usually more expensive, loan appraisals

The closing costs that are allowable as charges to the borrower are defined by FHA. Generally not allowed are all other costs, such as junk fees, which are usually paid by the seller. The allowable fees are as follows:

- Origination fee
- Credit reports (actual costs)
- Underwriting fee
- Processing fee
- Flood Certification fee
- Appraisal fee
- Attorney's fee
- Deposit verification fees
- Inspections fees
- Property survey
- Cost of title insurance
- Title examination
- Certification fees
- Document preparation (by a third party)
- Transfer stamps
- Taxes
- Recording fees
- Home inspection fees up to $200

If you're refinancing, allowable fees include:

- Fees to payoff bills
- Courier fees
- Wire transfer fees
- Reconveyance fees[50]

VA Loans

The U.S. government established a special program to give loans to service personnel and veterans of the armed forces. We are grateful to them for their services during war and peace and one way to show support for those who have put themselves in harm's way on our behalf is through the Veterans Administration Home Loan Program.

The Veterans Administration, often referred to as the VA, *guarantees a portion of the loan.* The guaranteed loans are made by private lenders and must be for the veteran's personal occupancy. *The guarantee means the lender is protected against loss if the borrower fails to repay the loan. The guarantee is based upon the veteran's entitlement – the amount the VA would repay the lender if the veteran defaulted on the loan.* It is not a gift and the applicant must qualify for the loan based on satisfactory credit, employment and income.

The veteran's basic entitlement is $36,000. The 2009 loan limit is $417,000 – this loan limit can change yearly. Visit www.homeloans.va.gov for your particular county's limit. A veteran can use his or her entitlement to borrow any amount a lender is willing to provide. Check with your lender regarding down payment requirements and lender guidelines.

In order to qualify for a VA loan veterans must be eligible as defined by the Department of Veterans Affairs. Contact the Department of Veterans Affairs to see if you qualify for a VA loan or apply with any mortgage lender that participates in the VA home loan program. Your lender will need to get a *"Certificate of Eligibility"*

---

[50] The *reconveyance fee* covers the cost of removing your current lender's lien from your property title. This only applies when you refinance

(COE) Form 26-1880 from the VA to prove that you are eligible for a VA loan. The lender will then process the loan and guide you thru the loan process. Visit the VA's website at www.va.gov for a detailed list of common closing costs or call the VA at 1-800-827-1000 with any questions.

A borrower has many *advantages* with a VA loan:

- There is no maximum VA loan amount. However, lenders will generally lend up to four times the amount of a veteran's entitlement without requiring a down payment
- There are no mortgage insurance premiums
- The mortgage is assumable. The new borrower must qualify for the assumption, but does not need to be a veteran
- The borrower may pay the loan off early without a prepayment penalty
- The VA offers assistance to veteran borrowers in default due to temporary financial difficulty

This is one of the strongest advantages in the current climate of foreclosures. To get a VA loan, you must be a veteran who can qualify for the benefit. The children of a living or deceased veteran are not eligible and the benefit cannot be passed on. The borrower cannot use a VA loan to get an investment property or vacation home.

The unmarried surviving spouse of a veteran, who died on active duty or as the result of a service-connected disability, is eligible for the home loan benefit. In addition, a surviving spouse who obtained a VA home loan with the veteran prior to his or her death - regardless of the cause of death - may refinance the loan through the VA-guaranteed program to receive an interest rate reduction.

Another advantage to the borrower with a VA loan is the veteran does not have to pay a mortgage insurance premium, but instead pays an up-front funding fee. The amount of the fee depends on the down payment, the status of the veteran, and whether the veteran has used the entitlement before.

The VA funding fee may be financed. Disabled veterans, spouses of disabled veterans and surviving spouses of veterans who died in service do not pay the funding fee. The VA also limits the amount veterans may be charged for other fees. Closing costs, however, cannot be financed into the loan amount.

We would recommend that you prequalify for the VA loan just like you would a conventional loan. This lets you know up front if you qualify or what you would need to do to qualify for the loan.

A borrower has a few *disadvantages* with a VA loan:

- There is a maximum VA loan amount. Without a down payment, in 2008, the maximum VA loan amount was $417,000, with 25% of that value guaranteed by the VA.
- The one-time funding fee ranges from 1.25% to 3%, depending on the length of the veteran's service, the amount of down payment and the number of VA loans he or she already has.
- The interest rates may or may not be better than a conventional loan.

Conventional Loans

A conventional loan is not backed in full by the VA or protected by the FHA. Conventional loans meet the guidelines set forth by Fannie Mae and/or Freddie Mac, whose operations are guaranteed by the U.S. government. These two entities are very large mortgage trading companies who do not make loans, but provide the guidelines and lending limits for lenders who make the loans. *Fannie Mae and Freddie Mac were formed by the federal government to provide liquidity in the mortgage marketplace. Conventional loans are often referred to as conforming loans and are sold to other banks, mortgage companies, Fannie Mae, or Freddie Mac.* These loans are packaged into securities and sold on Wall Street. These securities have become a commodity and this buying and selling of mortgages has created what is called the *secondary market*.

The secondary mortgage market allows lenders to sell their mortgages to other banks and large investors, which then frees up a lender's money to provide more mortgages to yet more borrowers. If banks had to keep these mortgages full term - 15 or 30 years - they would soon use up all their funds. Home buyers would then have a more difficult time acquiring mortgages.

The rise in foreclosures in 2007 and 2008 had a significant impact on Fannie Mae and Freddie Mac, and is responsible for new legislation to strengthen them. The Federal Housing Finance Regulatory Reform Act of 2008 established a new, independent regulator for Fannie Mae, Freddie Mac and the Federal Home Loan Banks.

Here are some of the *advantages* of a conventional loan:

- Lenders may be willing to keep conventional loans in their own lending portfolios, thus allowing more underwriting flexibility because the loan will not have to conform to secondary market guidelines
- Lenders have more flexibility to negotiate or eliminate certain loan fees
- A lender may be willing to finance non-realty items with the real estate loan, such as furniture and appliances not included in the home
- If the loan is held in a lender's portfolio, appraisals will only need to meet the lender's guidelines instead of the strict appraisal standards of FHA or VA loans
- If the borrower is short on cash, the lender may fund a portion of the closing costs in exchange for a higher loan interest rate
- Lenders can raise the loan limits in high-cost areas to 150% of the standard conforming loan limit. This would make it $625,000 or $938,250 in high cost areas[51]
- Legislation exists which requires the enterprises to serve a variety of underserved markets

Some of the *disadvantages* of a conventional loan are:

- Interest rates vary with each lender and can exceed those of FHA and VA loans

---

[51] *High cost areas* are Alaska, Guam, Hawaii and the U.S. Virgin Islands.

- Conventional loans generally require a minimum down payment of 5%, as compared to government-backed loans, which are often at 3.5%
- Origination fees and other costs are determined by individual lenders and may be higher than those of other programs
- Because mortgage documents for conventional loans vary by lender, certain clauses can be included in a mortgage contract; for example, a prepayment penalty, or an acceleration clause[52]
- Loans greater than 80% of the loan-to-value (LTV) require the borrower to purchase Private Mortgage Insurance (PMI) to protect the lender from default. However, there are ways in which to eliminate or cancel this added expense:

  o Paying down your mortgage loan to 78 percent of the value and being current on your loan.
  o Proving to the lender that the policy is no longer needed due to an increased property value of 25% or more of the loan amount.
  o Putting 20% or more as a down payment on the property.
  o *Getting a second loan from another bank for part of the remaining 20% if the primary lender agrees.*

With this last method, the risk is spread out among two lenders. This method is better known as the 80/15/5 or the 80/10/10. The three numbers refer to the amount each of the three entities (two banks and the borrower) has contributed to the purchase price of the home. The lender who loans 80% is in first position, meaning in the event the borrower defaults, the first position lender will be paid first from the sale of the home. The second position lender would be paid next, if the foreclosure brought in any money beyond the 80%. The borrower contributes the third number in the series as his down payment. Thus, in a 80/15/5 loan, the first bank lends 80% of the amount needed for the borrower to purchase the house, the bank in

---

[52] An *acceleration clause* is language in the mortgage note, also known as the notes payable document, which details how a loan may be required to be repaid early if the borrower defaults on other clauses of the contract.

second position pays 15% and the borrower contributes a down payment of 5%.

So, you ask, why would any bank want to take a second position? In a word, profit. Borrowers pay much higher interest rates to the second position lenders. The 80/15/5 and 80/10/10 loan programs benefit everyone because the monthly payments on the two mortgages are still lower than paying one mortgage with PMI. Plus, the homeowner has the advantage of mortgage interest being tax deductible. Ask your lender to discuss which options are available to you. Be sure to note that *not* putting down 20% means you will have to meet the additional guidelines of the mortgage insurance company. If that company denies you, your only choice is to consider one of the other options, such as the 80/20, 80/10/10 or the 80/15/5.

Non-Conforming Loans

Non-conforming loans do not conform to the standard guidelines for conventional loans. Jumbo loans, for example, are considered "non-conforming" because they exceed the maximum loan limit for conventional loans. Sub-prime loans are considered non-conforming because they do not meet the credit guidelines established for conventional loans, and the rates for these loans are typically higher because they are riskier.

Jumbo Loans - If a borrower wants a large, expensive home, he or she needs a jumbo loan, and is usually required to make a down payment of 5% - 10%. Larger down payments may be required for loans over $1 million. Lenders may also require higher income streams, strong credit and a show of reserves for a certain period of time as well. Guidelines are a little bit tighter now and each loan is considered on a case-by-case basis.

The major disadvantage, however, of a jumbo loan is the lender will most likely charge a higher interest rate. Also, not all lenders offer jumbo loans.

In 2008, Congress temporarily increased jumbo loan limits through the end of the year. Fannie Mae and Freddie Mac, the government-sponsored mortgage finance companies, could buy loans worth as much as $729,750, a large increase over the previous $417,000 loan limit. The move was aimed at helping struggling homeowners refinance large mortgages at lower interest rates. It also allowed the Federal Housing Administration to insure loans in expensive markets. For 2009, the revised maximum conforming limit is $625,500. Higher rates on Jumbo loans mean there is little opportunity to refinance, and falling home prices make it even more difficult to refinance as equity disappears.

Sub-Prime Loans - Much has changed since we wrote the first edition of this reference guide. Finding a mortgage, particularly in the sub-prime market, has become much more difficult and expensive. With so many sub-prime lenders going out of business in 2007 and 2008, many have found new life by migrating over to the Federal Housing Administration and originating FHA loans. The FHA is fast becoming the "new sub-prime." Sub-prime lenders are blamed for causing the current financial crisis because of their high foreclosure rates.

Fixed vs. Adjustable Rates

Interest rates fit into two categories: fixed and adjustable. A fixed interest rate remains the same over the course of the loan, while an adjustable rate changes during the life of the loan. Fixed interest rates typically come in the form of 30-year and 15-year mortgage loans. Some lenders have also introduced the 40- and 50-year mortgage.

30-Year Fixed Mortgage - This product's interest rate stays fixed for 30 years. The advantage to the borrower is the comfort of knowing the monthly payment (principal and interest portions) will remain the same every month for 30 years. A 30-year fixed has lower monthly payments than a 15-year fixed rate, because the borrowed loan amount is amortized over 30 years rather than 15. The disadvantage of this type of product is that market interest rates may go down, but the borrower is locked into a higher rate.

15-Year Fixed Mortgage - The 15-year mortgage is similar to the 30-year except the borrower builds equity faster; the mortgage note is paid off sooner and the monthly payment is higher. However, lenders charge a lower interest rate on a 15-year, compared to a 30-year note, since they get their money back sooner. One of the disadvantages of this type of mortgage is that you must have a higher annual income to qualify.

Adjustable Rate Mortgages - The adjustable rate mortgage product is the most confusing and most dangerous product of all. It may easily be termed a "time bomb loan," and we talk about this later in the chapter. It is one of the great contributors toward the explosion of foreclosures we began experiencing in 2006 and which continued well into 2009. ***Think of an ARM as a mortgage product with variable moving components.*** The components are:

- initial rate period
- index
- margin
- adjustment period
- rate cap
- lifetime cap
- interest rate (fully indexed or effective rate)

Let's take a closer look at each of these components of an ARM.

- The **initial interest rate,** or teaser rate, is the low interest rate offered in the beginning period of an adjustable-rate mortgage. It remains fixed for a certain period of time. It is also the rate lenders use to lure borrowers to this product.
- An **index** is a guide lenders use to measure and implement their own interest rate changes on their adjustable-rate products. The most common indexes are tied to 1-, 3-, and 5-year Treasury Securities, but there are many others. The interest rate – and your payments – are periodically adjusted up or down as the index changes.

- The **margin** is the lender's markup. *The index plus the margin equals your interest rate.* Lenders may sometimes try to confuse you by referring to the interest rate as a fully indexed rate or effective interest rate. Commonly, margins range from 2.00% to 2.75%. For example, if the 1-year treasury index is 4.25%, after adding the lender's markup to the index, the interest rate becomes 6.25% with a 2.00% margin.

- Changes in an index generally take place over a pre-determined period of time, known as the **adjustment period**. Adjustment periods can change monthly, bimonthly, annually, etc., depending on the chosen product. The index rate may adjust up or down. If it declines, the payment amount will also decline. See the next section for more information on how to understand what type of ARM you're being offered.

- The **rate cap** is how high your rate is permitted to change each adjustment period. It limits the amount your monthly interest and principal payment can increase.

- Be sure to get the most important cap of all: the **lifetime cap**. This cap states that, over the life of the loan, the rate can never go past a stated maximum rate. If your lifetime cap is 11%, and in the seventh year the index value plus margin equals 12%, your lifetime cap will stop the rate increase at 11%. It cannot go over 11% at anytime during the life of your loan.

- The **interest rate,** as it pertains to an ARM, is often referred to as the **fully indexed** or **effective interest rate**. This rate takes into account all the components at different time periods of your loan's life, to determine the interest rate that's needed to calculate your 30- or 15-year note fully amortized.

Understand Your Adjustment Periods with an ARM

An ARM with a rate that changes once a year is called a one-year ARM, and these are the most common. You may see an ARM described with numbers such as 1/1, 3/1, and 5/1. The first number in each set refers to the period of time the interest rate stays fixed. For example, a 3/1 ARM will stay fixed for three years before adjusting every year thereafter. Therefore, the second number is the adjustment period, showing how often adjustments can be made to the rate after the initial rate period has ended. You may also see an ARM described with such numbers as 2/28 or 3/27. A 2/28 ARM is a mortgage with a fixed rate for the first two years, and then the interest rate adjusts for each of the next 28 years. A 3/27 is an ARM in which the rate is fixed for the first three years, and then adjusts for each of the next 27 years.

These products are often offered to people who have plans to move within two to three years or have credit issues. Many loan officers sold borrowers on the concept of using the first two or three years as a time to clean up credit issues. Refinancing was then the solution to lower the monthly payment in the future.

Mistake # 25: *Not paying attention to the actual terms of your loan*

Advantages and Disadvantages of an ARM

An adjustable rate mortgage is attractive to borrowers who initially need a lower monthly mortgage payment. It's also presented as a great product for those who want to qualify for a higher loan amount than they can now afford because of an ARM's initial lower interest rate, or if a borrower plans to move when the fixed portion of the product expires.

To decide if an applicant has enough income to meet the monthly payment obligation, lenders usually use the initial interest rate, or minimum payment, on an ARM to calculate the monthly payment. And that's where the problems really begin. ***Though the interest rate may rise after the initial rate period, the underwriting requirements are based on the low initial interest rate of the ARM, as opposed to the fully indexed rate.*** This makes it easier for some borrowers to qualify for the mortgage. However, after the initial low interest rate (teaser rate) term expires, the interest rate can often jump to higher than market rate (to make up for the low initial rate), which frequently makes the loan no longer affordable. This is why so many homeowners were unable to afford their homes once their ARM rates adjusted to reflect the fully indexed rates.

Mistake # 26: *Falling for a teaser rate*

Many sub-prime lenders lead with this type of ARM product. It is an easy product to sell to the uneducated borrower because of the lower, teaser interest rate. It can be dangerous because it does not take into account the potential – and likely – increase after the initial rate period is over. Also, the moving components attached to this product, which we listed several pages back, make understanding the product difficult. This is why an ARM can be so dangerous for the average borrower.

Interest-Only Mortgages

An interest-only mortgage requires the borrower to pay only the interest portion of the monthly mortgage payment, with nothing toward the principal portion of the loan. The terms for these loans are usually for a period of 5 or 10 years. When this time is up, the borrower then has the option to refinance, pay the balance in a lump sum, or start paying off the principal. Borrowers can always apply additional payments toward the principal at any time, but it is not required. Since there is no payment made to the principal, the principal balance remains unchanged. For example, if you took out an interest only loan on $300,000 and made payments for 10 years, at the end of the 10 years you would still owe $300,000.

This product is *advantageous* to borrowers who:

- Want a smaller monthly payment for a higher loan amount
- Have sporadic earnings with income in the form of commissions or bonuses
- Consider themselves savvy investors who use the savings from the principal to invest in other investment vehicles

One of the disadvantages of interest-only products is that most borrowers will not invest the extra principal savings, but spend it instead. Also, many borrowers anticipate income growth, but when the increased monthly payment of principal and interest comes due, they fall short and have difficulty paying the higher payments. Many times, loan officers push the benefits of interest-only loan programs, but they neglect to tell borrowers about the disadvantages.

In all of these scenarios, ask questions and make sure you understand how your payment works for you. There are so many different products on the market today that it's hard to come up with steadfast rules. If you are not comfortable at the 30-year fixed rate and want to consider other types of programs, ask questions. Know how your payment could change throughout the life of the loan.

In Summary, the mortgage industry is changing every day. There are a variety of loan programs on the market, ranging from conventional to non-conforming to FHA and VA. Ask questions of your loan officer and investigate all your options. If you select an ARM, make sure you understand how and when your loan will adjust, and by how much. More importantly, determine a comfortable monthly mortgage payment for you and your family to handle, then stick with it. If it means waiting until you are financially able, than do that!

Pass The Knowledge On!

CHAPTER 13

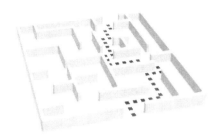

FINDING THE RIGHT MORTGAGE LOAN

In this chapter we'll explain how to select the best mortgage to meet your needs, and explain the tools you now have at your disposal to make this decision. We'll examine all the costs associated with a mortgage loan, and look at the choices you'll have for terms of the loan. And even though you've learned by now that some of the best rates come from prime lenders, please remember there is more to choosing a mortgage than a rate! In fact, choosing a mortgage loan product without taking into consideration the overall cost of the loan could easily cost you thousands!

So how do you do this? Well, you've made a start. You already decided on which loan officers you want to consider. We gave you numerous ideas on how to determine who makes the cut in Chapter 9.

Next, it's important to remember that there are settlement costs to go along with whatever great rate you find. Let's discuss those settlement costs for a moment.

Throughout this book we have used the terms "closing costs" and "settlement costs" interchangeably. Closing costs are one of those general terms in real estate often used to define *the total cost* of closing your loan. However this is *only partially true* so it's worth noting. *Closing* is defined as the point in time when the actual title of the real property[53] owned by the seller is conveyed to the buyer, per the terms of the real estate sales contract. Typically there are a variety of costs associated with the transaction that are incurred by both the buyer and the seller. These costs are typically paid at the time of closing and are known as **closing costs**. These costs, however, should not be confused with your **prepaids and reserves,** which are also collected at closing and make up the total settlement costs.

Mistake # 27: *Not paying attention to your GFE, TIL and HUD-1*

We'll use the Good Faith Estimate to better understand these terms, since they impact a borrower's total funds needed to close. And let's also look at the Settlement Statement and the Truth in Lending Disclosure Statement, too, since they explain other crucial aspects of your mortgage loan.

1. **The Good Faith Estimate (GFE)**, which you receive three days after you have submitted your loan application, is designed to tell you the following:

- What your *estimated* settlement costs will be
- An *estimate* of how much money you will need to bring to closing
- If you will require closing cost assistance from the seller or others

2. **The Settlement Statement (HUD-1)** is similar to the GFE except it's the document you receive 24 hours before the day of closing, along with the *actual* settlement costs based on the *actual* closing date. The GFE was the preliminary document to this final document.

3. **The Truth in Lending Disclosure Statement (TIL)** is designed to provide you early on in the home-financing process with the *truth in lending* as it pertains to your loan. You receive this form at the same

---

[53] *Real property* is also known as real estate.

time as you receive your GFE, and again at closing when all the numbers are final.

The TIL also explains the **Annual Percentage Rate** (APR), which is a uniform measure of the cost of the loan from the first year to the end of the loan period, assuming you pay consistently for the term of the loan. *When you see the APR, it will be higher than your quoted interest rate because it includes the cost associated with closing your loan.* Here's why: When lenders advertise rates, they must follow the federal Truth in Lending Laws, which state the APR must be posted next to the quoted interest rate. The concept behind this is to prevent lenders from luring borrowers into unsuitable loans by hiding fees and up-front costs behind low, advertised interest rates. *You will know whether or not the loan officer included the closing cost fee in the APR when you see a check mark (√) under PFC (Prepaid Finance Charge) on your GFE.* The rules for calculating the APR are clearly defined, however, the APR will be different from lender to lender, depending on which fees and charges are included in the calculation. Problems arise when a loan officer does not include in the calculation a fee that was √ on the GFE. This skews the APR, making it more challenging for the borrower to compare to other APRs. Essentially, the loan officer has cheated the system, and if you are unaware of this, you may make a decision based on inaccurate data. Visit our website at www.MakeNoMistakes.com for a list of items that should be included in the APR calculation. Click on **"Real Estate Forms"** for "APR Calculation Table" (enter code 550 in the book coupon field). The list is also located in the back of this book.

Ask your prospective loan officer for a clearer understanding of what's included in the APR. Based on that person's answer, you may choose to disqualify this loan officer early on.

When you talk with various loan officers, *you will receive the GFE and the TIL within 3 days of submitting your application. These are the two forms you will use to compare mortgage loan programs.* You might be wondering why, if the Truth in Lending form is supposed to tell me the truth about the terms of my loan, you can't just compare these forms to determine the best deal? The answer to this is: Loan officers make mistakes and their mistakes could cost you thousands!

How to Use Your Lender Comparative

To fill this need, *we've designed the Lender Comparative worksheet as a tool to compare various loan products you're considering for a specific property purchase*. Find an example in the appendix. It will help you see what you are truly being charged for, and it will help formulate your questions. If you can, go to our website at www.MakeNoMistakes.com and select the *Lender Comparative* tab to use this tool. Note: When you order the Make No Mistakes™ System, you will receive a workbook which includes *all the excel spreadsheet* tools and checklists in excel format so you can download, save and print a copy. Whichever route you use, you'll want one handy while we discuss it.

Notice there is space next to each row for your own comments. Make notes to yourself here to highlight the advantages or disadvantages of each loan, or any other info you need to help you make a decision. For example, Lender A is not charging me for this, so why is Lender C? Or, why is there such a big difference in the amount of monies Lenders A and B would have me bring to closing? Arm yourself with the answers to these questions, as they are the criterion you should consider when shopping for the loan. It's not easy comparing different loan programs.

Don't forget that the mortgage rate is only one part of a mortgage product. There are also points and fees to compare between the different loan officers. Loan officers tend to make this confusing because they have different names for what amounts to basically the same fees. They'll also waive fees and then add others to make up for the loss of the fees waived. And to top it all off, depending on who you go to for financing, you may receive the Good Faith Estimate in different formats!

This tool allows you to look at all the loans you're being offered. You can then ask better questions objectively. Review your options and converse intelligently about your mortgage loan choices. Also, by going through this exercise and asking questions of your loan officer, he or she will know that you are shopping around for the best deal and are knowledgeable on the subject.

Also, feel free to share the results of this form with your real estate agent or loan officer to gather their comments about your options. This form is only available at www.MakeNoMistakes.com.

Don't be overwhelmed by the Lender Comparative. Once you start examining our sample, you'll see how logical and self-explanatory it is, and just how helpful of a tool it can be.

To get started you must have the Good Faith Estimate (GFE) and the Truth In Lending (TIL) forms in hand from each of the loan officers to accurately compare mortgage loans. Then go to the Lender Comparative, which is in an Excel spreadsheet format. *Next, enter the amounts from each lender in each line in the appropriate columns on the GFE. This will make it easy to compare the loan officers' information.* Note: When you order the Make No Mistakes™ System, you will receive a workbook which includes *all the excel spreadsheet* tools and checklists in excel format so you can download and save your own information, and return to it at your leisure.

We suggest using a highlighter or pen to mark off on your hard copy each time you enter a cost into the Lender Comparative so you know that you have accounted for it. Remember, you can get a spreadsheet that's already set up in an easy-to-understand format by visiting our website, www.MakeNoMistakes.com. Simply clear out the numbers we've used as examples and add your own information. Sections of the Comparative are discussed throughout this chapter.

Here are the categories we'll examine together in this chapter:

1. Items Payable in Connection with the Loan (Section 800)
2. Title Charges (Section 1100)
3. Government Recording & Transfer Charges (Section 1200)
4. Additional Settlement Costs (Section 1300)

The sections above make up the ***Total Estimated Closing Costs***, which we'll cover in detail.

5. Items Required By Lender to be Paid in Advance (Section 900)
6. Reserves Deposited with Lender (Section 1000)

The sections above make up the *Total Estimated Settlement Charges* (Sections 800 – 1300).

The Total Estimated Funds Needed To Close includes *the down payment and all other charges such as the ones listed above.*

The section numbers are not in chronological order, so don't be alarmed. They do, however, follow the same format of both the GFE and Settlement Statement. We will go into great detail and define each of these two forms' line items in Chapter 21 since they almost always correlate line item by line item.

For now, simply take note of the differences between the loan products that the loan officers are offering. These should prompt you to ask questions and watch for more inconsistencies.

On the Lender Comparative worksheet, you'll notice we placed several comment bars that resemble red triangles. Click on these for explanations of the line items, or to find out what information is requested for that box. The comment boxes will look similar to these below:

LENDER COMPARATIVE				
LENDER	**Lender #1** **ABC**	**Lender #2** **DEF**	**Lender # 3** **GHI**	**COMMENTS**
TERM	30	30	30	
PROGRAM	FIXED	FIXED	FIXED	
Sales Price	$ 313,183.00	**Melissa Walters:**		
% Down Payment	20%	If you're considering a two-loan program, such as the 80/15/5, enter the 80% loan amount here		
Down Payment	$ 62,636.60			
1st Loan Amount	$ 250,546.40	$ 250,546.00	$ 250,546.00	

Let's first start with the loan terms and the proposed mortgage payment itself. Here is that section of the Lender Comparative with sample dollar amounts filled in so you can see how it all works together.

LENDER COMPARATIVE				
LENDER	**Lender #1 ABC**	**Lender #2 DEF**	**Lender #3 GHI**	**COMMENTS**
TERM	**30**	**30**	**30**	
PROGRAM	**FIXED**	**FIXED**	**FIXED**	
Sales Price	$ 313,183.00	$ 313,183.00	$ 313,183.00	
% Down Payment	20%	20%	20%	
Down Payment	$ 62,636.60	$ 62,636.60	$ 62,636.60	
1st Loan Amount	$ 250,546.40	$ 250,546.00	$ 250,546.00	
2nd Loan Amount				
1st Interest Rate	**6%**	**5.75%**	**5.875%**	
2nd Rate				
1st Principal & Interest	$1,502.15	$1,482.07	$ 1,483.61	
2nd Principal & Interest				
Monthly	**$1,502.15**	**$1,462.12**	**$ 1,482.07**	
Hazard Insurance	$ 143.92	$ 143.92	$ 143.92	
Taxes	$ 629.00	$ 629.00	$ 629.00	
PMI				
HOA	$ 83.33	$ 83.33	$ 83.33	
Monthly Mortgage Amount	**$2,343.53**	**$2,318.37**	**$2,338.32**	

After referring back to a previous page for our list of seven categories that explain Total Estimated Settlement Charges and Total Estimated Funds Needed to Close, let's start with the first category.

1. Items Payable In Connection with the Loan

These items will be all the charges identified on the Good Faith Estimate as line items in the 800 series. See our sample section below of a Good Faith Estimate. Specifically, it itemizes fees the broker and lender charge the borrower to complete the loan. These charges could include any number of fees, ranging from loan origination to wire transfer. This is the most common area to find "junk fees," which are defined as the extra fees that some loan originators charge which may be frivolous and unnecessary.

GOOD FAITH ESTIMATE

Applicants: **CUSTOMER SAMPLE**	Application No: lender 3
Property Addr:	Date Prepared: **10/27/2008**
Prepared By: **1st Financial Services Ph. 281-679-1074**	Loan Program: **CONVENTIONAL - 30 YEAR**
1650 US HWY 6 #350, Sugar Land, TX 77478	

The information provided below reflects estimates of the charges which you are likely to incur at the settlement of your loan. The fees listed are estimates-actual charges may be more or less. Your transaction may not involve a fee for every item listed. The numbers listed beside the estimates generally correspond to the numbered lines contained in the HUD-1 settlement statement which you will be receiving at settlement. The HUD-1 settlement statement will show you the actual cost for items paid at settlement.

Total Loan Amount $ **250,546**   Interest Rate: **5.875 %**   Term: **360 / 360** mths

800	ITEMS PAYABLE IN CONNECTION WITH LOAN:			PFC S F POC
801	Loan Origination Fee	1.000%	$	2,505.46 ✓
802	Loan Discount			
803	Appraisal Fee			350.00 ✓
804	Credit Report			35.00 ✓
805	Lender's Inspection Fee			
808	Mortgage Broker Fee			
809	Tax Related Service Fee			105.00 ✓
810	Processing Fee			400.00 ✓
811	Underwriting Fee			
812	Wire Transfer Fee			
	FLOOD CERTIFICATION			26.00

If you are dealing directly with the lender instead of using a broker, the 800-section fees should not be estimates; they should exactly match your HUD-1 Settlement Statement fees. However, if you are using a broker, he or she may not have access to what the lender will ultimately charge. At the time the Good Faith Estimate is produced, the loan officer may not yet know which lender will actually handle the loan package. Therefore, the broker or loan officer will usually estimate a fee on the lender's behalf.

Notice how we took the numbers from the GFE and entered them in the Lender Comparative above. Remember that loan officers may have different names for basically the same fees. They may even have a different format for their Good Faith Estimate. Don't let that get in your way! Your objective is to simply add each charge into your Excel spreadsheet, the Lender Comparative. At the end, when everything is totaled up, you will be able to truly compare the loan products and see the differences. Trust us. A little work now will save you headaches and the wrong decision later. Be sure to use the *comments column* to write down your thoughts and comments.

2. Title Charges

These charges will be everything identified on the Good Faith Estimate as line items in the 1100 section, with costs related to conveying the title of the property or any attorney charges for completing the transaction. Attorney fees are usually established up front and split between the borrower and seller. You can negotiate these fees *at the time the offer on the property is drafted by you and your agent.*

1100	TITLE CHARGES:		PFC S F POC
1101	Closing or Escrow Fee:	$	250.00
1105	Document Preparation Fee		150.00
1106	Notary Fees		
1107	Attorney Fees		150.00
1108	Title Insurance:		225.00

In this section, loan officers might use different amounts for the same service, however, the fees here should be the same among all the lenders since the fees are dictated by the title company or the attorney's office – not by the lenders. Rather than a loan officer calling the title company to confirm the charge, a loan officer will simply estimate. We suggest you or your agent contact the title company or closing attorney office in order to get accurate fees. Meanwhile, for comparison purposes, simply notice if there is a blaring or significantly higher figure than all others. Otherwise, make all the numbers here the same based on your research. See our example below.

TITLE CHARGES				COMMENTS
Closing/Escrow	$ 250.00	$ 250.00	$ 250.00	SHOULD BE THE SAME
Doc. Prep-Title/Closing Agent		$ 150.00	$ 150.00	SHOULD BE THE SAME
Attorney Fee	$ 365.00	$ 150.00	$ 150.00	SHOULD BE THE SAME
Title Insurance		$ 1,649.00		SELLER PAYS FOR TITLE POLICY - BUYER ONLY PAYS FOR LENDER POLICY
Courier /Express Mail		$ 30.00		NO COURIER FEE???
Lender Title Insurance	$ 280.00	$ 225.00	$ 225.00	SHOULD BE THE SAME
TOTALS	$895.00	$2,454.00	$ 775.00	

3. Government Recording and Transfer Charges

These charges are identified on the Good Faith Estimate as line items in the 1200 series. They should be the same for all lenders in your area, as they are jurisdiction-dependent and thus not set by a lender. These fees are *not negotiable*. They include title recording fees with your government entity (usually municipal or county), and city/county/state tax stamps, as relevant to your property.

1200	GOVERNMENT RECORDING & TRANSFER CHARGES:		PFC S F POC
1201	Recording Fees:	$	120.00 ✓
1202	City/County Tax/Stamps:		
1203	State Tax/Stamps:		70.00

Here, different loan officers might use varying amounts for what you know to be the same service, or they'll leave off a charge entirely. The fees here should be the same among all the loan officers since they are dictated by the government and only vary based on sales price. You can confirm these charges with the title company or closing attorney's office. See our example below.

GOVERNMENT				COMMENTS
State Tax Stamp	$ 70.00	$ 70.00	$ 70.00	SHOULD BE THE SAME
Recording fees	$ 120.00	$ 120.00	$ 120.00	SHOULD BE THE SAME
TOTALS	**$ 190.00**	**$ 190.00**	**$ 190.00**	

4. Additional Settlement Costs

These costs will be all the charges identified on the Good Faith Estimate as line items in the 1300 series. They are the additional settlement charges, otherwise known as miscellaneous fees. These fees are usually *negotiable* with the seller.

1300	ADDITIONAL SETTLEMENT CHARGES:		PFC S F POC
1302	Pest Inspection	$	75.00
	SURVEY		380.00
	HOA TRANSFER		
	HOA PRO RATED		
		Estimated Closing Costs	4,841.46

Here, loan officers add such items as inspections, homeowners' association fees (HOA) and other third-party charges. The loan officers may even have different charges for their survey and inspections. HOA fees should be the same among all lenders. The problem in this section is that, more often than not, loan officers forget to account for the HOA fees. You can confirm these charges with the title company or closing attorney's office since they are the entity that eventually puts together the final Settlement Statement. This means that they are in contact with all parties who plan to charge for any and all services. See our example below.

ADDITIONAL SETTLEMENT COSTS				COMMENTS
Survey	$ 514.19	$ 380.00	$ 380.00	What is Lender # 1 including in its survey that Lender #2 & #3 are not?
Termite/Pest Inspection	$ 100.00	$ 75.00	$ 75.00	Why is Lender # 1 not requiring a termite inspection?
HOA Transfer Fee	$ 125.00			Lender # 2 & #3 forgot to charge HOA fees.
HOA Pro Rates	$ 200.00			Lender # 2 & #3 forgot to charge HOA fees.
TOTALS	$ 939.19	$ 455.00	$ 455.00	
Estimated Closing Costs	$ 5,493.65	$ 7,573.19	$ 4,841.46	

These four sections added together amount to the Total Estimated Closing Costs.

So far, we've explained four of the six items needed to produce the Total Estimated Settlement Charges. The other two sections are funds that have a cost but are paid on behalf of the property's owners, as opposed to a cost associated with putting the loan together, i.e., creating all the loan documents. Hazard insurance, and mortgage insurance and interest are costs that most lenders require be paid in advance. The payments go directly to the service provider, that is, the insurance company that provides the homeowner's insurance and the lender who provides the mortgage loan.

5. Items Required by Lender to be Paid in Advance

Items required by the lender to be paid in advance by the borrower are known as prepaids. Typically, but not always, prepaids are time-period-related. For example, homeowner's insurance is billed for coverage of a specific, *upcoming* time period. Homeowners are usually required to pay this bill in advance.

900	ITEMS REQUIRED BY LENDER TO BE PAID IN ADVANCE:						PFC S F POC
901	Interest for	10	days @ $	40.8877	per day	$	408.88 √
902	Mortgage Insurance Premium						
903	Hazard Insurance Premium						1,726.80
904							
905	VA Funding Fee						

The Prepaid for the interest-only is always prorated to the estimated day of closing. For example, if you are closing on the twentieth of the month, you will pay for 10 days of Prepaids if the month ends on the thirtieth. In other words, you will pay interest on the loan from the day you take ownership to the end of the month. Borrowers always pay for one year of homeowner's insurance in advance, and the insurance policy goes into effect the day of closing. In our example above, homeowner's insurance is referred to as hazard insurance and the one-year premium is $1,726.80. The same calculation applies for mortgage insurance premiums and for the VA funding fee, if the borrower is applying for a FHA or VA loan, respectively. We've added this section and reserves together on our lender comparative simply to consolidate costs.

ESTIMATED PREPAID ITEMS / RESERVES				COMMENTS
Prepaid Interest (To month end)	$ 417.58	$ 400.18	$ 408.88	
Hazard Insurance (1 year in advance)	$ 1,727.04	$ 1,727.04	$ 1,727.04	
Hazard Insurance (3 months in advance)	$ 431.76	$ 431.76	$ 431.76	
County Taxes (3 months in advance)	$ 1,887.00	$ 1,887.00	$ 1,887.00	
Estimated Total Prepaids/Reserves	$ 4,463.38	$ 4,445.98	$ 4,454.68	

6. Reserves Deposited with Lender

In addition to the Prepaids, most lenders require borrowers to deposit reserves[54] in an account, often referred to as an escrow account, for such things as:

- Homeowner's insurance
- Mortgage insurance premiums
- Taxes

1000	RESERVES DEPOSITED WITH LENDER:			PFC S F POC
1001	Hazard Insurance Premium	3 months @ $	143.92 per month	$ 431.76
1002	Mortgage Ins. Premium Reserves	months @ $	per month	
1003	School Tax	months @ $	per month	
1004	Taxes and Assessment Reserves	3 months @ $	629.00 per month	1,887.00
1005	Flood Insurance Reserves	months @ $	per month	
		months @ $	per month	
		months @ $	per month	
		Estimated Prepaid Items/Reserves		4,454.68

Lenders require money be placed in reserve accounts to ensure these items are always paid, which diminishes the risk they took in loaning money to their borrowers. The money deposited into this account is – technically – still yours until it's used to pay your insurance premiums and property tax invoices when they're due. ***Your reserve account is also referred to as your escrow account.***

On the other hand, if the Reserve sections of your GFE are *blank*, you have decided *not* to escrow. In that case, you should expect the seller to issue a tax credit at closing. We discussed the risk associated with not escrowing, as it pertains to closing costs, in Chapter 4.

---

[54] A *reserve* is monies paid in advance for your real estate taxes and insurance premiums.

What Happens to Your Reserve Account When Taxes or Insurance Increase?

Beware! Anytime your insurance premiums or real estate taxes increase – which could be once a year – your lender can ask you to put more money in your reserve account. There are typically two ways to accomplish this.

- Pay a lump sum to cover the additional costs
- Increase your monthly payment to include the additional costs

Lenders don't usually give you a long time to make this decision and then to pay the additional money; 60 days or less. Keep in mind that if you choose to ignore the lender's request, and continue to make your same monthly payment, the lender will return your check to you. At that point, it's considered late, and will appear as a late payment on your credit report.

7. Total Estimated Funds Needed To Close

This is the last area on the GFE, and it's located near the bottom of the page. This is where all the sections are calculated to determine how much money you will need to bring to closing. In our example, the home's purchase price is $313,183.00. The borrower is putting 20% down, which makes the down payment $62,637.00. The amount the borrower wants to finance by the lender is $250,546.00. We'll get to the amount the borrower needs to bring to closing in a few minutes.

In our example, there were *no seller contributions.*[55] We discuss seller contributions in several chapters, so review the book's index for more information on the subject.

---

[55] *Seller contribution* is when the seller of the property contributes monies towards the buyer's closing cost as an allowance or an incentive to purchase the property.

The option fee is the fee given directly to the seller at the time the contract is executed. The fee acts as an insurance policy to protect the earnest money for a period of time while the buyer has inspections performed on the property. The option fee can be for any amount that both the buyer and seller agree on but it's certainly just a small fraction of the earnest money amount.

The earnest money, the amount that's negotiated at the time of the contract, serves as a good faith gesture to the seller that the buyer is serious about purchasing the property. It is typically a small percentage of the total purchase price of the property and is applied toward the down payment needed at the time of closing. The earnest money check is made out to the title company, cashed and held in an escrow account until closing. Neither the buyer nor the seller has access to these funds until closing unless there is a mutual agreement to release the funds.

At closing the borrower is given credit for all monies applied to the property prior to closing. These credits show up as subtractions to the total amount due at closing. **In this example the borrower will need to bring $68,833.14. This amount should correlate to the amount stated on the GFE.**

LENDER COMPARATIVE				
LENDER	**Lender #1 ABC**	**Lender #2 DEF**	**Lender # 3 GHI**	**COMMENTS**
Purchase Price	$ 313,183.00	$ 313,183.00	$ 313,183.00	
Loan Amount	$ 250,546.00	$ 250,546.00	$ 250,546.00	
Down Payment	$ 62,637.00	$ 62,637.00	$ 62,637.00	
Estimated Closing Costs	$ 5,493.65	$ 7,573.19	$ 4,841.46	
Estimated Total Prepaids/Reserves	$ 4,463.38	$ 4,445.98	$ 4,454.68	
Total Estimated Settlement Charges	$ 9,957.03	$ 12,019.17	$ 9,296.14	
Seller Contribution (Amount Paid by Seller)	$ -	$ -	$ -	
Option Money	$ (100.00)	$ (100.00)	$ (100.00)	
Earnest Money	$ (3,000.00)	$ (3,000.00)	$ (3,000.00)	
Total Estimated Funds Needed to Close	$ 69,494.03	$ 71,556.17	$ 68,833.14	

If, after reviewing your good faith estimate, you find you are short of the funds you need to bring to closing, here are your options:

- Reduce the amount of house you hope to purchase
- Ask for a gift from family or friends
- Choose to not buy the house now, and save until you have enough funds
- Ask the seller for a seller contribution toward your closing costs
- Look into down payment assistance programs

Down Payment and Closing Cost Assistance

If you qualify, there are many home buyer assistance resources available for individuals and families. Qualifications are usually based on income, size of family and the location of the property. For some people, it seems impossible to even begin to save enough cash without some form of *down payment assistance*. Many programs will assist borrowers with down payments and/or closing costs. Look at such organizations as The American Housing Program, which facilitates federal, state, county and city assistance programs, including the U.S. Congress Emergency Housing and Economic Stimulus Act. There is a $250 home buyer education/admin fee at time of closing. Visit the American Housing Program's website at www.housingprograms.org for more information. Or simply check the internet for other down payment assistance programs with the name of your state and you will find several sites you can investigate including our website!

But even if you already have your down payment, why not keep your money? It may make more sense to NOT use your own funds as a down payment if you can qualify for assistance. Just make sure you understand the terms that come with assistance. For example some programs want 50% of your profits when you sell. This may be ok, if the assistance was worth it to you.

Additional Information You May Need From Your Loan Officer

Last, but not least, the detailed Lender Comparative prompts you for additional information you may need to obtain from your lender:

- Is escrow required?
- Will there be a tax credit?
- Is there a prepayment penalty?

ADDITIONAL INFORMATION YOU MAY NEED FROM YOUR LENDER				
LENDER	**Lender #1 ABC**	**Lender #2 DEF**	**Lender # 3 GHI**	**COMMENTS**
Escrow Required	no	no	no	
Tax Credit *	n/a	n/a	n/a	
Prepayment Penalty	no	no	no	
APR	**6.138%**	**5.922%**	**6.009%**	

The first question has to do with whether or not escrow is required. This may not require a decision from you if you are not putting a down payment on the property of 20% or more. If your answer is *yes*, you will be required to set up an escrow account. You should expect the lender to request a minimum of three months of taxes and insurances as previously explained.

If your answer is *no*, and you're choosing to *not* escrow, *you will receive a tax credit from the seller for the months that they occupied the property.* For example, if you are closing in June you will receive approximately six months of taxes for the period that you did not own the property.

Mistake # 28: *Falling for the TV infomercials' cash-at-closing claims*

Be very careful! We've all seen the infomercials with the excited home buyer who says, "I got this house with no [or little] money down!" Or maybe you've seen the one of the borrower who says he *bought a house and put $3,000 in his pocket at closing.* This is not in reference to the concept of flipping,[56] but rather, the simple concept of a *tax credit,* which is money a buyer receives from the seller for the period of time the seller owned the property in the current year. For example, if you purchase the property on July 13, the seller pays you for 194 days of property taxes, which covers January 1 to July 13. The buyer receives this prorated tax money at closing, and it is first applied toward the total closing cost. If there are funds left over, then yes, it is cash back to the buyer – but only for a short time, and it's not the borrower's to keep! As a result, the column called *Total Funds Needed to Close* will be decreased by the amount of the tax credit. Yes, the buyer does receive a tax credit of $7,930.72, but remember: the borrower must now pay the taxes for *the entire year* ending December 31, because the seller gave the borrower the prorated sum at closing.

---

[56] *Flipping* is the term used to describe the act of an investor buying a house and selling it immediately for a profit.

Using the daily tax rate found on line item 901 of the GFE, this is how our example was calculated:

194 days
X $40.88 (daily tax rate)
= $7,932.72

The $7,930.72 goes to the buyer, but it goes back out again soon to pay for the real estate taxes, which is why the seller gave it to the borrower in the first place. *So don't believe everything you see in those real estate infomercials on TV! This is a perfect example of why it pays to ask questions, and not take any information at face value.*

In real life, the challenge with this tax credit is that it's usually not explained clearly to the borrower. As a result, the borrower forgets about it! The borrower is so focused on getting in the house and by doing so with as small an amount of money as possible, it's a total surprise when the invoice for the property taxes comes in the mail. This can be a bad situation. If you don't have the money to pay property taxes, you could lose your home even if you are current with the principal, interest and insurance parts of your mortgage payment.

Next, be sure to ask if there is a prepayment penalty for the loan. A prepayment penalty is a charge or penalty to the borrower when part of or the whole mortgage is paid off before a certain period of time elapses. A lender would charge this fee to avoid having significant losses due to a borrower paying off the loan early, either because of refinancing the house or selling it. A lender expects to make a certain amount of money from each loan it has; if the loan goes away earlier than anticipated, the lender wants to be compensated for this loss of revenue. Two pieces of good news here: a prepayment penalty is usually for a loan's first few years, not the entire life of the loan; and prime loans usually do not come with prepayment penalties.

The Annual Percentage Rate (APR) is a great tool to compare the cost of a mortgage loan over the term of the loan. It includes any charges payable by you that are imposed by the lender as a condition for the extension of credit. Charges included in the APR calculation should be indicated as Prepaid Finance Charges on the GFE as previously discussed in this chapter.

Another question you may want to ask each of the loan officers you're interviewing is about locking in an interest rate. Normally this is not done until you have found a property and decide to move forward with buying it. ***Locking in a rate has its advantage and disadvantages.*** Obviously, if you lock in and the rates go up, then you've made a great decision. On the flip side, however, if the rates go down, you're unable to take advantage of the new lower rate without paying more money to buy it down. You could just let the rate expire, but that poses other challenges.

If you decide to lock in a rate, be sure to have the loan officer give you a copy of the lock confirmation from the lender so you don't have to hear later that you never told him to lock it! Along with the confirmation, you should see the date the locked interest rate expires. This allows you to write language in your contract to protect your interest rate in the event the seller causes a delay in closing. See page 246 for sample language in special provisions.

How Do You Decide On A Lender?

Understanding yourself, your budget and your financial circumstances will help you decide on the best route for you. We will use our sample information on the Lender Comparative to demonstrate the thought process you might consider. It's always best to discuss your options with your loan officer and real estate agent too. Remember, they deal with buyers and sellers everyday so they should be able to provide varying perspectives.

Consider asking yourself these questions before you start making a decision:

- What interest rate am I being offered?

- What is the maximum monthly payment I am comfortable making, taking into account my current debt? In our example there is not a big difference in the monthly mortgages. Lender #2 offers the lower mortgage note, although Lender #3 costs the borrower $19.95 more a month. Does this difference warrant paying more in closing costs?

	Lender #1 ABC	Lender #2 DEF	Lender # 3 GHI	COMMENTS
Monthly Mortgage Amount	$2,343.53	$2,318.37	$2,338.32	

- Do I see my income increasing in the future? If so, when and by how much? Should I consider looking at a 15-year mortgage that would give me a higher mortgage payment but allow me to pay it off quicker?

- Do I have all the money for a down payment? Will I need down payment assistance?

- Do I have enough to cover my closing costs? Will I need the seller to contribute to my closing costs? Knowing what the estimated costs are of borrowing money before you start searching for your property will help determine if you need to look or ask for assistance from the seller. This will also let the real estate agent know how to negotiate on your behalf and how to structure your contract.

	Lender #1 ABC	Lender #2 DEF	Lender # 3 GHI	COMMENTS
Estimated Closing Costs	$ 5,493.65	$ 7,573.19	$ 4,841.46	

- In our example, there was a difference of $2,731.73 in total closing costs between Lender #2 and Lender #3. Would it make sense for me to consider paying more in closing costs to have a lower mortgage payment?

- How long do I plan to live in the house? More than 11 years? We often encourage borrowers to look at this simple scenario:

It cost you $2,731.73 in additional closing costs to save $19.95 a month. Divide this savings ($19.95) into this cost ($2,731.73) and you'll find it would take just over 136 months to recoup this additional outlay of cash. These 136 months equate to a little more than 11 years. So the question then becomes, "Do I plan to live in the home as long as 11 years?" If not, then it's not worth the extra cost to save $19.95 a month. If you were to stay in the home for the entire 30 years of the loan, then Lender #2 would be the better deal because of the lower APR and the lower interest rate.

This should conclusively illustrate that choosing a product based solely on the best interest rate is seldom, if ever, the right thing to do. In this case, choosing lender #3 makes more sense because the homeowner does not plan to live in the home more than eleven years.

	Lender #1 ABC	Lender #2 DEF	Lender # 3 GHI	COMMENTS
1st Interest Rate	6%	5.75%	5.875%	
APR	6.138%	5.922%	6.009%	

In summary, we can't stress enough how important choosing the right loan is to your future and peace of mind. Consider your loan choice – and its terms – just as important as choosing the right home. Know your loan's advantages and disadvantages, and don't be intimidated by the complexity of the mortgage programs presented. Do your homework and make a decision that meets your needs.

That's why you have to interview loan officers and put together a comparison spreadsheet of the programs presented to you via the Good Faith Estimates and Truth in Lending disclosures. Remember, our Lender Comparative Worksheet is a great example – and tool – you can use to guide you on your path of comparing loan options. Obtain a copy of the Lender Comparative by visiting our website.

It is important to make an educated decision based on the facts, not just an interest rate. You need to look at the whole program, including mortgage insurance, prepayment penalty and down payment requirements. Review all the features and line items on your GFE so you can decide if any or all of these products meet your needs. If you need advice or can't make a decision, consult a mortgage professional who will take the time to educate you. Use this guide and any other sources you may have to verify what you were told and to help you formulate questions.

Pass The Knowledge On!

CHAPTER 14

SEARCHING FOR A HOME

In this chapter you will learn that it is important to *start* the process of searching for a new home already knowing *what you want at the end* of the process. Not staying focused can cost you thousands!

Buying real estate is unlike any other purchase you will ever make. It's a psychological journey. The process to find the right property takes energy, time and having an idea of what you want. Once you find the right property, you just may become obsessed! You start sending pictures of the property to your family and friends, and driving by everyday and then – bam!!! You're emotionally attached and you lose most of your ability to think rationally and now, no other house, in your mind, will do.

This concept is very similar to falling in love at first sight. We know you are saying that this couldn't happen to you. We would be willing to bet, however, as you start your search and find what you believe to be the perfect home, you will remember this part of the book and laugh.

We had two clients who needed more space because they were expecting another mouth to feed within a few months. Their current home was a three-bedroom, three-level townhome in which the third bedroom served as both an office and guest bedroom. They needed to move into a four-bedroom home with a study. We started searching for a home in their desired location that would meet these qualifications.

One day we toured a beautifully-decorated home that looked as though an interior designer must live there. It was just fabulous! Our buyers had to have this house. They began to convince us that this was the perfect house for them, even though there was not enough closet space and the fourth room could only serve as a study.

Though we agreed that the home was beautiful, we also had to remind them that they were not buying this home's furnishings or accessories. That meant that this home would look different with their own furnishings in it. We also mentioned that once they moved in, they would be calling us in another two years to sell it because this house didn't really meet their needs.

As their real estate agent, my duty was to keep them from becoming emotionally attached to a house that did not meet their needs. It was easy for me to see the difference between what they shared with me in their initial interview and what they saw in a beautifully-decorated but smaller home. My clients passed on the home after I reiterated the importance of paying attention to the location, flow and structure of the home – and not how well it was decorated. Soon after that, we found what was truly the perfect house for them, and they told us they appreciated our help earlier when we had urged them to keep looking.

Mistake # 29: *Falling for a staged home*

Today's sellers recognize that "staging" helps to sell their homes for top dollar and much more quickly. Staging is decorating, fixing, and positioning furniture and accessories to make the home more appealing to the market, similar to that of a model home. Just turn your television to HGTV (Home Garden TV) and watch the many programs that show the *before* and *after* shots of homes. Buyers may have no real interest in buying the home, but after the owner updates, paints and positions furniture differently, the same home becomes worth fighting over.

Builders uncovered these secret years ago, and this is the reason they spend so much money decorating model homes. They recognize that people, in general, are not visionary; many of them have difficulty seeing how a home can look unless it is furnished. That's why builders and now more sellers spend so much time and money on decorating; playing on buyers' impulses and emotions. Once you see it, you have to have it.

Mistake # 30: *Buying too much house*

The search process can be short and sweet or it can be long – depending on how realistic your wants and needs are. Working with a good real estate agent pays off. A good agent should sit down with you, take the time to interview you and ask a series of questions. It's important that you are realistic in your wants and desires. While most buyers determine a price they don't want to exceed, nonetheless, the most common criteria to change during a search is the *price*. You look at everything within your price range but nothing seems to grab your attention. So you inch your way up to your top approval amount. Here's the problem. You have to be careful to not put yourself in a position where your mortgage payments are so high that you end up working just to pay for your home. Unless, of course, you know you won't get sick, and don't mind eating at home most of the time, not going out with friends, not trading in your car for a newer model, and not taking vacations.

Must Haves vs. Desires

Below is an example of the *Home Search Criteria Checklist*. There are four columns: Features, Must Have, Desire and Comments. The features simply list the criteria by which you are making your decisions. Things that you *must have* are four bedrooms, three baths, and two stories, for example. *Desires* are items you would like to have but the lack of them would not prevent you from making an offer on a house. Examples of desires are granite countertops, hardwood flooring in the study and things you want but are not deal breakers. We have also added a box to allow you to detail your goal in the home search process.

Your goal should be realistic and achievable. This means if your budget only allows for a $200,000 property, your searches and time should not be spent looking at $300,000 homes. Last but not least, think about what your *true goal* is in this whole process. When you have identified why you want to purchase a home it will keep you focused on achieving it, particularly if the process gets a little stressful and emotional. There is a blank sample of the *Home Search Criteria Checklist* on the website for your use at www.MakeNoMistakes.com. Use your pass code 550 to access it.

FEATURES	MUST HAVE	DESIRE	COMMENTS	X
GOAL	To be able to purchase a single family home in the Lamar school district for the betterment of my children's education and safety. Seeking a seller who is willing to sell for 400,000 or less and pay up to 3% of all closing costs.			
REQUIRED MOVE IN DATE	12/31/2008	NOV. 30, 2008		
TYPE OF HOME: SINGLE FAMILY, CONDO, TOWN HOME	SINGLE FAMILY			X
PRICE	$ 400,000.00	$3000 MONTHLY	Approved up to $450,000	X
DOWN PAYMENT	$ 80,000.00		Have over $110,000 in available funds	X
SOURCE OF DOWN PAYMENT			SAVINGS ACCOUNT	X
INTEREST RATE			Not to exceed 7%	X
CLOSING COSTS	$ 14,000.00	$ 2,000.00	Want seller to pay up to 3% of closing costs	X
APPRECIATION SEEKING	5%		5% COMPOUNDED ANNUALLY	X
MAINTENANCE LEVEL	Medium		Utilities and operation of home should not exceed $1000 a month	X
RESALE	YES		Want to sell in 5 years in order to purchase a larger home in 5 years	X
TERM - HOW LONG DO YOU PLAN TO LIVE IN THIS HOME	5			
LOCATION	CLOSE TO THE LOOP, SAFE NEIGHBORHOOD		Greenway Plaza Area, Mid Lane Subdivision, The Galleria	X
SCHOOL		LAMAR	PRIVATE SCHOOL NOT AN OPTION	X
EXTERIOR FEATURES:	Brick on all 4 sides		WANT A TRADITIONAL STYLE HOME	X
AGE OF HOME			NO MORE THAN 20 YEARS OLD	X
STORIES	2			X
GARAGE	2		Detached	X
POOL			Yes - Ok with building our own	X

Mistake # 31: *Buying in the wrong location*

Where do you want to live? Where can you afford to live? Would you consider a master plan community,[57] or the suburbs or the city? These are very important factors. In Houston, living "inside of the loop" is prized because of the accessibility to downtown, transportation, shopping, restaurants, nightlife, sports, etc. But there is a cost associated with this location that not everyone can afford.

Have you heard the saying "location, location, location" as it pertains to opening a business? This saying also applies to home ownership. *Location* can be as detailed as where your home is located within a subdivision. For example, is the home located within a cul-de-sac or is it on the corner of the main road? We have seen beautiful homes stay on the market a long time due to their undesirable location. There are many reasons why the location of the property should be important to you. One of the biggest reasons is the ability to resell the property quickly for a profit. Be sure your agent takes this into consideration when conducting the search.

Buying Within a Certain School District

Do you have children of school age? It is a fact that every home is assigned to a specific school district. You contribute to the school in the form of property taxes whether you have children attending the schools or not. Homes in better school districts tend to be priced higher because of demand – parents want their children to receive the best education possible. We often see parents sacrifice their lifestyles and themselves for the love of their children. Because they put their children's education first, they sometimes buy homes that they may not necessarily love just to get into the school district. So find out which school districts are the best and determine if those areas make sense for you.

---

[57] A *master plan community* is self-contained with most amenities within the community, including hospitals, supermarkets, etc.

Know Your Property Tax Rate

Property taxes are something you need to look into – and carefully. Taxes often increase every year unless you live in a city that places certain *caps* on all or part of the total taxes. It is important to note what you will be paying for: is it better schools, better roads, access to lakes and quality municipal utility districts[58] (MUD), or is it the prestige of being able to say you live in a particular area?

Mistake # 32: *Not paying attention to the property tax rate*

Also, you'll need to know your tax rate. You would be surprised how many people don't pay attention to this aspect of the purchase process. You will need to note the status of the sellers' tax base. Are they retired senior citizens? Is the property their homestead? Perhaps an investment property for them? Their rate may be different than yours will be, depending on your age or what your use of the property will be. If it's your intention to purchase the property as an investment property; you will typically pay higher taxes than if you are claiming the property as a homestead. Be sure to investigate this aspect of the taxes, particularly if you are purchasing it to create cash flow each month. The tax debt may not take effect until the year after you've purchased the property, leaving you with less cash flow.

> *A young married couple who were clients of ours purchased a home in an older neighborhood where many of the homeowners were retirees. Many of them benefited from a lower tax rate because of their age. In that state, when homeowners turn 65, their tax base rate stays fixed. When the young couple bought the home, it was reappraised a year later and taxed at a new higher rate. The outcome was an additional $425 a month for the new owners. Had we not paid*

---

[58] A *municipal utility district* (MUD) is an entity that provides water, sewer, drainage and other services to homes and businesses within its boundaries through the use of bonds, which are paid back by the neighborhoods using the services.

attention to the tax records and recognized that the taxes were based on a senior citizen tax rate, this would have gone unnoticed and the buyers would have calculated their budget wrong. Fortunately, they were prepared.

Therefore, check the tax rate and what property tax exemptions[59] are currently in place. You may or may not qualify for the same ones. Contact the county appraisal district where the property is located.

Designs, Floor Plans and Features Not Easy to Resell

The design, floor plan and features of a home are key attributes to the ability to resell it in the future. A home will sell based on how it feels, flows and looks to a buyer. A home that flows well, even if it is not decorated well, sells well – and that's what you want. You never know when you may have to sell this home. Today, buyers want comfort, low maintenance and style. Think about your lifestyle.

Here are just a few design ideas that will start you thinking about what may sell well in your market:

- Is the entry and curb appeal inviting? Or do buyers just keep driving past and don't bother to look at the rest of the house?
- Does the dining room have straight access into the kitchen?
- When you come home with groceries, what path will you take from the garage? Is this path tiled or carpeted?
- After you've finished taking a shower, do you have to go outside of the bathroom to get the towel?
- Do you have to walk naked across the bedroom to your closet to take out and put on your clothes?
- Where is the master bedroom located in respect to the other bedrooms? Is it on the first floor or on the second with the rest

---

[59] *Property tax exemptions* allow you to reduce your tax liability based on specific qualifications, i.e. veteran, over 65, primary residence. These qualifications differ by state.

of the bedrooms? If all bedrooms are on the same floor, are the secondary bedrooms on the other side of the house, away from the master?

- Do you enjoy entertaining? If so, where will your guests congregate? Does the kitchen extend into the family room or is it closed off and away from the other entertaining areas?

How a home is set up is important. Do you prefer the master bedroom downstairs instead of upstairs? Do you really need a living room which you never use? Every city and state seems to have their preferences. Know what they are. Again, one of your goals should always be to appeal to the market you are purchasing in. This will make it easier to sell when you need to.

Size, Square Footage, Lot Size

Size, square footage and lot size of the home are all aspects of the home that you are buying. We never suggest that you buy the biggest, most expensive house in the neighborhood. You'll seldom get the same amount of *value* as you would with some of the smaller- or middle-sized homes in any given neighborhood. When we say "value" in this context, we are referring to your resale potential.

Other items to consider are whether you want a single, two- or three-story home with a large backyard? Do you want the home positioned in a cul-de-sac? Must the bedrooms be a certain size, or the yard large enough for a pool? Be sure to share all your ideas with your real estate agent, including your likes and dislikes.

Resale Value

Resale value expectations are key considerations, especially if you know this is *not* the last home you are going to buy. Resale value is the ability to sell your home with an expectation of a profit. As investors, we always look at every property from the standpoint of whether or not we could turn a profit on this property whenever we choose to sell it.

Mistake # 33: *Not sharing your resale value expectations with your agent*

Setting your expectations as it pertains to resale value is an important factor to share with your real estate agent and loan officer. Your expectation might be to stay in your home for a short period of time or sell it in order to buy something else. Keep in mind that nothing is guaranteed or written in stone.

From a financial standpoint you want to think about whether it makes sense to buy into a particular neighborhood and whether it will support a profit after five years. Or do most homes in the neighborhood sell for close to what they sold for five years ago?

Your real estate agent should be able to give you the following historical information on any given subdivision that is more than a couple of years old:

- The average square footage of most homes in the neighborhood
- How long the homes tend to stay on the market
- The home sales trend in that neighborhood for the past few years

This information should all play into your decision-making process.

Pro's and Con's of New Construction vs. Resale

New construction may not be an option in the area where you want to live, but if it's any consolation, we are not big proponents of new construction. Why? Resale values on established homes, in established neighborhoods, are already established! You can check the resale sales history of your home or others in the neighborhood. If your neighbor doesn't cut his lawn, more than likely that is not going to change too much – unless they sell to someone who will. Though neighborhoods can change, there is enough information you could gather from the internet, a neighborhood newsletter, by driving around and from a nearby police station. Let's not forget about the nosy neighbors who can give you great insight as to the ins and outs of a neighborhood. You could attend a homeowners' association meeting to hear the homeowners' issues and complaints. Another good website to check is www.familywatchdog.us, which will let you know if there are sexual offenders in or around the neighborhood.

New construction is like investing in a business you don't know much about. Let's begin by dispelling some of the myths. *The first and foremost myth is: new does not mean 'no problems.'* Any home built by man has the potential to have problems. Also, new construction can quickly deplete much of your cash. Items such as blinds, gutters, sod in the backyard, and a refrigerator are a few items which may not necessarily come with your new home. A home that's not newly-built will probably have most of these items already, and you can live with them until you are financially able to upgrade. These days, builders are making efforts to become more competitive with resales (i.e., homes already built) by offering very creative incentives to buyers. Many items are negotiable.

The other downside to new construction is buying too soon into a subdivision. Builders sometimes reduce the prices of their homes partway through the sales process, which means the early buyers ended up paying more than others did. Then again, if the neighborhood turns out to be a success you may have made a great decision. The risk is up to you.

New construction, as with anything else, just requires buyers to do their research. Understanding how builders work is crucial to making a wise purchase. We have seen buyers who, in the beginning, say they don't want the cost of their homes to go past a certain limit. Yet time and again, after dealing with the builder or the design center, buyers walk out tens of thousands dollars over budget because they chose expensive upgrades.

Also, beware of many builders who change their names frequently or who have reputations that are not always first-rate. The best way to learn more about a builder is to ask your real estate agent to get a list of referrals of homes the builder constructed in the past. Call these homeowners and ask questions about their business dealings with the builder. Or find other real estate agents who have sold the builder's property while representing *the buyers*. These agents will be happy to share their buyers' experience, both before and after the buyers moved in. You can easily find these real estate agents by searching the MLS historical records. Focus your questions around quality, service and warranty issues. Ask such questions as:

- How did the builder handle change orders?
- Was the builder organized?
- Was the builder professional?
- Was the quality of the work good and completed on time?
- Did the builder discuss expectations, both yours and theirs?
- How does the company handle warranty issues after 30 days? Within a year? After a year if the foundation and roof need addressing, for example?
- Who handles warranty issues? The builder or a third party?

The servicing or warranty of the property is a very important factor. Our experience shows that builders often act as general contractors for the properties they build. In a nutshell, they get the building plans from the architects, and engage third-party vendors and contractors to complete various tasks. Then they follow up and inspect the job through to completion, making sure everything will pass inspections, including those of the city. This process continues until the home is complete.

These vendors, or tradesmen ("trades," for short), are independent of the builder's company and are not employees. When you take ownership of your new construction, the builder should provide you with a list of contact numbers for the trades that worked on the house. Some of the challenges as a homeowner are when you have a warranty issue. Some builders put the responsibility on you to contact these third-party vendors. Unfortunately, we have witnessed vendors who don't believe in honoring their warranty work, especially if they no longer do business with the builder and there is no financial incentive for them. There is nothing more frustrating than dealing with a house that is relatively new yet aspects of it don't work properly. You're then forced to decide if you want to fight the third-party company and/or the builder to honor a warranty.

It sometimes can be easier to deal with builders who plan on being in the community a while because they are building a few more hundred homes. However, if you have chosen to go with a smaller custom builder consider negotiating *additional builder coverage*. Go to your state or local builder association and get a list of companies they recommend.

Do not get a builder warranty confused with a home warranty. A builder warranty is for new construction only, as opposed to a resale. The builder warranty should address, at minimum, such issues as:

- Performance standards
- A definition of the terms of a builder's warranty obligations to the home buyer
- Establishing a fair dispute resolution system
- Informing home buyers of their rights under state law and
- Provide a warranty document that assigns responsibility for certain maintenance items of the home

Another important factor to find out is how the builder handles special requests and change orders, because buyers change their minds hundreds of times! If you have never been through the process of building from scratch, it can be nerve-wracking, time-consuming and hard on your budget. Also, you may have certain expectations and when you don't see the process coming along, it begins to feel alarmed and stressed. The process of building can take anywhere from four months to much longer, depending upon the size and complexity of the project. So patience is a virtue you will certainly need. More importantly, know everything you want done upfront and negotiate it into your deal. If you change your mind, you can give the builder an opportunity to earn much more money from your lack of knowledge.

Our best suggestion is to get a copy of the floor plan you are interested in and walk-through it in your mind. Visualize all that you see, from landscaping and furniture placement, to wiring for audio inside and outside, to dimmer switches, etc. Write it down or sketch it all out. Discuss it with others. Go over the plans and requests several times. Walk through your existing home and note the things you love about it. You will then be better prepared to know what you want.

Mistake # 34: *Believing new construction is a home without problems so you don't need an inspection*

Also, keep in mind some builders don't build well-made homes. Buyers tend to find out after the fact because they don't spend the money to get them *inspected*. There will be more on this subject later, but *understand that when you buy new, you are at the mercy of a warranty department to fix things that could have been discovered and repaired before your purchase.* Don't assume because the house is new it doesn't require an inspection.

Pro's and Con's of a Fixer Upper or Foreclosure

These types of properties are always an option and always available. Just decide if you have the temperament to deal with what comes with a fixer upper or a foreclosure. If you aren't handy around your home or apartment, be very careful with fixer uppers. Also, if a house went into foreclosure, it was probably because the owners didn't have the money to properly care and maintain it. Perhaps the utilities were turned off, causing damage, such as mold. In addition, the chances of you getting a sellers' disclosure that tells you all that is wrong and right with the house is slim. *The key is to not get caught up with wanting to purchase a home simply because it's a foreclosure and you've heard that foreclosures are bargains.*

Mistake # 35: *Underestimating the cost of repairs*

When you're inspecting these types of homes, be sure to have a sense of how much it will take to fix the property. Our experience with contractors has always been that you'll get a quote, but by the time they finish the job it's always over budget. This is especially true if you don't know what you don't know, or rather, if you lack knowledge. Also, contractors and tradesmen can be unreliable. They commit to the job and then don't show up, often because of scheduling changes on their end. Ask your real estate agent to assist you with finding reputable contractors or subcontractors.

Foreclosures are properties that are now owned by the lender, who is holding the mortgage because the homeowner couldn't pay it. The lender then tries to sell the home and earn back the amount still owing on the mortgage. There's usually a lot of paperwork involved, and sometimes a loss for the bank. A bank is in the business of selling money, not houses. Their goal is to get their money as quickly as possible from the highest bidder on the house, so they can start the process again by loaning out their money and earning interest on the loan.

Again, it is important to do your research before you bid on a foreclosure. Don't think just because it's a foreclosure it's a good deal. That's a myth. Don't fall for it. Do your homework and look at the comparatives that are similar to the foreclosure property. More importantly, determine how much of your cash you'll need to improve the property so it meets your expectations.

Multi-Unit Properties

Multi-unit properties are wonderful if you buy them correctly. It's important to determine two things when you're buying a multi-unit property: if rentals in this area are common, and the property's history with keeping the units leased. The beauty of multi-units is you're able to spread your risk around. For example, if you're the landlord of a single-family house and your tenant doesn't pay rent for a month, you have to come up with 100% of that amount to make your mortgage payment on time. With a multi-unit, the amount you need for your mortgage payment is spread over all the units, so one tenant not paying rent one month doesn't have as much impact on you. Hopefully, your payment is low enough – and the rents you charge are high enough – that the multi-unit property "cash flows." This means the rents collected each month are more than enough to make the mortgage

> **Tip:**
> *If, at the time of purchase, a unit has tenants, be sure to collect the security deposit from the seller along with existing contracts.*

payment, and you're able to build a reserve for the times when you have a vacancy, a late-payer or a repair to the building.

In Summary, we've outlined in this chapter just a few of the characteristics you should consider as you start your search for the perfect home – for you. You have plenty of choices, which also mean a lot of decisions. Don't expect to have all the answers right away, all on your own. Remember, you're not alone: Your real estate agent/coach is there to offer expertise, ideas and advice throughout the entire process.

A real estate purchase is usually an emotional one, although you'll want to try to focus on the facts, keep your lists of must-haves vs. desires in mind at all times, and ask plenty of questions. Coming in prepared will lead you to the right property quickly. Use the *Home Search Checklist* in this book and on our website as a starting point. It will help you to see if your expectations are unrealistic or if they can inspire you to consider a new idea. Either way, being prepared and knowledgeable will get you what you want, faster, at less cost, and with fewer mistakes.

Pass The Knowledge On!

CHAPTER 15

PURCHASING A FORECLOSURE

In this chapter you will learn whether purchasing a foreclosed home is truly for you. We will discuss the various processes and options that are available to you as you buy a foreclosed property as either your homestead or as an investment.

There are always foreclosures available to purchase in any market, strong or weak. The only difference may be the *number* of foreclosures available.

It's been said that someone's misfortune can be someone else's gain. Purchasing a home in foreclosure can be very profitable. It can also turn out to be one of the easiest ways to lose thousands!

First, it's important to understand why a homeowner may allow his or her home to go into foreclosure, which is usually caused by a failure to pay the mortgage note, property taxes or HOA dues:

- Job-related: Laid-off, fired, quit or was transferred to another state
- Health-related: Inability to continue working due to medical condition
- Finance-related: Excessive debt and mounting bill obligations
- Marital-related: Divorce

- Wrong mortgage product: Can't afford payment because of Adjustable Rate Mortgage

Ways to Purchase a Foreclosure

One way of purchasing a foreclosure is by negotiating with the homeowner prior to foreclosure. If you ever attempt to purchase a foreclosure directly from a seller, you should know that foreclosure proceedings vary from state to state. In states where mortgages are used, homeowners can end up staying in the property for almost a year; whereas in states where trust deeds are used, trustee sales give a seller about four months before they need to vacate the property.

Many of us have heard stories of just such families who are finding it difficult to pay their mortgage payments. They receive a knock on the door, and there is someone willing to relieve their misery. That person could certainly be you. Often times the person making the offer is prepared to make a financial contribution to the homeowner in return for a signed quitclaim deed.

Before the foreclosure process is actually underway, a Notice of Default letter must be sent to the homeowner and/or recorded at the county clerk's office. During this time period, the seller still has the right to sell his or her home. Real estate agents refer to this period as a *pre-foreclosure.*

What Is a Quitclaim Deed?

A quitclaim deed is removing your rights – by law – to redeem the property and *quit claiming* any interest, at any time, in the property as it passes claim to another person. However, the mortgage loan can remain with the original homeowner unless that, too, is purchased or assumed by the new homeowner.

Most states offer a redemption period to a homeowner who loses his property to foreclosure. This means the seller has an irrevocable right[60] during a certain length of time to cure the default, including paying all foreclosure costs, back interest and missed

---

[60] An *irrevocable right* is impossible to retract or revoke.

principal payments, in order to regain control of the property. We strongly suggest that you contact a real estate attorney who can guide you through your state's proper process, since the exact process varies and may require buyers give certain disclosures to sellers. If borrowers fail to provide those notices, or to follow the guidelines about preparing offers on the required paperwork, borrowers can be hit with fines, lawsuits or even a revocation of the sale.

Mistake # 36: *Purchasing a home without a title policy*

Title companies are reluctant to issue title insurance based on a quitclaim deed, so you should think hard before purchasing a property with no title insurance protection. Essentially, you're taking a chance no one will come out of the woodwork and make a claim to the property in the future. This can also include mechanics' liens for work done to the property prior to your taking possession, which may add costs associated with courts or attorneys to prove the sale occurred. Title companies are just not willing to take on these risks.

The quitclaim deed is intended to be a simple means to transfer property from one family member to another, or to add a family member or spouse to the title of a property. You often see quitclaim deeds used when there is a divorce and one spouse is signing the property over to the other by using the quitclaim deed.

In the case of a divorce, for example, the property may have been purchased jointly, with both names responsible for paying the mortgage note. Now, one spouse will get the property in the divorce by court order. The spouse who is giving up an interest in the house signs a quitclaim deed to the spouse who is keeping the house. Both spouses are still responsible for the mortgage note until it's refinanced into the other's name, or sold.

Often, both spouses' names are on the title of the property, which shows that both have an interest in it, but for whatever reason, just one spouse's name is on the mortgage note. In this case, the spouse who's giving up interest – and who's not responsible for the mortgage note – would have to be paid for his or her contribution toward the property, most likely from selling or redistributing other assets, or by awarding that spouse with a home equity loan (which takes some of the equity out of the home).

At no time does a letter explaining this, and asking for one spouse to be removed, suffice with the lender. Not even sending copies of the divorce decree awarding the property to one spouse, the notarized quitclaim deed, or even something from the city or county showing that the property is now in just the one spouse's name – none of that is enough for a lender to remove a person's name from a mortgage loan. Lenders do not care who is and who is no longer responsible for the loan; they just want their payments, and they want to make sure they're covered if something happens to a borrower. Think about it – prior to the divorce, the borrowers paid the mortgage on time. Post-divorce, there is much less income available, either because it's split between two households or because one spouse is helping to support the other. Either way, there's a greater risk the loan will default. The lender will want every resource at its disposal to try to get the mortgage paid on time. So there's no way the lender will agree to remove half of the payment source (one name) if, legally, the lender doesn't have to. There's a large disincentive, in fact, to remove one name.

Purchasing a Home at an Auction

Purchasing a property at auction is an excellent opportunity to buy at undervalued prices. *"At auction" is when the homeowner has been unsuccessful trying to sell the property on his own, or even through a "short sale," which is known as pre-foreclosure.* By the time a property goes to auction, the lending institution tries to recapture its losses by auctioning the property in a public sale to the highest bidder.

The proceeds from the sale are disbursed (paid) first to the mortgage lender who initiated the foreclosure action, and then, if there are any additional funds, to settle any remaining obligations of the homeowner associated with the home. Some examples of this are unpaid personal property taxes, civil lawsuit judgments and state and federal tax liens. Beyond that, if any money remains, the homeowner will receive the difference.

If you take ownership of the property without having verified that your winning bid will cover and clear any liens, other than a mortgage, you become the responsible party. Which means the only way to sell or refinance the property is to pay off all the liens – regardless of whether you created the debt or not! This would be a costly mistake.

Note that the opening bid (minimum amount of the first bid) is determined by totaling the remaining loan balance, court costs, loan interest and back taxes, legal fees and other liens, all of which is normally paid by the winning bidder.

Again, it's important to *not get emotional* and thus find yourself in a bidding war. It is wise to approach this process knowing your best and highest offer, so you will stop once the bidding reaches that point. This means you will have researched the market price at which the house can be sold, subtracted the total cost for the fix-up, liens and other issues, to determine your profitability and if it's worth your time.

A potential downside to purchasing a home at auction means you need to be prepared to bid using cash, or have quick financing arranged. If you are the winning bidder on a property, a five to ten percent deposit is required at the end of the auction, with the balance of the purchase price due within a few days and usually not more than 30 days. Deposits are non-refundable and all sales are purchased in "as is" condition.

Another downside to purchasing this type of home is a buyer is not often allowed to inspect the house before making an offer. Purchasing a property sight unseen makes it difficult to calculate how much it will cost to improve the structure or bring it up to livable standards. You also run the risk that the current occupants will retaliate and destroy the home, particularly if you need to evict them from the premises. The process of eviction can be costly. Also, these auctions can be very chaotic and intimidating to you the first time you go down to the county court house to bid. We suggest that you go to a couple of them first before trying to participate. Certainly the best time to go is when the weather is bad and the majority of bidders choose to stay home. More importantly, take a class on this process before attempting it yourself.

Note that the previous owner may still have the right to purchase the property (redemption period) back from you, depending on what state you purchase in. This is unlikely to happen, because if the owner was in a financial position to buy back the property, he probably would not have defaulted in the first place, but you never know. Therefore it is important for you to be aware of this before putting too much capital into a property, not knowing if you will have to sell it back. Again, please contact your local real estate attorney for the rules and regulations of your state. There are some states that do not have a redemption period.

Short Sales

A mortgage lender may consider a *short sale* on the property to prevent a home foreclosure. A short sale is when the mortgage lender agrees to discount the remaining loan balance due to:

- An economic hardship for the homeowner, for which they must qualify
- A slow real estate market climate
- The belief that the short sale would result in a smaller loss than foreclosure would.

The homeowner then has the ability to sell the property for less than the outstanding balance of the loan. The goal is to sell it quickly. The remaining proceeds of the sale, after all closing costs have been paid and including any past due taxes, go to the lender in full satisfaction of the debt. However, it is usually up to the financially-strapped homeowner to initiate this discussion with the lender. The borrower will need to fill out lengthy paperwork to prove financial hardship, but a short sale is usually worth it.

Not all lenders allow short sales. In fact, lenders who offer this option have to get approval from several different levels of credit management. This process requires patience and consistently following up with everyone involved. We have seen it take over six months to close on a short sale property. If you're in a hurry, we strongly suggest you don't bother with this route. In today's foreclosure-laden world, the mortgage-lending department managers are dealing with hundreds of properties. Don't expect them to get back to you quickly; it's rare when it happens.

Mistake # 37: *Assuming all foreclosures are great deals*

Buying a home that's in foreclosure can be a great deal, but you can't just assume it is. Not every foreclosure deal will meet your needs, and some aren't worth a second glance.

HUD and REO Homes Are an Option Too

HUD[61] and REO[62] foreclosed homes, if purchased correctly, offer great savings. They come with clear titles, and there usually aren't any surprises once the title is yours because both HUD and REO homes are closed with title policies.

A HUD home is a 1- to 4-unit residential property HUD acquired because of a foreclosure action on an FHA-insured mortgage. HUD becomes the property owner and offers it for sale as a way to recover from the loss on the foreclosure claim. Visit www.hud.gov for more information on the rules for purchasing a HUD home. A REO, or Real Estate Owned property, is one that failed to sell at a foreclosure auction and is now owned by the bank. Many times these homes are not listed in MLS. Please remember, just because the property is described as a foreclosure does not make it an automatic deal! Check out the following websites that consist of both government and banking institutions that offer lists of properties in foreclosure.

---

[61] A *HUD* (Housing of Urban Development) home is a 1- to 4-unit residential property acquired by HUD as a result of a foreclosure action on an FHA loan. HUD becomes the property owner, and offers it for sale as a way to recover the loss on the foreclosure claim.

[62] *REO* stands for Real Estate Owned, which is a term lenders use to describe the properties in their possession because of a foreclosure or forfeiture.

Bank of America REO:
http://bankofamerica.reo.com/search /

BB&T REO (Branch Bank and Trust):
http://www.bbt.com/applications/specialassets/search.asp

Beal Bank Commercial REO:
http://www.bealbank.com/Content.aspx?ID=13

Citibank REO:
http://www.citimortgage.com/Mortgage/Oreo/SearchListing.do

Compass Bank REO:
https://www.compassbank.com/appforms/properties/index.jsp

Country Wide REO: http://www.countrywide.com/purchase/f_reo.asp,

Fannie Mae REO:
http://www.mortgagecontent.net/reoSearchApplication/fanniemae/

FDIC Real Estate Owned:
http://www.fdic.gov/DRRORE/

Freddie Mac REO:
http://www.homesteps.com/hm01_1featuresearch.htm

GRP Financial Services Properties:
http://www.grpcapital.com/properties/index.php

Homes for Sale by the U. S. Government
http://www.HomeSales.gov

HSBC REO:
http://www.banking.us.hsbc.com/

HUD REO:
http://www.hud.gov/homes/index.cfm

Indy Mac Bank REO:
http://apps.indymacbank.com/individuals/realestate/search.asp

JP Morgan Chase Bank REO:
http://mortgage.chase.com/pages/other/co_properties_landing.jsp

M&T Bank REO:
http://services.mandtbank.com/personal/bank_owned_prop.cfm

National City Mortgage REO:
http://www.ncmcreo.com/

Ocwen Financial REO:
http://www.ocwen.com/reo/home.cfm

People's Bank REO:
http://www.peoples.com/im/cda/multi_elements/0,,1355,00.html

Regions Bank Properties:
http://realestate.regions.com/servlet/Ore/ForeclosedPropertySearch.jsp

Sallie Mae Financial Services Properties:
http://www.grpcapital.com/properties/index.html

SBA Properties:
http://app1.sba.gov/pfsales/dsp_search.html

SunTrust REO:
http://www.suntrustmortgage.com/reo.asp

Wells Fargo REO:
https://www.pasreo.com/reo/

Finding the Right Foreclosure for You

Often times there are multiple offers on this type of property, even while your offer is being considered. Again, it is important to *not* get emotional, but to do your homework on how much the property is really worth based on its present condition. The lender will take the best offer with the highest success of the property closing. That's usually a cash offer, as opposed to mortgage financing. Don't get frustrated if your offer is not accepted: simply move on to the next deal.

You are allowed to order an inspection. Get one! Do not risk purchasing a home without a thorough inspection. Often times, foreclosed properties have been sitting empty for a long time, and mold, rodents, thieves and even drug traffickers could have set up in the property. Since foreclosed properties are sold "as is," there is no seller's disclosure, no home warranty and no survey. As a result, the total cost of fixing the property must be assessed up front.

If you are considering a home as an investment because you plan to turn around and sell it, then you must contend with the cost of "carrying the costs of property" until you sell it. From the time you take ownership to the time it is sold, the clock is ticking. You must pay the monthly mortgage note, fix the property yourself, and/or deal with contractors who may under bid and under deliver, and then you have to sell the home. If your projections are off in any of these areas, you suffer the financial consequences.

Again, it's important to *not get emotional*, especially if you find yourself in a bidding war. This can happen just as easily online as in person. It's wise to approach this process knowing your best and highest price offer so you will stop once the bidding reaches that point. Again, this means you have researched the market price at which it can be sold, subtracted the total cost to fix it up, took other issues into consideration, determined profitability and determined if the project is worth your time.

You don't want to be in a situation of not closing on time. Closing beyond the date stated in your contract will cost you money. Many banks charge a *per diem* if you are not ready when they are. They don't accept excuses; they expect to close on or before the closing date of the contract. A *per diem* rate usually runs about $100 a day.

You must complete all of the bank's requirements before you submit an offer. A requirement may be specific language in the contract which they will not change. Don't debate with them unless you really don't want the house. If you are unwilling to abide by their terms and sign all documents, they usually move on to the next best offer without even giving you notice.

Keep your offer simple and clean. Banks will not accept your contract if it is littered with contingencies. In fact, they value *cash* offers more so than those being financed. Cash offers less of a risk since there is no borrower's lender to deal with, and cash offers a shorter close period. Loss Mitigation departments want to do as little work as possible, since time is money – and they view foreclosure properties as deals they have already lost money on.

In Summary, purchasing a foreclosure can be profitable, but it can also be very costly if you project incorrectly. Worse, if you don't do everything in your power to verify the house has a clean title, it's very possible you'll end up owing money to companies or laborers who worked on the house before you even bought it! So who has to pay the contractor? You do! *Not* the previous owners, even though they contracted to have the work done. Have patience with the process.

If you're not sure about buying a home in foreclosure, consider your other options: pre-foreclosure, HUD and REO homes, and "at auction." Do your research. No matter which route you take, don't assume that all foreclosures are good deals. And don't forget to get an inspection *before* committing to move forward.

Pass The Knowledge On!

CHAPTER 16

NEGOTIATE YOUR BEST DEAL

In this chapter you will learn how to negotiate and how to not leave money – YOUR MONEY – on the table. We'll show you the psychology behind your offer and behind the seller's acceptance of that offer. How you and your agent approach the other side will dictate how successful you are in this real estate transaction. Negotiating badly can not only cost you your deal but thousands too!

Once you have found the right property, it's time to start the negotiating process. Regardless of whether your property is new construction or a resale, *everything* is negotiable.

Mistake # 38: *Negotiating without understanding your leverage*

Let's agree that, in negotiating, you must gather as much information upfront about the property as you can. One of the first and easiest things your real estate agent should do is research the sales history of the area where you plan to buy. He or she can easily access this information. The data is very specific, and you should use it to compare the house you're interested in to others that are similar. "Similar" means the number of bedrooms and baths, square footage of the home, the size of the lot, the year built, certain interior features, the condition, if there is a pool, etc. This document is known as a Comparative Market Analysis (CMA) and it provides historical data of the sales activity in the neighborhood. We discussed CMAs in detail in Chapter 2.

As you can see, the available information can go back several years, depending on how long the Multiple Listing Service (MLS) retains the data. This local database lists all the available properties marketed by agents who participate in MLS.

When we first started selling real estate, a friend of ours shared her difficulty in selling her house and asked if we would come by and take a look. When we walked through the door we thought we were in the home once owned by the Brady Bunch! Absolutely nothing in the home had been updated since the early '70s. We also noticed the kitchen counters were quite low. She was 5 feet tall, so we guessed it felt OK to her. She mentioned that the home had previously been owned by a disabled person who needed low counter tops. During the four years she owned the home, the only change she made was to replace the flat roof, which cost $4,500.

We agreed to take the listing, knowing we had to do something drastic. We hired a previous client who was an interior decorator to work with us to get the home looking like a model home. We went to Pier 1 and purchased $800 worth of accessories, paint, materials and cleaning products. Over a weekend, this home was turned from a throwback-to-decades-past into a beautiful villa on an island paradise.

A potential buyer came in and fell in love with the house. We actually believe he fell in love with how it was decorated. He was 6'5" and should have noticed those counter tops that were customized for the former homeowner! The buyer came unrepresented without a real estate agent, immediately made an offer and the home was sold!

Because he was without representation, he approached this deal from a disadvantage. The home sold for $147,000, yet the seller paid $77,000 four years ago and the house had been on the market over seven months prior to us listing it. A good real estate agent would have discovered those facts, shared them with the buyer and told him what these facts meant.

Also, the seller was willing to accept a much lower price for the house – as low as $120,000 – because she was in a hurry to move out. She had already signed a contract to buy and move into a new home that was completely done and ready for her, but she needed the funds from the closing of her existing home to afford the new house. The buyer had leverage and did not know it; consequently, he overpaid and was led by emotions instead of the business facts. Not a good place to be when negotiating.

Looking at the Comparative for Clues

Using the story above, the buyer could have easily accessed the information listed below with the help of a real estate agent. Think how having this information would have affected the outcome!

1. The ability to see how much the owner paid for the property four years ago.

2. The ability to see pictures and the description of the home four years ago, giving him insight to any upgrades that might account for a significantly higher price.

3. The ability to know how long the property was on the market, known as DOM, or days on market. Days on market tells you how long the property has been open to the public for viewing. It is usually fair to say that the longer the property is on the market, the more willing a seller is to negotiate. Sellers get tired of staging and cleaning their homes for every viewing, not to mention feeling frustrated if they are paying two

mortgages while waiting for the current house to sell, or being anxious if they need the money now.

4. The ability to see how sales have been financially structured for other homes in the subdivision within the last year. An example would be to notice if sellers have been contributing towards buyers' closing costs and giving repair allowances.

5. The ability to see if there were seller contributions[63] made towards closing costs or reduced real estate agent commissions for other houses recently sold in the neighborhood. These things would impact the comparable homes' sales prices, which could have caused the sales price of this house to be higher or lower.

6. The ability to have a second set of eyes call attention to certain structural or mechanical concerns in the home that might pose a problem, e.g. low counter tops.

7. The ability to see that the home was overpriced.

8. The ability for the real estate agent to assist the buyer in formulating a negotiating strategy.

9. The ability to see the pricing trends of the neighborhood or subdivision. This is done by simply creating various search criteria and comparing them. Let's use the example of a two-story house with 4 bedrooms and 3.5 baths, a two-car garage, and that is 2,500 square feet and sits on a 10,000-square-foot lot. The real estate agent would search for similar sales from January 1, 2008 to December 31, 2008, then January 1, 2007 to December 31, 2007 and so on, to see what the averages are doing. Are the prices of the homes going down or up? By what percentage?

---

[63] When the *seller contributes* part of their funds to assist the buyer with closing or repair costs.

10. The ability to see what other properties are selling for in the neighborhood and if there was a similar but smaller floor plan. If so, compare its listing or sold price.

The Psychology Behind the Deal

In any negotiations, one of the first rules is to understand what you have going *for you* vs. *against you*. This is another example of understanding the psychology behind the deal. You want to know as much as you can about who possesses what, the advantages and disadvantages, and the pro's and con's, in order to set up your game plan. We call these items "leverages." As we mentioned early on, acquiring real estate is like playing a game. It's crucial to understand both sides: what you have going for you and what the sellers have going for them. This is called *leverage*. Understanding your leverages, along with your Comparative Market Analysis, will prepare you and your real estate agent for negotiations.

Your goal, of course, is to purchase the home at the best possible price without compromising your standards. Here is how you determine your leverage:

- What are your thoughts about the seller's asking price?
- What is the current market condition of the area you're considering purchasing in? Is it a buyer's or seller's market?
- What does the appraisal district (taxing authority) say about the property's value?
- What is your real estate agent saying about the sales price?
- What is the DOM saying? (If the home just came on the market, the sellers may feel confident it will sell soon, so they would probably want their asking price or even more. However, if the house has been on the market awhile, the sellers' confidence may not be high so they may be more open to negotiating with a buyer.)
- Have other real estate agents attempted to sell this property prior to its current listing? (MLS should have a history of this. Knowledge is power, and knowing the seller had it listed

before tells you the seller may be very frustrated and anxious to sell.)

- What does the listing agent say about the property?
- What type of feedback is the listing agent receiving from other agents who come in and show the property?
- What are the agent's comments in the MLS? Is the comment "seller is motivated" there, or something similar?

We usually like to ask the seller's real estate agent a few questions, too:

- How did they arrive at their asking price? Which comparables did they use? (Some agents may feel uncomfortable or get an attitude behind these questions; however, we have always found that if agents price their listings too high, and they know it, they are usually inclined to comment on it. For example, "the seller insisted on the list price" which means the agent suggested a lower sales price. You can learn a lot about the seller and his agent's pricing psychology from asking these questions.)

- Why are the sellers choosing to sell?

- What type of feedback are you receiving from other agents who previously showed the property?

- When can the sellers move out?

Mistake # 39: *Talking too much*

Through the investigation process of trying to find out as much about the property as you can, you may come across the seller. The tendency may be to talk to them in hopes to find out as much as you can about the property. However, while you're talking the seller is learning more about *you*! This information could backfire and impact your negotiations. Sometimes home buyers talk too much. It is best that you let your "good" real estate agent do their job and negotiate on your behalf.

Sometimes the seller's real estate agent will talk too much and offer more information than you expected. That is why having a list of questions to ask the selling side can pay off; the more questions you ask, the more they talk. Newer real estate agents sometimes feel empowered when they have a listing and so they'll divulge information you can use to your advantage.

Know Your Leverage

Refer to your *Identify Your Leverage Checklist to* compile questions that bring up any differences that could be to your benefit. For example, if you noticed that the average price per square foot of a home in the subdivision is $99, but the sellers want $102, a great question might be, "we noticed the average home similar to yours is going for $99 a square foot, yet your seller is asking $102? What are they basing this on?" Keep in mind that every property is different, so there are no canned questions.

We also suggest you use your *Property Viewing Checklist* to help you notice the physical aspects of the home, and to get you thinking beyond your emotions. By using this checklist, you can determine which items might need addressing prior to the inspection. In other words, if there are additional terms you'll need but aren't found in a standard contract. ***List these terms as part of your offer price, as opposed to doing so after the inspection results.*** We will explain more about this in Chapter 17. At this point, you'll have most of your leverages *if* the house has been on the market for a while and *if* the seller is not entertaining multiple offers at the same time on this one property.

Below are other questions you should consider researching. Use the checklists we developed to formulate your final list of questions and thus formulate your negotiation strategy:

- What are the neighbors saying about the house? You would be surprised what they have to share.

- Is the lot size larger or smaller than most in the neighborhood?

- Are the room sizes larger or smaller than most in the neighborhood?

- Are there more or fewer rooms than the neighborhood average?

- What does the appraiser say about the property? (Ask your loan officer to ask the appraiser about the neighborhood and the seller's asking price. Oftentimes an appraiser will do preliminary legwork before going to the property, to make sure the asking price is reasonable before wasting his time or the client's money.)

- What is the condition of the home? Good, fair or poor?

- What was your first impression when you walked in the door?

- How did it smell? (We've helped clients get homes for a steal because of overpowering interior odors. Homeowners are usually aware of and embarrassed by these smells, and are very willing to negotiate. Some smells, such as cigarette smoke and certain cooking spices, can be unwelcoming, although with the right treatment, they can disappear forever.)

- Are there repairs or renovations that need to be done? If so, how many? Who will do them? Will there be an allowance for them or will they be something you plan to negotiate?

- How much earnest money are you willing to put down? The seller perceives that the more you put down, the more serious you are. Keep in mind; however, this is also the amount of money you may be willing to risk in the event something goes wrong, such as not getting financing.

- How will you finance the home? Obviously, cash is always the easiest, but very few people pay cash for a house. If you can show you have gone through the pre-approval process, this adds more strength to your negotiations.

- Are you asking the seller for seller contributions? This can sometimes have a negative impact on your leverage. On the other hand, they are becoming more common. They're usually used to reduce the amount of cash a buyer needs to bring to closing. Asking a seller to contribute toward your closing costs means that he is walking away with less profit. He is taking part of the home's appreciation and/or equity to help you buy it. In January, 2009, the maximum allowable seller contributions on primary residences and second homes with the buyer putting less than 10% down is 3% on conventional loans.

Mistake # 40: *Failure to include an option period in your contract.*

- How much *option money* are you willing to put down? Also known as an *option fee*, this is money that protects your earnest money for a period of time. It allows the *buyer to terminate the contract for any reason* during that time, which is typically 10 to 15 days in Texas, for example. It's during this time that the buyer hires an inspector. If the inspector's findings aren't what the buyer expects, the buyer has a way out of the contract without losing the earnest money. Since the option fee is usually only about $10 a day ($10 for 10 to 15 days is only $100 to $150), and earnest money is usually 1% of the purchase price ($2,000 on a $200,000 home, for example), option money is a great way to go. Option money can be used for more than just an inspector's disappointing findings; buyers can also use it for something as simple as buyer's remorse. Information on how to include this contractual language in your contract can be found in the next chapter.

- Can you use the closing date as leverage, if the seller needs to move out soon? This could be an advantage if you're offering a quick sale. Inquire about the seller's needs and show that you are flexible; it may be to your benefit.

- How does the home curb appeal compare to the rest of the neighborhood?

- Is the home decorated nicely? Home décor can impact your emotions, which can skew your decision to purchase, particularly if the home is decorated in a way that appeals to you. Beware what most people fail to understand that once the seller removes all their furnishings, the home will completely look different. Don't buy into their dream, buy into your own!

- Is the home in move-in condition? Will you need to do work, such as painting, cleaning, carpet replacement and repairs, to feel comfortable living there? This all needs to be considered.

- What are the sellers taking with them and excluding from the deal? In other words are they taking certain things out the house that could essentially impact the value? These could be such items as a chandelier which truly makes the dining room; custom draperies for a particular window, or a mirror in the bathroom that appears attached but is actually removable.

- Who's paying for what? There are closing costs associated with both selling and buying. Such costs are the title policy, any attorney fees, the real estate agents' commissions, surveys, membership in homeowners' association and home warranties, to name a few. We'll cover these items in more detail later, and explain who typically pays for what.

- What are the sellers' reasons for moving? Are they in a pre-foreclosure situation or in the midst of a divorce? What do their closets say? Do you see both the wife's and husband's clothing in the closet? Try to find out why the seller is moving. Again, the nosy neighbors and the inexperienced real estate agent can tell you a lot.

The most important factor here is to keep a level head. Try to look at this experience as a business deal, and keep your anxiousness at bay! Then, let your real estate agent do the rest: negotiate, negotiate, and negotiate!

Stop Looking, and Make an Offer!

Once you have asked yourself the above questions to determine your leverage, the terms you'll propose in the offer, and the price, you or your real estate agent will make the call to the seller and/or the seller's agent. Buyers often struggle during this time; they get buyer's remorse, or they fear a confrontation or maybe just the unknown. Remember, the seller is committed to selling, but you, as the buyer, have the option to buy or not to buy the property.

> *Tip:*
> *Be sure to review all "Sellers Disclosures."*

If you are in a market that is known as a "seller's market," meaning there are more buyers than sellers, much of your negotiating leverage may go out the window. The sellers know if you don't give them close to their asking price, they will just wait until someone does – and they won't have to wait long.

A Seller's Market

Here are the general characteristics of a seller's market:

- There are many buyers looking to buy homes and a low number of homes on the market.
- The community is experiencing a booming local economy, with new companies opening their doors and looking for workers to fill positions. Those workers will need homes, and they're eager to buy.

- Sales prices of homes are escalating, with annual appreciation in double digits even though the national average is about 5% to 7% a year.
- Sellers are less likely to assist with buyers' closing costs; and higher down payment amounts become the norm.
- Homes can often sell higher than the asking price because of multiple offers made on the same property at the same time.

A Buyer's Market

Here are the general characteristics of a buyer's market:

- There are not enough buyers so homes stay on the market longer, creating a higher inventory of homes from which buyers can choose.
- Job growth is easing and jobs are fewer due to businesses downsizing, failing or moving out of the area.
- Builders with a higher inventory of homes can't sell them so they offer additional incentives to buy.
- The number of foreclosures increases and short sales become another option for sellers.
- Home prices begin to depreciate and some home owners will find themselves "upside down" – owing the banks more than the property is worth. They might have made a poor purchasing decision to start with, or they're unable to wait for the market to change in their favor, for some reason.
- Sellers are willing to offer assistance with buyer closing costs.

Your Offer Should Include:

A good, experienced real estate agent can explain the psychology behind your offer and the anticipated reaction of the seller. Make sure you discuss this, along with your negotiating strategies, before either of you submit your offer.

Your offer must always be in writing and supported with the following items:

- Copy of your earnest money check
- Copy of your option check
- Copy of your pre-qualification or pre-approval letter

Personally, we do not entertain verbal offers, which we view as noncommittal. If you are truly interested in the property, you will take the time to do the right things and put together a real offer – in writing.

In Summary, purchasing real estate can be highly emotional, even to the point where you find yourself compromising certain characteristics you initially defined as "must haves." Doing your homework upfront, before beginning negotiations, and by using your *Comparative Market Analysis*, the *Property Viewing Checklist* and the *Identify Your Leverage Checklist* will help you to put your emotions in check.

Rely on what you have learned. Then, follow your agent's advice after you discuss all your concerns and the results of your research. Understanding the leverage each party has will position you to find the best deal and to ensure that you Make No Mistakes™.

Most buyers are concerned today that they're paying too much for the property. In a changing market, it is impossible to predict how much longer – or how much further – housing prices will fall. Don't forget to look at your *local* market, as it may be different from areas that are experiencing the biggest drops and that are in the news. Most importantly, figure out what you can afford, and make your offer based on historical data and trends.

Pass The Knowledge On!

CHAPTER 17

CONTRACTS

In this chapter you will learn what information and language are needed for a real estate contract in order to protect yourself and your earnest money. We will also point out who typically pays for which part of this multi-faceted real estate transaction.

You're ready to prepare an offer with your real estate agent or attorney. Before getting to this point, however, you've done your research and you have obtained your prequalification letter. You've stayed within your price range and found the property that meets most of your must-haves and desires.

The most important point we can make about your real estate contract is to make it as comprehensive as possible. The details should *always* be specific, clearly stated, and in writing. *Nothing* should be left open to interpretation. If you think it should be in the contract, it probably should.

Mistake # 41: *Leaving out specific details in the contract*

Your contract is not the place to leave out details. Following is a list of details you may need to include in this document. Review your contract against this list to make sure you have included everything relevant to your situation:

- **Names of parties involved**, such as the seller, buyer, real estate agents and attorneys.
- **Address** of the property.
- **Legal description.** Every property has its own unique legal description that describes where it is located. The description usually includes the terms *lot* and *block number and* can easily be obtained from your county taxing district.
- **Offer price.** The price you are willing to pay for the house.
- **Down payment amount.** How much money you will put down toward the purchase price of the home vs. how much you will finance.
- **Financing arrangements.** Identify which method you'll use: conventional, FHA, VA, cash or something else. The financing method you use is important to the seller because, depending on your method, there may be a cost to the seller. For example, if you are getting assistance through a grant program, the seller may be required to contribute monies to your closing costs. All of this plays into negotiations between the seller and buyer.
- **Title** to the property. Who will research the title in order to provide clear title? A title company or real estate attorney? The seller usually pays for this service, although it is negotiable between the buyer and seller.
- **Earnest money deposit.** How much will you put down to demonstrate your seriousness about purchasing this property? It is customary in most states to see 1% of the sales price. *The down payment and earnest money deposits are two different payments.* The earnest money is given with the contract and held in an account by a third party, usually the title company. The earnest money is in *jeopardy* if the buyer does not fulfill the terms of the contract. At closing the earnest money can be applied toward any portion of the down payment and closing costs.
- **Home inspections.** This service is contracted by the buyer. The inspector's role is to determine any necessary repairs to the home and land, and if there are any defects. In other words, the inspector provides the buyer an overall picture of

the condition of the home. The inspector's job is general in scope, and he or she may suggest you contact a specialist for a question, e.g., an air conditioner specialist if the inspector suspects issues with an air conditioning unit.

- **Disclosure Statements.** These documents disclose a variety of information about the property. The most common document is the **seller's disclosure**, which is filled out by the seller of the property. It contains information about the interior and exterior features of the property. It also reveals if there were ever any insurance claims filed against the property, or if it was ever flooded, or impacted by earthquakes, hail or tornadoes, or if anyone has ever died in the home due to unnatural causes. *Be sure to read this document thoroughly.* It could indicate signs of current or future maintenance and repair issues.

Mistake # 42: *Not asking for a copy of previously completed inspections*

The seller is required to provide copies of any inspections previously done on the property within the last four years in most states, although your state may differ. If you can obtain a copy, review and compare it to your recent inspection report. Look for items that showed up in both reports. In fact, if the current listing agent sold the property to the sellers to start with, have your agent ask the listing agent for a copy. Your local MLS system will list the agents involved when the current homeowner's purchased the property.

Once you have the data, question the inspector and the seller to see if the issue is a persistent matter that you will always have to deal with as the new owner. Share your thoughts with the inspector when you give him copies of the disclosures.

The previously completed inspection reports are a tool to help prepare your offer. Remember, part of the disclosure process is doing your own due diligence, so there is nothing wrong with asking questions about the property prior to submitting your offer. You just have to ask. Keep in mind that it is best and easier to ask for repairs, based on your own visual inspection and the seller's disclosure and past inspection reports, ***during the initial negotiations***. Many deals fall apart because buyers and sellers cannot come to an agreement about repair issues after the formal inspection is completed. Why does this happen so frequently? There are many reasons. Most are due to a breakdown in communications between the agents. Or the seller is betting that the buyer won't pull out of the deal because of a few inspection items; the seller knows the buyer is already emotionally tied to the home and has spent money on an inspection. We'll discuss inspections again in Chapter 18.

Lead-Based Paint Disclosure

If the house was built prior to 1978, this document must be filled out and signed by all parties. This form is designed to protect borrowers from exposure to lead from paint, dust, and soil. You are also required to receive, when you sign your offer, a pamphlet known as "Protect Your Family from Lead in Your Home," which is published by the Environmental Protection Agency (EPA). The seller or landlord must also disclose if and where there are any lead-based paint hazards, and the condition of those painted surfaces. If you did not receive the disclosure of information on lead-based paint hazards form if you bought pre-1978 housing, contact 1-800-424-LEAD (5323) or visit www.hud.gov/offices/lead.

Negotiate an Option Period

The option period is determined at the time the offer is drafted. It goes into effect after the contract is executed, or signed by both parties. It allows buyers to conduct their inspections, decide whether or not they truly want the house without risking their earnest money, and stops the seller from selling it to anyone else. Parties may mutually agree, in writing, to lengthen or shorten the time period for inspection. We usually see 10 days and our buyers typically pay $100 for this option, which is not returned if the buyer decides to walk away from the deal. Home buyers may waive this opportunity, but we do not advise it because there are many reasons – some unforeseen – you may need this time. If this is not a standard option in your state's contract, you can add it in your special provisions section by simply including a paragraph similar to this one:

> *For nominal consideration, Buyer agrees to pay seller $100 (option fee) within two days after the execution date of this contract, for which Seller grants buyer the unrestricted right to terminate the contract, giving notice of termination within 10 days after the executed date of this contract. The option fee will be credited to the Sales Price at closing. In the event the Buyer chooses to terminate during the option period, the option fee is forfeited and the earnest money is returned to the Buyer.*

The Right Language in Special Provisions

Special provisions in the contract allow you to write in conditions or provisions you may want the seller to adhere to in order for you to accept the terms of the *overall* contract. Listed below is language typical of what we usually include in the special provisions section.

- *Contract is voidable unless executed by_____ (a specific date and time, i.e. November 29, 2008 at 5:00 p.m.).*

"Voidable" means it's the buyer's discretion whether or not to void the contract if it goes past the date stated. The buyer has the choice. This also places a deadline on the seller so the seller doesn't hold on to your offer *and* entertain others that might come in.

- *Buyer retains right to restructure financing as long as there are no delays in closing or additional costs to seller.*

We think this special provision is important because, during the financing process, you never know when you may have to restructure your financing. You don't want the seller to be so rigid that he or she won't work with you. If a change in the original financing terms negatively affects how much the seller has to pay, the seller may use one of these options:

- o Consider the borrower in default of the contract term, or
- o Return the earnest money if the borrower is unable to secure financing based on the original contract, or
- o Add the difference in the form of additional buyer closing costs

Here's another.

- **If property fails to appraise for sales price, contract will terminate and earnest money will be refunded to buyer.**

Most of the contracts set forth by states usually have language to address this, but we always like to make it clear to the other side. Sometimes the seller doesn't understand why the buyer can't move forward in purchasing their property, when it's because the seller has overpriced it.

- **Seller will repair and provide "paid" receipts on all agreed items ___ days prior to closing.**

This avoids last minute repairs and also gives some leeway to address the work if it's not completed to the buyer's satisfaction.

- **All home warranties will be transferred to buyer at the seller's expense.**

This language asks that the seller gather all documents showing existing warranties. The age of the roof and major repairs are typically stated in the seller's disclosure. Your concern should be if the warranties are transferable. Foundation and roof work are often times not transferable *unless* a transfer agreement is paid for in *advance of the property being sold to the new owner.*

- **If the appraisal shows a difference of more than 1% of the stated square feet in MLS, buyer may terminate this contract** *by providing written notice to the selling party within 3 days after the terminating party receives the appraisal. If neither party terminates this contract or if the variance is more than the stated percentage, an adjustment to the sales price will be made based on the difference of the price per square feet.*

These sentences, though long, protect the buyer in the event the appraisal reflects a lower square footage amount. Sometimes sellers are truly unaware of the size of their homes; or that the information listed by the taxing authority is incorrect; or they just inflate the number of square feet in order to ask for a higher list price. This sentence will protect you if the variance is too great, and it will smoke out the potential for appraisal fraud.

- *If buyer's interest rate increases due to extension of contract beyond <u>30</u> days from effective date of contract, by no fault of buyer; seller will buy down buyer's interest rate to original rate of <u>6%</u>.*

This provision protects the buyer against a builder and/or the seller taking their time to close. It also protects the buyer from a higher interest rate due to no fault of his or her own. The seller may require a signed lock rate from the lender showing an expiration date before they agree to this term.

- *Seller will leave home in move-in condition with carpets professionally cleaned, floors polished, bathroom and kitchen cabinets cleaned. Landscape should be left freshly cut and trimmed 24 hours before closing.*

Need we say more? But please note: You must inspect what you expect! It's essential that you do a walk-thru on the day of closing, if possible. This way, if the home was not left in proper condition, the seller can either provide a cleaning allowance so you can have it done or delay closing until it's done. The choice is up to you and the seller as to how to proceed.

Mistake # 43: *Not knowing who pays for what during the contract stage*

Depending on individual states, your earnest money contract, the sales contract or the binder can vary in length. For example, New York and Florida's are three pages long, while Missouri and Texas have eight-page contracts, not including any addendums. These contracts are written by each state's real estate commission and are specific to the state in which you are purchasing. In fact, in a real estate transaction it is not uncommon to see fees that are state-specific. The following section will focus on costs and fees that are negotiable between the buyer and seller.

The Seller Contribution

This is the amount you negotiate with *the seller* to assist you, the borrower, in paying all or some of your closing costs. The funds are subtracted from the *seller's equity* at closing and are used as an incentive for the borrower to purchase the seller's property. This amount must be written in the contract and *cannot be agreed on without the lender's approval*. The concept of seller contribution is more common in markets where there are more sellers than buyers. As of this writing, the maximum allowable contribution on primary residences and second homes with less than 10% down is 3%. Check with your lender if you plan to put down more than 10% for your seller contribution limits. Investment property is limited to 2% seller concessions, or contributions, regardless of the down payment amount.

Hazard Insurance Cost

You are required to have one year of hazard insurance paid in advance. This is usually paid for *by the buyer*. Contact more than one insurance agent to provide you with price quotations and choices on the type of coverage. This insurance is designed to cover the lender and your property in the event of fire, wind and storms. Lenders often have minimum requirements, so it's very important to know the coverage you do and do not have. Many insurance agents will offer the bare minimum of coverage, which may or may not cover water damage from the *inside* of the home if pipes burst. On the other end of the spectrum, your insurance coverage may not cover you if water comes from such external sources as flooding. Depending on what part of the country you live in and whatever natural disaster is prevalent – earthquakes, hurricanes, tornados, flooding – be sure to understand your risks.

You may be able to reduce the amount of your insurance costs if your lender is willing to accept replacement cost coverage. Replacement costs are the expenses associated with replacing or rebuilding your house only, since you'd still have the land. This coverage is less expensive because it does not include the land value – you don't have to purchase new land. If the house burns down, for example, the land is still there.

Let's say you purchased your home for $250,000. The land is worth $120,000. Therefore you could take out a (house) replacement insurance policy of $130,000 instead of the full $250,000. This strategy could save you a few hundred dollars a year if your lender will let you do it. So ask your loan officer and insurance provider about it. And *insist* in talking directly with the underwriter if your loan officer can't seem to make it happen. The replacement value is found in your appraisal report.

You can also ask your insurance agent if the company participates in the Comprehensive Loss Underwriting Exchange (CLUE); that is, do they obtain CLUE reports that evaluate the history of a property for any prior insurance claims. This will let you know if the seller has made any claims regarding the property. If you find that the home has had a claim, be sure to question if the repair was made, take notice if the repair showed up on the seller's disclosure, and go examine the area that was repaired. Oftentimes, sellers don't make the proper repairs; they simply keep the insurance money.

The Title Policy

The title policy is typically paid for *by the seller*. Though every state differs, this is a one-time, prepaid insurance policy that the seller purchases on behalf of the buyer. The premium for coverage lasts as long as the new owner and the heirs own the property. It insures that in the future, should someone claim ownership of the property, the policy would defend the homeowner's ownership of it. The title company will only provide this to a buyer after researching the title and deed. *The title company also insures that all judgments and liens attached to the property have been cleared before they insure it.* Here are things the title company could uncover as they thoroughly research your property's title:

- forged signatures, fraud, duress, impersonation
- documents improperly signed, sealed, acknowledged, or delivered
- encroachments[64]
- surveys
- recorded documents affecting a property, such as easements[65]
- income-tax liens, and mechanics' liens
- title search errors
- others having rights arising out of leases, contracts

Title insurance rates vary by state. In some states the title company determines a competitive price while other states are regulated by that state's Department of Insurance and so the fees may not be negotiated – neither higher nor lower. In both cases, the premium fees are calculated on a per $1,000 rate and directly related to the value of the home. Ask your local title company about these fees and don't be afraid to ask for a discount.

If you are buying a home that has changed hands within the last several years, ask your title company about a "reissue rate," which is when the title company might accept a lower premium because a previous one was recently purchased within the last four years.

If you are buying a newly-constructed home, make certain your title insurance covers *claims by contractors* who may not have

---

[64] An *encroachment* is an intrusion of a building, an improvement or an object from a neighboring property onto another owner's property. Some examples are trees, fences, walls, driveways, garages etc.

[65] An *easement* is the right for someone other than the owner of the property to use the land for a specific purpose. Common examples include utility and cable access.

been paid by the builder. There are times when the builder's debt shows up after you have purchased the property. These claims are known as mechanic's liens,[66] and we discussed them in Chapters 15. These liens are attached to the specific property for the supplies and labor that improved the property. So regardless of who created the debt, the owner of the property at the time the lien is posted is responsible for paying the lien on the property. If the builder refuses to pay the debt and if the lien is not noticed prior to the new buyer taking ownership from the seller, then the subcontractor may get paid when the new seller sells the property again. How long a lien can stay tied to a property is also state specific. The length of a judgment depends upon the laws of the state in which the judgment is filed. Most judgments are valid from 5 to 20 years and some can be renewed at expiration.

The Mortgagee's Title Policy

The mortgage lender, in most cases, will require that the *buyer* purchase a "Mortgagee's Title Policy" for the lender's benefit. Like the title policy, this policy provides financial protection against hidden defects, adverse title claims or risk to the buyer and its mortgage company providing the loan on the property.

The Survey

This is also typically paid for by the buyer. It provides the footprint of the house and establishes the boundaries of the property; in other words, how the property you're buying sits on the surrounding land. Sometimes the title company and the lender will accept a survey the seller already has, depending on how old it is. This could save you a few hundred dollars if you decide to use it. *If you do, be sure to walk the land, and make sure there has been nothing added to the property*

---

[66] A *mechanic's lien* is placed on a property by contractors who have done work but who have not been paid.

to change the characteristic of the survey you have in hand, e.g. a pool added, an extension of a room, a patio.

> *Lisa purchased property and accepted the existing survey in order to save money on closing costs. She didn't realize that the seller had built a flagstone patio in the backyard that extended 2 feet into the utility easement. The utility company needed access to the cables underneath the ground, which meant destroying her patio to access the cables. The repair cost her more than the new survey would have to begin with.*

Management Transfer Fee

This fee is typically paid by the buyer and has to do with the property's homeowners' association, if there is one. The management company and the homeowners' association usually charge to transfer ownership of a home in the subdivision or development. The fee covers the paperwork to change names and to provide copies of the deed restrictions.

Contact Information

The contract requires contact information such as your name, address, telephone number and email address. The title company needs this information to send all the documents to you prior to closing. There are times, however, when this information is abused. Sellers sometimes decide to contact buyers directly, and vice versa. More often than not, a deal goes bad fast when this happens, and the issue of trust becomes a big factor in negotiations. We've seen sellers try to make side deals or make upsetting comments to the buyers who then want to back out of the deal. It's best to use your real estate agent's phone number and your personal email from a Yahoo or Hotmail account if you have one. If not, use your agent's information. Furthermore, we encourage you to get a money order or cashier's check from your bank if your own checks show your address or phone number. The objective is to not allow the other side to contact you directly. It's the reason you hired representation: your real estate agent.

The Closing Date

The *settlement date* is sometimes referred to as the closing date. This is the day all parties meet at the title company or attorney's office and sign all legal documents to transfer ownership.

Mistake # 44: *Not reviewing Murphy's Law*

However, "closing" and "funding" are two different terms. *Closing* is when all paperwork is signed, dated and notarized, and certified funds from the buyer are collected, if applicable. Then, the paperwork and copies of the certified funds are faxed to the lender. The lender reviews and officially accepts the documents, *then* prepares to wire funds to the designated escrow company on the borrower's behalf. This is known as *funding*: when all monies have been distributed according to the approved settlement statement. At that time, congratulations are in order!

The point we make is just because you signed all the paperwork, it doesn't mean the money is there waiting for you or for the seller. So if you are closing on a Friday at 4:00 p.m., more than likely the money will not arrive at its destination until Monday morning. Therefore, you may not be able to move into your new home over the weekend because the seller has not received funds or clearance that his old mortgage was paid. If that happens, it's unlikely the seller will release keys to the property. Keep this in mind when you're scheduling movers and switching the utilities to your name. In business, until the money is in the account, the deal is not done. This is why we ask you to review the *Murphy's Law Checklist:* so you are prepared for whatever could go wrong.

Temporary Lease

If you find yourself in the situation described above, it's very possible the seller will request a Seller's Temporary Residential Lease. This document allows the seller to continue living in the home after closing for a negotiated, short period of time – usually a few days (although we have seen it as long as 90 days). When we represent sellers, we usually request a temporary lease because it allows the sellers to move out of the home only after they know their money from the closing is in the bank. Too many times, we have seen sellers move out beforehand, yet the buyers' financing is delayed or just falls apart. The seller is then stuck having to start over again and go through the entire process of trying to sell the house. In the meantime, the sellers may have committed to another property. Now, they are faced with the cost of paying two mortgages, or with losing their earnest money and other cash outlays associated with buying another home. They had thought everything was going to work out, despite not actually receiving the funds from the sale of their home yet. At this point, you, as the buyer, may also have lost your earnest money and all the cash outlays associated with getting to this point.

Because of this potential for disaster, don't be surprised if the seller's agent asks you to agree to a Seller's Temporary Residential Lease, although it is not required to sell a home. It is a short, two page document, and is not meant to replace the full-length lease contract, which is used for leases longer than 90 days. It is also not uncommon for sellers to request a lease when they need a short while longer to get enough cash to actually move.

The opposite counterpart to the temporary lease is a document known as the Buyer's Temporary Residential Lease. In this case, the sellers become the landlord and the buyers become the tenants. This form is used when buyers wish to occupy the property prior to closing, perhaps because their existing lease is expiring and they anticipated being able to close on a certain date – which didn't happen. It's likely the agent representing the seller will advise the seller not to lease the property to you as the buyer, simply because the risk is high that something could go wrong, such as buyer's remorse, or, worse yet, a further delay in a closing that may never happen.

Imagine how complicated this would make the seller's ability to market and sell the property!

Both of these temporary residential lease agreements must contain the following items:

- Clearly identify the landlord and the tenant
- State the property address
- Explain the lease's term, including a start date and a termination date
- Establish a *per diem* rate. It is customary and usually fairly easy to get the seller's agreement to cover the costs of PITI, including any HOA fees, on a *per diem* basis. To calculate the *per diem* rate, simply divide your mortgage cost by the number of days in the given month
- Be sure to include a security deposit amount, which the tenant pays the landlord to cover damages to the property and/or to satisfy the tenant's obligations under the lease
- List the cost of the utilities, whether they are included or excluded
- Include information about pets, whether they are allowed or not
- Describe property alterations which are not allowed, such as nail holes
- Detail the current property conditions and mention how to address repairs
- List who handles and pays for repairs and/or maintenance expenses
- Make sure at least one party maintains insurance, although usually both parties will. As a tenant, be sure your contents are covered.
- Include an indemnification of the landlord from claims made against you by a third party
- Possession of the property by the buyer as a tenant may change insurance policy coverage
- Use language which addresses what happens in the event either party defaults

- Establish reasons for termination of the lease
- Describe any holding over, which are fees as damages for failing to terminate the contract

Remember, as real estate agents, we are not attorneys, so we always encourage you to consult one. And since this is a reference guide about buying – and not selling – it is our experience that your goal should be to protect the property after you become the owner of it. One way you can do this is to insist on a security deposit, paid on the day of closing, by the seller. It would certainly incent the seller to leave the property in good move-in condition when the seller does eventually move out.

One last thought on temporary leasebacks and temporary residential leases: As a buyer, be sure to consult your insurance agent about changes of ownership and possession for limited purposes.

In Summary, the contract is a tool designed to be very specific so that all parties understand their roles and rights. On the other hand, keep in mind that everything is negotiable! There is nothing written in stone that says the seller or the buyer must pay for something. We have just shared with you what is most commonly seen and accepted. But no matter who pays for what, be sure to include that information in the contract.

Do not get so friendly or assumptive with the seller and the seller's real estate agent during the process that you get lax and don't write specific language into the contract. Your agent is there to represent you and to protect your interest in the transaction.

Be open to asking questions. You'll learn a lot more about the property this way, and some of that information could save you hundreds or even thousands of dollars.

Pass The Knowledge On!

CHAPTER 18

THE HOME INSPECTION

In this chapter you will learn that not having an inspection on the property, regardless of whether it is a resale or new construction, is a huge risk and could cost you thousands!!!

It's time to get an inspection once you and the seller:

- Agree on the financial terms, based on what you know so far about the property
- Insert any special provisions in the contract
- Use your option period to secure time to terminate the contract for any reason
- Agree on how you will take possession of the house

Mistake # 45: *Not ordering a home inspection*

Keep in mind that the inspection is not designed as a way for the buyer to *renegotiate* the terms of the contract, though many buyers believe this. The primary purposes of an inspection are to understand what it will take to care for the property and to be assured that the property will be safe and dependable.

You can find a home inspector in the local yellow pages, on the internet or from your real estate agent. Bear in mind that most inspectors are licensed by a professional association, not the state government.

Just as you would ask questions of your real estate agent and loan officer, be sure to ask home inspectors questions regarding their capability to do their work. Some obvious questions might be how long they have been inspecting homes, and if they are familiar with homes in a particular area. For example, there may be areas in your city where homes were built in a certain era and they have characteristics that newer homes don't have. You certainly would not want an inspector who is unfamiliar with this type of home to inspect it. He or she might examine the home in the same manner they would a newer home – and that's just not going to be reliable. In turn, it could prevent you from moving forward with the property because it is being inspected on different criteria.

Also, find out the inspector's license number. In many states, the lower this number, the longer they've been licensed. For example, a license number of 457 means the inspector has been licensed longer than an inspector with the license number of 3851. However, keep in mind that just because a person is licensed doesn't mean they have been actively inspecting homes full-time over the years, or that a lower license number means less experience. This is just a guideline, not a rule.

One of the best forms of protection against a bad inspection is E&O insurance. *Errors and Omissions insurance is an insurance that most professionals in the real estate business carry in order to protect themselves against error, omission, or negligence during the property's physical inspection.* Not everyone carries this. The most common inspection claims are because an inspector failed to disclose a roof leak or foundation crack, for example. A quick call to your local Better Business Bureau is always prudent. And ask the inspector to see his or her E&O insurance certificate, too.

A general home inspection is very similar to a physical exam at the doctor's. The exam covers all the readily visible structural, mechanical, and sometimes the environmental components of the house. This includes the plumbing, electrical and heating systems, and the roof, crawl space and foundation. Sometimes an inspector will notice signs of termites and other pests. A pest inspection should be done by a licensed pest control professional. The inspector can usually provide you with a list of other relevant inspectors he has worked with.

The general inspection does not cover things that may not be readily seen inside of walls and ceilings. ***The inspection will NOT cover the following:***

- Geologic stability, lot lines, environmental hazards, zoning designations and code compliance
- Decorative, stylistic, cosmetic, or aesthetic aspects of a home, such as chipped paint
- Sprinkler systems
- Security systems
- Hot tubs and swimming pools
- Unattached appliances such as a refrigerator
- Environmental health hazards, such as radon gas, lead paint or asbestos
- Noise transmission between units, if purchasing a condo or town home
- Common areas of the subdivision

It is wise to contact a specialist to get an expert opinion on these issues if the general inspector has concerns. Whether you are buying a resale or new construction, you should get an inspection. But why do this on a new home, you might ask. Keep in mind that humans built that house, and humans are prone to cutting corners and making mistakes. If you buy a newly constructed house, move in and then a problem crops up, you're stuck waiting for the builder's warranty person to fix the problem. It's unlikely the builder will feel any urgency to fix your items. After all, the builder has already been paid. You are at the mercy of a warranty department.

Before builders get paid, however, they're motivated to fix any problems. They want the buyers happy and closing on time, so the builder can get paid. So always conduct an inspection on a new home – that's when you have the leverage, not after! And if you can conduct an inspection prior to the sheetrock going up, that's even better! Just being able to have your inspector check out the framing, wiring and plumbing will save you potential costs and headaches in the future. Then walk through every item on your punch list[67] to ensure the work was done to your complete satisfaction. If you find something you are uncertain about, call your inspector out again! A little bit of money spent at this stage will save a lot of money – and hassles – later.

One of our clients decided to purchase a beautiful new townhome in the downtown area. It was still under construction. During one of our walk throughs, we saw that, architecturally, this builder did a great job. However, his attention to detail was less than desirable. For example, much of the trim work along the ceilings and base of the walls were uneven or missing.

We expressed our concerns to our buyer and insisted he spend the additional money to order an inspection. The inspector found more items that weren't obvious. One item, in particular, was a stucco and drywall issue. We brought all these items to the attention of the builder, who was more than willing to make the fixes prior to closing. Sure enough, after our client signed on the dotted line and moved into the house, there were other items that needed to be addressed – items that could only be found after moving into the property and living there on a day-to-day basis. Our client had to take time off from work to meet trade workers who sometimes never showed up or were late arriving for the job. This story went on for months!

You might ask why the inspector didn't find everything that was wrong with the property. Keep in mind, it is the inspector's role to find as much as possible. However, inspectors are human too and sometimes things are overlooked. Or, they don't start becoming a problem until later, after the house is lived in for a while. It is always worth

---

[67] A *punch list* is a list of items that the builder needs to fix or replace.

the money to have an inspection because a good inspector can bring issues to your attention that could potentially cost you thousands, even in short-term ownership situation.

Mistake # 46: *Not inspecting what you expect*

It is a lot easier to get repair and replacement items addressed before closing than after. It is expected you'll find other items that need addressing once you begin living in your home. Let *these* be the items your home warranty[68] policy addresses, versus any major items that an inspector could have uncovered during an inspection. Be persistent in this area so you don't feel frustrated and wish you had never bought your home.

During the inspection, the inspector will follow a standardized list of items to inspect. You can expect the inspector to explain any deficiencies he may find and answer your questions while going through the home. Some findings may call for safety-related repairs, and the inspector is trained to identify if you need a specialist for further investigation. Inspectors can often offer suggestions to resolve problems, and they can also offer information on properly maintaining your house.

At the end of the inspection, you should have a "summary" discussion with the inspector. You'll go over the problems that were found, and the inspector will explain more about the items that will appear in the written inspection report. *An inspector will find something in all homes, even brand new ones.* The inspector sends copies of the report to the buyer and the buyer's real estate agent, via email or fax, within a couple of days of the inspection.

---

[68] A *home warranty* is an insurance policy that covers homeowners of new construction for repairs or replacements of many of the most frequently occurring breakdowns of home system components and appliances.

Mistake # 47: *Not attending the inspection*

Though it is not required that you and/or your real estate agent attend the inspection, we *strongly suggest* it. Here are the reasons why:

- It gives you another opportunity to go into the home, get a better feel for it and become more familiar with it.

- While inspectors try to be very clear in their written reports, sometimes the reports can be interpreted incorrectly. The conversations you have with the inspector are generally very valuable and will offer additional insights and suggestions.

- Inspectors often mention little things in person that might not warrant being included in the formal written report. They may also give you a range of costs on how much an item will cost to repair or replace.

- Being in the house again is another opportunity to decide if you really want to move forward with buying the home.

How to Use the Inspection Report

The inspection report can also be used in several ways:

- As a reference document while you work through the repairs and improvements in your new home.
- As a tool to negotiate with the sellers on how much they are willing to contribute toward the cost of repairing or replacing things in the inspection report.
- Many buyers see the results of an inspection report as a reason to go back to the seller to renegotiate the sales price. It's not! This has already been established before the inspection. Though there have been times when the sales price has been adjusted after the inspection, it is not the norm. In fact, it's more normal to see buyers walking away from the property

because the inspector found too many items that are potential headaches and very costly. If this happens to you, think twice! Is the price of the home worth these potential headaches? Do you have a professional who can address these problems?

Depending on how negotiations have gone to this point, the inspection can be the straw that breaks the camel's back. The whole negotiation process can cause enormous stress on both sides. Sometimes asking the seller to do work on the property that they have already detached themselves from can cause sparks. The biggest conflict comes when the seller feels the buyer has asked for too much. This is usually the phase when the deal can seize up or even break down. If that happens, the buyer has just spent $200 to $500 to inspect someone else's house. If this happens to you, however, count your blessings if the inspection report comes back with items you are just not willing to deal with and you choose to back out of the deal. The cost of the inspection was well worth it.

Recently, we became the listing agent on a property that was over 40 years old. It had been on the sales block for more than 400 days, and we were now the second agents trying to market this home. Our client, the seller, soon received an offer, although it was $7,000 less than his asking price. Nonetheless, he accepted the offer. When the buyers conducted their inspection and received their inspection report, they came back with a large list of items they wanted our client to fix.

Our client agreed to have the carpets professionally cleaned and to give the buyer $1,500 toward all the other repairs. The buyers wanted $4,500 for the repairs. As you can probably guess, this deal blew up because the seller thought the buyers were being unreasonable. The buyers knew they didn't have to buy this house, so if they couldn't get the property on their terms, they would move on – and they did.

The moral of the story is anything can happen throughout the process. And though the home was older, we knew it would take a certain kind of buyer to appreciate its character. We advised our clients that these were not the right buyers for this home. In fact, within a week of the first disappointing transaction, our clients received another, more satisfactory offer.

The Option Period

The option period gives the buyer the right to terminate the contract for any reason. The inspection report is not a basis to renegotiate, but a tool designed to inform the buyer of what repairs and treatments are needed. Therefore, prior to execution of the contract, the borrower should have *specific* language addressing any obvious needs for repair. Once the contract is executed and the buyer orders an inspection, the seller does not have to agree to address any items in your inspection report. *However, most sellers entertain the buyers' requests for repairs because they know they are in that probationary option period where the buyers have the right to terminate for any reason.* So, as a result, some sellers will opt to negotiate on repair items, not on sales price. However, nothing states the buyer cannot approach the seller on the sales price within the 10-day option period.

Sometimes sellers will write "as is" in the contract. This tells the buyer the property is being sold in the state it is currently in and that no repairs will be done. Upon signing the executed contract, the buyer then has to make the decision to take the home "as is" or to back out within the allotted time of the option period.

So let's assume that after the inspection you are still interested in owning the property. You would then go through the repair list to determine which items you would like the seller to address. One of your potential lenders might insist on all of the items being repaired. Like most sellers, however, the ones you're working with have already done as much as they want to do on the house. Having to do more is not on their agenda.

With this in mind, here are some possible scenarios of what the seller might choose to do:

- State they're not fixing anything

- Agree to fix some items, but not others
- Offer an allowance[69] for you to make the repairs as you see fit
- Offer a combination of any of the above

Your real estate agent needs to understand the technical aspects of a home. If not, he or she should at least know where to get the information in order to be able to explain and perhaps defend an item on the inspection report. Not knowing and, worse yet, not being able *to articulate the problem* could easily cost you the deal, particularly if the seller finds your request unreasonable or the cost of the repair prohibitive. Also, if the negotiations were already or become rocky, the sellers may decide they don't want to deal with you and so they intentionally sabotage the deal in hopes of finding another buyer.

> *Here's another story where we represented the buyer. Our buyer wanted to purchase an abandoned house that had the potential to become a beautiful home. The home had been picked up by a group of investors who had started to work on it. We began to negotiate with these investors, and were extremely aggressive with our offer.*
>
> *After we received the inspection report, we addressed the sellers' real estate agent about a problem with the roof. Fixing the problem was only going to cost the buyers about $2,000. But because of how she articulated and delivered the information to the sellers, it sounded as though it was a much larger problem. Because of the real estate agent's inability to identify that the roof problem was not really a major issue, her clients, the sellers, took $10,000 off of the asking price for this roof issue when $2,000 would have been acceptable.*

Another important point to keep in mind when asking for repairs to be completed by the seller is to ask for *paid* receipts and *transferrable warranties*. Showing that the work requested was

---

[69] An *allowance* is the amount of cash offered by the seller in lieu of making the actual repairs or replacements.

completed by a *licensed professional* is important. You don't want Joe Blow, who is really a painter, fixing the air conditioning unit just because he knows a little bit about air conditioning. ***Then, inspect what you expect several days before your final walk through.*** If the seller knows it is your intent to inspect the job several days before closing they are more likely to make the effort to complete it. If you set your deadline enough days before closing so that, if the work isn't up to snuff, the seller can and will have it redone before the closing date. If the seller knows this ahead of time, hopefully, he'll do it right the first time.

In Summary, paying for an option period in order to conduct your inspections is well worth the small cost. Having an inspection is a *must* if the property is new construction or a resale. An inspector will always find something, so the inspection is well worth the money. Having an extra set of trained eyes look specifically for signs of short-term and long-term repairs could save you thousands of dollars and several headaches. Having a good real estate agent who can articulate the issues reported in the inspection report is advantageous when you're negotiating or requesting items to be repaired, treated or replaced. Always inspect what you expect, including the paid receipts and transferrable warranties.

Pass The Knowledge On!

Section V:
Successfully Navigating
The Loan Process to Closing

CHAPTER 19

THE FINAL LOAN APPROVAL

In this chapter you will learn about the final leg of the loan process, *"clear to close,"* and how you get there. It's important to understand this process because it's a phase where many lose thousands of dollars – or their minds – or both!

So far, you have completed all your inspections, had all your specialists enter the home to provide you with varying bids, decided to move forward with your purchase and advised your mortgage professional that you wish to finalize the financing.

For those of you who followed our advice and have already been pre-approved, selected your loan product, locked your interest rate and supplied the requested documentation to your loan officer, great!

But if for some reason you're not at this stage of the loan process, you're taking a real chance leaving it for this late in the game. Why? Because in today's tough financial market characterized by strict credit guidelines, getting an approval is like winning the lottery – even people with great credit and who meet all the qualifications are having a tougher time getting approved.

Getting a mortgage can be long and stressful, especially if you don't understand how the whole process should work. Under normal conditions, you can plan on 45 days from the time you complete the loan application to the day of closing when you sign the final papers.

Sixty to ninety days, however, is not abnormal and it depends on the market in which you are buying in. The process is always shortened when everything is completed on time.

When you apply for your loan, ask the lender what the company's average processing time is. The lender should be able to tell you when you can expect to close on your loan. There are five steps in the loan process:

1. Loan application
2. Pre-Qualification or Pre-Approval Phase
3. Loan processing
4. Underwriting and analysis of the loan
5. Closing

Steps 1 and 2 were already discussed in Chapter 6. So let's continue on to step 3 and first look at who is involved in the loan process.

Who's Involved in the Loan Process

The entire loan process is sometimes lengthy and confusing. It is important to understand that, from the beginning to the end, many different people have a task to complete in order for your mortgage to get *funded*. So that you can get a picture of how many people are involved in providing information or completing a specific task, here is a list:

- Borrower (and Co-Borrower)
      Employer(s)
      Banks and Creditors
- Real Estate Agent
- Mortgage Broker/Banker
      Credit Bureau
      Loan Officer
      Processor
      Lender
      Underwriter

Risk Department
Appraiser
Mortgage Insurance Company
- Inspector(s)
- Surveyor
- Homeowners' Association (HOA)
- Hazard Insurance Agent
- Title Insurance Company
    Closer
    Escrow Officer
    Settlement Attorney
    County Clerk Office
    Taxing Authority
- Seller

Each of these entities plays a part in the approval, processing, and closing of your loan.

Lenders work like an assembly line: When one person is done with a task, the file is passed on to the next person on the line. Trying to circumvent any step will just throw the whole process off. It only takes one person on that assembly line to miss a step or fail to complete a task on time to slow up the entire deal. If this happens, it's often a major problem, particularly if contracts are date-sensitive.

In addition, minor problems can occur along this assembly line, from a missing document to a missing signature. Something this small can take little or no time to correct, but can quickly lead to a major delay. If your file is missing something it is taken off the assembly line and put to the side. As a borrower, you are most likely under the impression that the file is still moving along. When you later realize it's not, the situation can get stressful. Your file depends on people – people doing their part, caring enough to complete their tasks and constantly checking on the status of the files that were bumped off the assembly line.

The borrower can be the worst offender by not supplying the necessary information on time. The clock keeps moving; no one waits for you. Whoever is working on your loan just moves on to the next complete file. The *seller* can also do things to cause delays in the closing. Just make sure you understand your role and responsibilities as stated in the contract. Don't make a mistake by causing delays due to your inaction.

This stage of the loan process can also be stressful because many borrowers think everyone is ready and waiting to serve them, and that the people involved in securing the loan will drop whatever else they're doing when they receive the information they requested from you. In reality, this is seldom the case. Just remember, nearly everything takes 24 hours. If you supply the document today, it will be looked at tomorrow at the earliest. Lenders are busy, and do things based on their own internal systems. They will work on completed files first and get back to your incomplete file when they finish the completed ones. The moral of the story is to do your part and be responsive. There are too many other people involved in your success to close on time so just make sure you do your part.

Once you've decided on a loan officer and executed a sales contract you will be required to supply documentation supporting your application. See the *Borrower's Paperwork Checklist* in the back of this book for a list of documents you will need to gather and submit to the loan officer. Or, visit our website and click on "**Real Estate Forms**" to download a copy of the Borrower's Paperwork Checklist. Access this section of the site by entering code 550 in the book coupon field.

You'll then sign off on all the disclosures required by the state and RESPA, including a revised Good Faith Estimate (GFE), Lock in Agreement and the Truth in Lending (TIL). As we discussed in an earlier chapter, RESPA (Real Estate Settlement Procedures Act) is a statute that requires borrowers be given disclosures of closing costs. RSEPA also prohibits kickbacks that may increase the cost of the mortgage loan to the consumer. As previously mentioned, these disclosures are designed to inform homebuyers about how to become better shoppers in the home-buying process. This statute is enforced by HUD, whose mission is to increase homeownership, support community development, and increase access to affordable housing.

Once the loan package is put together, it moves on to the processor, and a process like the one diagrammed below unfolds.

Flow Chart of the Loan Process:

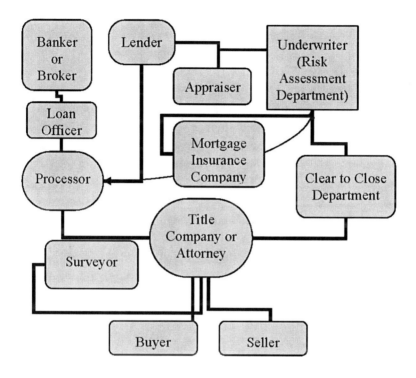

The Processor's Role in Getting You Approved

Once the loan officer has completed your loan package, he or she submits it to the processor. The processor's role is the quality assurance department for the broker or banker. The processor makes sure all the documents and verifications gathered by the loan officer and client are valid and in good order. Below are just a few examples of tasks the processor does before the file is forwarded on to the lender:

- Verifies your salary with your employer
- Verifies your account balances with your bank
- Verifies your rental history
- Orders another credit report if necessary

- Ensures all documents are filled out and signed correctly
- Follows up on the title commitment with the title company or closing attorney
- Gathers and prepares all the documents needed to complete your file

A processor is also familiar with the way certain lenders like to see the files. A careful processor will structure the files so as to give an underwriter fewer reasons to deny or question the file.

Sometimes the processor will call you directly and ask for certain documents that support your application and credit report. It is important that you supply them as quickly as possible. If not, you'll lengthen the loan process, thus taking the chance of losing your rate lock and having your credit pulled again, both of which could complicate the process.

The processor will also arrange to have your property appraised, call the title company to order the survey, and provide the preliminary title commitment.[70] This will take a couple of weeks to complete and return.

Ordering the Appraisal

Most real estate transactions require an appraisal to secure financing. An appraisal is a document prepared by a licensed appraiser who determines the market value of a property. Other situations that may require an appraisal include the removal of private mortgage insurance (PMI), taxation purposes, divorce, estate settlement, or proposed construction or remodeling projects.

Prior to 2009, appraisals were ordered directly by the broker, *but are now ordered directly by the lender on most files in order to reduce fraud* of overinflated appraisal values. This is also done to reduce the number of second appraisals ordered simply because the broker did not receive the price value he needed to complete the loan

---

[70] A *title commitment* is the promise to provide a title policy if all the criteria is met by both buyer and seller of any given property.

package. To learn more about the Home Valuation Code of Conduct of an appraiser, go to www.efanniemae.com.

How Do Appraisers Determine The Value?

The appraiser first searches for all properties sold recently (up to 3 to 6 months) that are similar to the property being appraised. The appraiser then looks for sale prices that are in line with the requested value. Next, they inspect the property's physical condition and any upgrades made to the interior and exterior of the property. Factors such as physical condition, proximity to services, and overall neighborhood values are also taken into account. There are two general approaches to determining residential value:

1. Cost approach
2. Cost comparison approach

The cost approach, also referred to as *replacement cost,* is the value of the land, plus the cost of reconstructing a substitute house on a similar lot, in similar condition. This approach is most often used for properties in which it is difficult to find recently sold comparable properties in the local market.

The most commonly used approach to determining value in the residential market is the *comparison approach.* In this instance the appraiser looks for properties that sold in the last three to six months that are comparable to the subject property. This approach gives buyers a reasonably good idea of how the house compares to others. And in relation to the comparables, the appraiser adds to the value for special items the house has, or deducts from the value for items that the house lacks.

This comparison approach gives the most accurate estimation of the value of the house. If the appraised value comes back higher than the sales price, it will not affect the loan. Remember, the appraisal's purpose is to simply inform the lender of the value of the property.

Here are some of your options if the appraisal *does not equal or exceed* the sales price you offered on the contract:

- The borrower and seller can negotiate for a lower sales price
- The borrower can terminate the contract
- The borrower can increase the down payment amount to make up the difference between the appraised value and the purchase price

In today's market, lenders will not loan more than the appraised value of a home. The industry had a problem with appraisal inflating in the past, but most lenders have systems in place to prevent this from happening now. One common example of this is an in-house review appraisal department charged with the task of reviewing an appraisal before the loan is approved. Sometimes the lender will even send out an employee-appraiser to review the property vs. sub-contracting it out, as has been the traditional route. Don't be surprised if your loan gets delayed in this department.

Mistake # 48: *Not reviewing or asking for a copy of your appraisal*

There are many ways a buyer can lose money in real estate. One less conspicuous way is by not bothering to review the appraisal report. Often buyers just want to know what the home was appraised for and as long as the value is greater than they're paying everyone is happy and no one bothers to look at the report. In fact, many mortgage fraud tactics could not be committed without an inflated appraisal value, so be sure to ask for a copy of your appraisal. Not asking for a copy of the appraisal once it has been completed is a *huge* mistake. Under federal law, the borrower is entitled to a copy of the lender's appraisal three days *before* closing. You should look at the homes they used to compare your property. These comparable properties should be similar in square footage, age, location, style of home, number of bedrooms and baths, and have other similar amenities.

An important factor to consider is the appraised square footage of the property. This number is easily overlooked and should be compared to that listed in the *MLS listing*. Be wary of MLS listings that overstate the square footage. They do this in order to give off a *lower price* per square foot, which may help the house sell. For example, the MLS listing may show a home is 3,000 square feet when in fact the appraiser measured it as *2,900* square feet. If the home is priced at $150 a square foot, a mere 100 square feet of missing space can actually cost you an extra $15,000! This tactic is common and easily overlooked by buyers and their agents. Sometimes, it becomes a dispute as to whose measurements are correct, that of the appraisal district, the appraiser, the builder or the sellers.

Underwriting and Analysis of the Loan

The lender's approval process is known as *underwriting*. Loan underwriting involves analyzing the borrower's property, credit information and any required additional documentation.

The Role of the Underwriter

The broker, banker, loan officer (the "originator") and processor, in most cases, do not have the authority to approve your loan. Their roles are to put together a compelling package for the lender's underwriting department to review and approve. *Specifically, the role of the loan officer is to sell you on the rate and terms of the loan. The processor's role is to sell the file on paper to the underwriter, who then determines the level of risk the lending company is willing to take.*

Mistake # 49: *Believing you have an approval without a "Clear to Close"*

However, there are times when both the originator and the processor have to be able to verbally sell your file. They must be able to articulate well enough to convince the underwriter to look at a situation from different perspectives, if need be. That is, they must be able to overcome any objections the underwriter might have, based on the guidelines he or she has to follow.

Even though you may have followed all of our advice from the *"Things Not to Do While Applying for a Mortgage Checklist,"* you might still receive a list of conditions from the underwriter to fulfill in order to get a final loan approval. In terms of approving or denying your loan, the underwriter will make one of the following decisions:

- Approve the loan
- Approve the loan with conditions
- Application returned for additional documentation and resubmission
- Deny the loan

If the underwriter decides to *approve your loan,* he or she will package the paperwork in preparation for selling the loan on the secondary market. However, if the underwriter *approves the loan with conditions,* don't freak out; this is common. Just get busy and get it done. Depending on how busy the underwriting department is and how quickly you can give them the information they need, it could take up to four additional days to complete your loan.

To help you be better prepared, here are a few more examples of conditions:

- Buyer must prove that child support payments are up to date
- Buyer must show proof and source of funds for the down payment
- Survey of the land needs to be done
- Property must be insured by a title policy
- Buyer must show a copy of the discharge papers from a bankruptcy
- Buyer must subscribe to private mortgage insurance
- Buyer must supply hazard insurance
- Buyer must payoff certain debt
- Approval value must meet or exceed sales price

If the underwriting department needs additional information, they will contact the processor with the list of conditions that need to be met before the borrower receives a "Clear to Close." This process can go in circles for a long time if the borrower and the processor are unable to present the information the way the underwriter wants to see it. Often, this part of the process causes everyone a lot of stress. The additional information the underwriter requests might be perceived as trivial or inconsequential in the whole scheme of the loan. But keep in mind the underwriter's guidelines require this information; his hands are as tied as yours. It can be very frustrating if you cannot readily get your hands on the information and you are supposed to close within days. The best attitude to have during these trying days is an understanding one and make sure through all of your preparing to move you still can readily access your important papers.

Automated Underwriting Systems

Today, most of this process is still manual, but the industry is moving to a more computerized, automated underwriting process. If you are a prime borrower, someone with little or no credit problems, with cash in the bank and sufficiently documented income, you may be able to get a mortgage quickly. In fact, with today's computerized mortgage underwriting, you may be approved in less than an hour and have the mortgage funded in less than two weeks! Computerized, automated underwriting looks at the same factors as manual underwriting does, but not as many of them. They are statistical models which compare data about loan applications to data from several hundred thousand loans made over the last few years. *The computer systems predict how likely it is for your loan to be repaid based on how loans with the same characteristics have been repaid in the past.* These fast mortgages are underwritten using one of two electronic programs, which allow the primary market lenders to quickly get an answer on your loan application.

- Freddie Mac's *Loan Prospector* software
- Fannie Mae's *Desktop Underwriter* software

If you're not a prime borrower, call your loan officer or visit www.fanniemae.com to see if you meet the guidelines for automated electronic underwriting.

Some lenders have used an automated underwriting system since the 1990s, but today almost all prime lenders use them. Everyone benefits because an automated system speeds up the loan process. Another benefit is that Fannie Mae and Freddie Mac set the guidelines, so there is much less subjective interpretation of the rules.

Typically, an automated underwriting system will provide one of the following recommendations:

- Approve
- Accept
- Refer
- Refer with caution

If the lender receives an "approve" status, it means Fannie Mae or Freddie Mac agrees to buy the loan from the lender. About 95% of the time, the secondary market buys the primary market lenders' mortgage loans.

If the response is "accept," they will want the loan to be *manually* underwritten, which means someone manually reviews the file. This slows down the process, so be prepared to supply ASAP all necessary documents the underwriter requests so you don't delay your closing any more than it already is.

"Refer" or "Refer with Caution" means the agency (Freddie Mac or Fannie Mae) won't buy the loan unless there are extenuating circumstances. A borrower with a "referred" rating will most likely not get a loan or will get one at a higher interest rate. A lender charges a "referred" mortgage loan holder a higher interest rate because the lender will either have to keep it in its own portfolio of loans or sell it to a private company that will charge more to take it off your lender's hands. Either way, it will cost the lender more money if Fannie Mae or Freddie Mac can't buy the loan. And, by the way, Fannie Mae and Freddie Mac together hold about half of our country's outstanding home loans.

If you are denied credit, the lender will send you a letter stating the reason or reasons why. At that point, talk with your loan officer about what to do next. Be sure to let your real estate agent know the status of your loan request.

The system looks for: equity, credit history and liquid reserves. For example, the system likes borrowers who have money in the bank after closing, to make payments if necessary. They also like borrowers who have more invested in the transaction, such as a higher down payment. The upside of these systems is they have some flexibility. The system allows for the underwriter -- who is trying to get the loan approved – to quickly deal with workable issues and to get the loan done. Underwriters simply have to meet the criteria set by the system. *Another upside is that the system is blind to an applicant's race and ethnicity, promoting fair and consistent mortgage lending decisions.* These systems' objectivity assures consumers their applications are fairly evaluated. Seems easy, doesn't it? It is, but that doesn't mean you don't have to provide documentation. You still have to provide what the software program says your file needs.

Factors Used to Determine Risk

The lender uses many factors to assess if the borrower is likely to pay back the loan, i.e., if the borrower is a good risk. These factors include:

Borrower Information

- Length and type of employment
- Income from employment and any other sources
- Expenses and debts, and the ratio of debt to income
- Type and amount of assets
- Age and number of dependents
- Insurance coverage, such as disability and life
- Purpose of the loan, such as purchasing a primary residence or a second home or income property, or to refinance a property

Property Information - The property is used as collateral for the loan. In case the borrower defaults on the loan, the lender wants to ensure the property's value is equal to or greater than the borrower's outstanding obligation, i.e., the amount the borrower wants to borrow.

The lender evaluates a variety of data, usually with the assistance of third-party vendors. Here are a few examples of what's commonly evaluated, and who typically helps the lender do this:

- The property's legal description and location - Title company
- The title information, including the type of ownership interest – Title company
- Any liens, encumbrances, or claims, including mechanic liens, placed on the property – Title company
- Improvements made to the property and its property value – Appraiser
- Information on the transfer history, such as the last purchase price and the purchase date - Title company
- Tax assessments, zoning– Taxing authority
- Restrictions and covenants, and dues – Homeowners' Association
- The assessed and market values, and corresponding trends of similar real estate properties which sold recently - Appraiser
- A net income analysis for several previous years (for investment property) – Appraiser
- The property's ability to be insured – Homeowner Insurance Company
- The boundary lines for the property, exterior improvements, easements and building setback lines – Surveyor

Any problems or negative results stemming from any of these vendors can slow up the process until the issue(s) are resolved.

Credit Analysis - The lender uses the borrower's history of paying other installment debt, and the size and extent of this debt, to determine the borrower's likelihood of repaying the mortgage loan. Factors the lender considers in the credit analysis include:

- credit history
- employment history
- amount of money in savings
- amount of money in checking accounts

- banking history (how well the borrower handled checking and savings accounts, how long of a banking history the borrower has, and if there are any red flags in the borrower's banking history)
- character of the borrower

Closing -When the processor fulfills all the conditions and the materials are stamped "approved" by the underwriter, *then* your loan moves to the "clear to close" department. At that point, your file is checked to verify it contains all the documents necessary to close, e.g., insurance survey and title policy. Your loan documents are prepared – often referred to as "drawn up" – and delivered to the title company or attorney's office for you to sign.

Mistake # 50: *Signing your loan documents without reading them*

The amount of paperwork home buyers sign at *closing* is astounding. Most of the documents are generated by the buyer's lender. Unfortunately, most buyers sign them without reading them. After all, there are a lot of papers and it can take buyers an hour or more to go through them. While we understand the temptation to get in, sign the papers and get out, we certainly don't recommend speeding through your closing appointment.

Mistake # 51: *Review the legal description on all legal documents*

Jose and Patricia purchased a property using cash. A year later, when they approached the idea of building another structure on their property, they were told that they did not own the property in its entirety. On further investigation they found that the deed of trust did not include the legal description for one of the lots. This meant that, although they believed they had bought the entire property (based on what was advertised via the MLS), their sales contract actually reflected something different. When Jose and Patricia contacted the owner of what they thought was their property, the owner was agreeable to transferring the title into the couple's names. This situation could have turned out much worse; instead of an expensive legal battle, Jose and Patricia had only the cost of transferring the title into their names. So something as simple as not noticing the legal descriptions in the sales contract and the deed of trust could cost buyers thousands!

Jose and Patricia made several mistakes: They came unrepresented at closing so they only had themselves to rely on to verify the paperwork. They also failed to double check the legal description against what was being advertised for sale in the MLS, and against the survey and the tax records. If they had, they would have noticed the discrepancy. Because Jose and Patricia had very little experience in purchasing real estate, they didn't understand how important it is to check the legal descriptions.

The legal description shows up on the three most important documents: the **notes payable**, the **deed of trust** and the **Settlement Statement (HUD-1),** along with other supporting disclosures, such as the sales contract and the survey. Pay close attention to any and all documents that state the legal description and require your signature.

Notes Payable

The **notes payable** document is easy to identify. It details the type of loan you have, such as a fixed, interest-only or adjustable rate mortgage. It also details your *interest rate* and *terms*. The notes payable will also tell you if there is a *prepayment penalty* involved which, as you've learned, is important to know about if you have one. None of these items should come as a surprise to you at closing, since these are the terms you agreed on with your loan officer when he or she presented your loan options.

If there is something that's unclear, don't be afraid to ask for an explanation. ***If there is a change, it should certainly not come to*** *your attention at this stage; that would be a sure sign your loan officer or lender is trying to pull a fast one.*

Deed of Trust

A **deed of trust** is the document or security instrument that transfers ownership of the property, and is recorded in the public records. The deed is often characterized by title companies as the "if you don't pay, you don't stay" document. It contains the following signatures:

- The previous owners, which are the sellers
- The new owner, which is you (you may also be referred to as the borrower or trustor in the paperwork)
- The Beneficiary, which is the lender
- The Trustee, which is a third party who represents neither the borrower nor the lender; it's usually the title company or an attorney
    - The Trustee holds the Power of Sale[71] in the event of default
    - The Trustee also delivers the deed of trust when it has been paid in full

In the event of a default, the trustee files a Notice of Default; however, in most instances, the trustee will substitute another trustee to handle the foreclosure under a Substitution of Trustee.

- After the 90-day period in the public records, and a 21-day publication period in the newspaper, the trustee then has the power to sell the property on the courthouse steps without a court procedure.
- During the three months following the recording of the Notice of Default, the borrower can redeem the property by making up the back payments and paying the trustee's fees.

---

[71] The *Power of Sale* is a clause commonly found in the mortgage note and deed of trust. It gives the lender the ability to advertise and sell a property based simply on the borrower defaulting on his or her mortgage, and without the lender having to go through the court system for an order to sell.

- Once the trustee sells the property at a Trustee's sale, it is final.

We used to be surprised by how many people would just sign off on all of these documents without reading them. *Closing is a tedious process with what appears to be thousands of documents to read and sign, but reading them carefully – and asking questions when you don't understand something – will save you headaches and money down the road.* And maybe even sooner than you think. Keep in mind that these documents are, for the most part, written to protect the lender. It's your responsibility to read them and understand not just your rights, but the lender's too.

Pay careful attention to these key areas in the Deed of Trust. Make sure that:

- Your name is spelled correctly
- The name of the lender is listed correctly
- The loan amount is correct and your last date of payment is accurate
- The correct type of loan you are receiving is indicated
- An accurate legal description of the property, including the address and county, is listed in the section known as Transfer of Rights
- The repercussions of non-payment are clearly listed in the section called "Payment of Principal, Interest, Escrow Items, Prepayment Charges and Late Charges"
- You understand the repercussions of failing to adequately sustain property insurance, since they are spelled out clearly and are significantly higher than your own policy

Property Insurance. Borrower shall keep the improvements now existing or hereafter erected on the Property insured against loss by fire, hazards included within the term "extended coverage," and any other hazards including, but not limited to, earthquakes and floods, for which Lender requires insurance.

…

If Borrower fails to maintain any of the coverages described above, Lender may obtain insurance coverage, at Lender's option and Borrower's expense. Lender is under no obligation to purchase any particular type or amount of coverage. Therefore, such coverage shall cover Lender, but might or might not protect Borrower, Borrower's equity in the Property, or the contents of the Property, against any risk, hazard or liability and might provide greater or lesser coverage than was previously in effect. Borrower acknowledges that the cost of the insurance coverage so obtained might significantly exceed the cost of insurance the Borrower could have obtained.

The deed of trust is also clear on how and when you should occupy the property

Occupancy. Borrower shall occupy, establish, and use the Property as Borrower's principal residence within 60 days after the execution of this Security Instrument and shall continue to occupy the Property as Borrower's principal residence for at least one year after the date of occupancy, unless Lender otherwise agrees in writing, which consent shall not be unreasonably withheld, or unless extenuating circumstances exist which are beyond Borrower's control.

Mistake # 52: *Not reviewing the loan application again at closing*

At closing, you need to review your loan application again. This version will be typewritten, and one that your loan officer created based on the information you provided. This is your second and final chance to review and confirm the information in your statement. We've witnessed loan officers inflating the borrowers' income in order to qualify them for the loan, so be sure to read it thoroughly. Don't assume any of it is correct. Any falsification could result in prison – for you!

Borrower's Loan Application. Borrower shall be in default if, during the Loan application process, Borrower or any persons or entities acting at the direction of Borrower or with Borrower's knowledge or consent gave materially false, misleading, or inaccurate information or statements to Lender (or failed to provide Lender with material information) in connection with the Loan Material representations include, but are not limited to, representations concerning Borrower's occupancy of the Property as Borrower's principal residence.

Joint and Several Liability: This paragraph discusses a situation where another party, such as a spouse, is involved in the ownership of the property but is not liable for the mortgage note. The language here states that as long as the spouse does not sign the Notes Payable, he or she is *not* personally obligated to pay this loan. If you are involved in this situation, please consult an attorney – which we are not. If your Settlement Statement's wording differs from what we've shown here, or if you're worried that some of it may apply to you, please confirm all interpretation of legal language with an attorney.

Joint and Several Liability; Co-signers; Successors and Assigns Bound. Borrower covenants and agrees that Borrower's obligations and liability shall be joint and several. However, any Borrower who co-signs this Security Instrument but does not execute the Note (a "co-signer"): (a) is co-signing this Security Instrument only to mortgage, grant and convey the co-signer's interest in the Property under the terms of this Security Instrument (b) is not personally obligated to pay the sums secured by this Security Instrument; and (c) agrees that Lender and any other Borrower can agree to extend, modify, forbear or make any accommodations with regard to the terms of this Security Instrument or the Note without the co-signer's consent.

Change of Loan Servicer: When you signed the Servicing Transfer Disclosure Form with your loan officer, you agreed to allow your lender to sell the mortgage note to another mortgage company. If your loan is sold, you'll be notified and given a new address to send the mortgage payment. This is common. You're simply sending your mortgage payment to a different loan servicing company. It does not change the amount, terms or interest rate of your original mortgage loan. Selling your loan is a means by which a lender makes money in order to loan more money. This process has no reflection on you as a borrower, nor do you have any say in it.

Sale of Note; Change of Loan Servicer; Notice of Grievance. The Note or a partial interest in the Note (together with this Security Instrument) can be sold one or more times without prior notice to Borrower. A sale might result in a change in the entity (known as the "Loan Servicer") that collects Periodic Payments due under the Note and this Security Instrument and performs other mortgage loan servicing obligations under the Note, this Security Instrument, and Applicable Law. There also might be one or more changes of the Loan Servicer unrelated to a sale of the Note. If there is a change of the Loan Servicer, Borrower will be given written notice of the change which will state the name and address of the new Loan Servicer, the address to which payments should be made and any other information RESPA requires in connection with a notice of transfer of servicing. If the Note is sold and thereafter the Loan is serviced by a Loan Servicer other than the Purchaser of the Note, the mortgage loan servicing obligations to Borrower will remain with the Loan Servicer or be transferred to a successor Loan Servicer and are not assumed by the Note purchaser unless otherwise provided by the Note purchaser.

The Settlement Statement is always the first document you receive at closing. It's prepared by the title company and *approved by the buyer's lender*. Because you should have reviewed this document 24 hours in advance of your closing, all your corrections should be noted and *all the fees are finalized*. Know that most real estate agents are truly unable to read a Settlement Statement so unless you know your agent is different than most, don't count on your agent to help you interpret the Settlement Statement. ***Unfortunately, most buyers just look at the bottom line and if the numbers are within reason they will not bother to question any of the other numbers.*** This is why it's so important to get a copy of as many of these documents as possible *beforehand* so you have time to review them for accuracy!

In Summary, remember that the loan process is complex. Many people are involved in it and you, the borrower, are the most important one. It starts with you, and it ends with you. You might be involved in mid-stream, too, because if the information you supplied earlier is not complete or you're not responsive enough to the requests for more information, the process can go downhill. Don't procrastinate when it comes to supplying information someone requests, especially the underwriter.

As you have learned, the underwriter is the only person who can approve your mortgage loan. After you have the "Clear to Close" approval, you'll sign a large number of documents, which you'll have to do if you want your house. You'll feel comfortable signing them because you'll have previewed the documents (including the legal descriptions on all documents) within the previous 24 hours, communicated any inaccuracies, asked your questions, and are now in full agreement with the revised (if necessary) forms in front of you. If you're still unsure, have your real estate agent, mortgage broker or loan officer, or attorney review them for you.

Pass The Knowledge On!

CHAPTER 20

CLOSING PROCEDURES

In this chapter you will learn how the role of the closing agent is pivotal and what you can do – or not do – to work with this agent and increase the efficiency of your closing meeting.

During the closing phase of the financing process, there's a good chance that either the buyer or seller could lose thousands of dollars. Remember, a borrower should pay attention to the three most important closing documents: the deed of trust, the notes payable and the Settlement Statement (HUD-1). Closing practices vary from one location to another, and even within the same city or county. In some areas, closings can be conducted by lending institutions, title insurance companies, escrow companies, real estate brokers, or settlement attorneys for either the buyer or seller.

The main role of a closing agent, regardless of who conducts the closing, is the same. For the purpose of this reference guide, we will refer to the title insurance company as the settlement agent, or escrow officer. No matter which of these three names this agent goes by, he or she acts as a neutral party who will handle the transaction on behalf of all parties involved. This person's role is the most encompassing of all the people who have worked on your real estate purchase.

One of the settlement agent's tasks is to distribute the Settlement Statement to all parties. Unfortunately, it is not uncommon for you to receive the three most important closing documents on the day of closing. If this happens, you risk losing a lot of money, perhaps thousands of dollars. Here's what can – and does – go wrong:

- *Carelessness* on the part of the mortgage broker, loan officer, lender, title company representative, seller, private mortgage company or escrow company – basically, anyone involved in the financing – might have caused inaccurate information. The expensive part happens when the bad info concerns fees and, since there are a lot of them, there's a good chance someone will transpose a number or overlook a change that was written in an amendment. Even one mistake can cause nearly every paper you'll review and sign to be inaccurate.
- *Title company rushing through the closing process.* We have seen settlement officers look at their watches, prodding buyers to hurry through the process, because they have signers for another transaction sitting in the waiting room and the settlement agent is running behind schedule. Imagine the pressure that puts on the borrower! And what happens if the borrower has any questions, perhaps about a fee? The question might need to be researched, and it could require the title company to get lender approval again.
- Don't let yourself get in this situation. Be sure to use the 24 hours you're entitled to, and request your Settlement Statement and as many other of your papers as you can. Look them over, and make sure the correct names and addresses and other details appear correctly. Also, make certain you understand where the numbers on the Settlement Statement are coming from. Use your GFE, executed sales contract, disclosures[72] and any amendments to the contract.

---

[72] *Disclosures* are any documents that are part of the sales contract that inform you about the property, such as the seller's disclosure, information about a HOA, if the property is in a MUD district, etc.

Role of the Title Company

Some states use an attorney instead of a title company for the pivotal role of closing agent, but either way, it's important to choose a good one. Because they represent all parties, they must make sure all parties' instructions are carried out and are in compliance with state and federal laws.

The buyer has the right to request the title company of his or her choice. Check out RESPA's Provision Sec. 2608, which states:

(a) *No seller of property that will be purchased with the assistance of a federally related mortgage loan shall require directly or indirectly, as a condition to selling the property, that title insurance covering the property be purchased by the buyer from any particular title company.*

(b) *Any seller who violates the provisions of subsection (a) of this section shall be liable to the buyer in an amount equal to three times all charges made for such title insurance.*

Your real estate agent will usually suggest a title company if you don't have a preference. There is usually no financial benefit to the real estate agent other than choosing one who does a great job and doesn't slow down the process.

But let's back up a bit and review the title company's entire responsibility. Earlier in the home-buying process, when the buyer and seller agreed on a price and terms and then signed ("executed") the contract; it was delivered to the title company, along with the earnest money. The title company assigns it a transaction number, known as GF #. The title company deposits the earnest money in an escrow account[73] for safekeeping, and they notify the seller that the buyer has deposited the funds as stated in the contract. The title company then

---

[73] This *escrow account* is just an account that sets aside funds until the buyer and seller agree to how it's to be used at closing or in the event the buyer or seller defaults. It differs than that of the reserve account that holds your prepaids, which is also referred to as an escrow account.

acts in a fiduciary[74] capacity until the final Settlement Statement is compiled and distributed.

After the GF # is assigned and the earnest money is in an escrow account, the title company will "open title," which means it will examine and research the history of the ownership of the property. The county clerk's office stores this information. It will show the following:

- If the sellers are the legal owners
- If there's an open mortgage, any judgments, or any other type of lien that will affect the sale
- If there are any existing restrictions, easements, public utilities, etc., which may limit an owner's rights to the use of the property, or grant any rights to others who are not property owners
- If property taxes and other public or private assessments are current and paid in full

In addition to the documents found at the county clerk's office, the title company may ask for other documents. The title company's goal is to decrease the risk of unforeseen claims to the property before they place title insurance on it. Here are a few examples of other documents they may request:

- A copy of a divorce decree showing which party(ies) holds ownership in the property
- A copy of a death certificate to prove a spouse has passed and is no longer entitled to ownership

When both the lender and the title company have gathered and *approved* all their supporting documents, the closing date and time can be set. By this time the lender has submitted the documents to the "Clear to Close" department and the title company's attorney has reviewed all their documents.

---

[74] *Fiduciary* means to act, by law, on someone's behalf in a trustworthy manner. In this case, in a way that protects both the buyer and seller's interests.

Once these tasks have been completed, "Clear Title" can be conveyed. This means there are no clouds[75] hovering over the title which would stop the transfer of ownership. The title company then issues a title policy, known as a "Commitment of Title Insurance," or the *owner's title policy*. This document lists any exceptions or other issues that need to be satisfied prior to the issuing the title policy. In other words, it details everything that both the buyer and the seller have to do in order to complete the title transfer, for example, pay the asking price of the seller or pay off an existing mortgage. This means the commitment is a *temporary policy,* or a *binder of the actual title policy* to come. You and your real estate agent will receive a copy of this commitment. Since time is of the essence, you should review it for anything that may affect the title. You can expect the permanent title policy to be delivered *at or after closing.*

The property's sale cannot take place if the title is not cleared. If, by chance, you're purchasing the property outright (without a mortgage loan), you should still close with a title company so they can ensure clear title. If you buy property and somehow skip over using a title company, it could mean you also take over *any and all* judgments tied to the property.

The title company will maintain close contact with the mortgage lender, real estate agents and any attorneys to obtain whatever documentation is still necessary for closing the transaction. Here are the steps the title company takes once the lender's "Clear to Close" department sends the closing instructions and legal documents to the title company's escrow officer.

1. All parties will assemble at a prearranged time for the closing.
2. The escrow officer is responsible for creating and submitting the final Settlement Statement (HUD-1).
3. At that point, the officer notifies the buyers and their real estate agent about the amount of money, in certified funds, they need to bring to the closing.

---

[75] A *clouded* title means there is at least one issue that prevents transfer of ownership.

4. The seller and their real estate will also know his or her financial position.
5. The escrow officer will compile and present the closing documents and fees.
6. All parties review and execute the papers.
7. The escrow officer will collect all monies from all parties.
8. The escrow officer will deliver the executed documents to the lender and in return receive a wire transfer of funds borrowed by the buyer.

The title company assumes responsibility for:

- Collecting all funds necessary for the transfer.
- Distributing monies in a prompt and accurate manner.
- Ensuring that the legal documents have been filed for record.
- Verifying that the mortgage lender's requirements have been fulfilled.
- Making certain all of the necessary paperwork has been returned to the lender.
- Paying all outstanding liens, such as any previous mortgages, that may have existed on the property.
- Ensuring that the title policies are mailed to the buyer.

In Summary, the role of the settlement agent, also referred to as an escrow agent, is to act as a neutral party for everyone involved in the transaction, and to present all the facts to the parties at closing – and earlier, if problems crop up. From the buyer's perspective, the title company determines if the property is clear of all claims. From the seller's position, the title company verifies the buyer has all the funds ready to pay the amount shown in the executed contract. From the perspective of the lender, the title company determines if the buyer is willing to sign off on the terms of the loan. All of this is specified in two documents: the Notes Payable, detailing the interest rate and terms, and the HUD-1 (Settlement Statement), detailing how the monies will be divided among all parties. You must be prepared to ask questions, especially because you have only 24 hours to review this and other documents before closing. Chances are, there is a mistake in there somewhere, and you can easily identify it if you compare the closing documents to your Good Faith Estimate (GFE), sales contract, disclosures and amendments.

Pass The Knowledge On!

CHAPTER 21

ERROR-FREE SETTLEMENT STATEMENT? NOT LIKELY!

In this chapter you will learn how to read and understand a Settlement Statement, also known as a HUD-1. Almost 90% of the time, you'll find at least one error in the Settlement Statement. Sometimes these errors can total thousands of dollars! It is very important that you understand how to read your Settlement Statement, or at least be sure to ask questions, since *you* are ultimately the one paying the fees. Many real estate agents do not know how to read a Settlement Statement, yet they may be the only representation you have at closing. Remember, most loan officers don't show up for closing. The responsibility is really yours – to understand and/or to ask questions.

Hopefully, you're receiving your Settlement Statement in advance of the closing appointment. Under law, you're entitled to receive and review it 24 hours in advance. Be sure you do this! It's much easier to read through it, referring to your Good Faith Estimate, this reference guide and other reference materials we provide for you, if you're doing it in the comfort of your own home or office and at your own speed. You'll also have time to make phone calls to verify information or fees that concern you. No matter what, be sure to bring your file of other papers regarding this real estate transaction to your closing appointment.

Both the buyer and the seller need to review their own columns and make sure that the monies are accounted for correctly. See *a sample copy of a Settlement Statement* on our website under **"Real Estate Forms."** Enter 550 in the book code field for an example of this three-page document. Be sure to print these pages on 8½" x 14" paper.

Settlement Statements have three pages of information:

1.   The first page *summarizes:*

    a.   Summarizes all the fees posted on pages two and three
    b.   Lists the legal description of the property
    c.   Lists all parties involved in the transaction
    d.   States the settlement and funding dates
    e.   Shows the loan amount that is being borrowed
    f.   Shows taxes paid for the current year by the seller and given to you, the borrower
    g.   Shows the borrower's deposits:

        i.   Earnest money
        ii.   Option money

    h.   Reflects the seller's contribution towards the buyer's closing costs, *if* it's not reflected on the second page
    i.   Posts how much money the buyer will need to bring to the closing in the form of a certified check

2.   The *second page is critical because it details all the fees*, which are broken down into seven categories:

    a.   Total Sales/Brokers' Commissions – usually paid by the seller
    b.   Items Payable in Connection with the Loan
    c.   Items Required by the Lender to be Paid in Advance – the buyer's Prepaids
    d.   Reserves Deposited with the Lender

e. Title Charges – fees charged by the title company
f. Government Recording Fees
g. Additional Settlement Charges

3. The third page usually has space for the signatures, along with the breakdown of fees that were summarized on page two.

You will need to refer to the sample copy of a *Settlement Statement* located on our website in order to understand the detailed descriptions that follow. The Settlement Statement is a standard document from HUD. Therefore, no matter what state your transaction is in, you will use this exact form.

Detail Page of the Settlement Statement (Page Two)

When the escrow officer goes over the Settlement Statement with you, he or she will usually start on page two because it is the breakdown of what is summarized on page one.

On page two there are two columns of fees. The first column is the borrower's side and it is identified as *"Paid from Borrower's Funds at Settlement."* The seller's side is the second column and it's identified as *"Paid from Seller's Funds at Settlement."* Everything listed in these two columns is what the buyer and seller are responsible for paying. *Please note that the numbers listed in all the rows on your Settlement Statement may not coincide with the numbers listed in our example. The title company will customize the second page as needed.*

So let's begin on page two at line item:

700. Total Sales/Broker's Commission:

This is the total dollar amount of the real estate broker's sales commission, which is usually paid by the seller. This commission is typically a percentage of the selling price of the home and any added bonuses. It usually represents the total commission for the real estate agent(s), if applicable. If there are two agents involved they will usually split the commission.

701. Lists the real estate agent's commission to the listing agent.

702. Lists the real estate agent's commission to the buying agent.

703. Total commission paid at settlement. This fee is usually paid by the seller, so it will be reflected in column two.

800. Items Payable in Connection with Loan:
These are the fees that the Brokers/Bankers/Lenders charge to process and approve the mortgage loan.

801. Loan Origination. This fee is usually expressed as a percentage of the loan, and sometimes referred to as a "point" or "points." Each point equals one percent of the loan amount. This fee will vary among lenders. For example, if a lender charges two points on an $180,000 loan, this amounts to a charge of $3,600. This fee is usually paid by the buyer unless otherwise negotiated.

802. Loan Discount. Also referred to as "discount points," this is a charge by the lender or broker to lower the interest rate. You will hear people refer to this as "buying down" the interest rate. For example, it may cost you a point to reduce the interest rate from 7% to 6.75%. Remember, a point is usually 1% of the sales price. You should be aware of this additional charge. If you don't remember asking to "buy down" your interest rate, ask your loan officer about this.

803. Appraisal Fee. This charge pays the appraiser for the appraisal report your lender ordered. The amount sometimes appears in the description column with POC, "paid outside of closing." This means that, prior to closing, you paid for the appraisal with your own funds. Therefore, these types of fees will not be added into the column but instead are identified on the Settlement Statement to the left of the borrower's column as a POC.

804. Credit Report Fee. This fee covers the cost of a credit report. It is usually paid by the buyer unless otherwise negotiated.

805 – 813: Various fees based on where you live. *These are often the junk or extra fees charged.* Be sure you're clear on these. More importantly, ask why they are necessary. If the escrow officer hesitates it may be a sign of a junk fee. Ask for it to be removed prior to closing.

814. Mortgage Broker Fee. Fees paid to the mortgage brokers or the actual lender may be listed here. Check your GFE, because this is an area where extra, unnecessary fees are added after you receive your GFE. Make sure you bring your GFE with you to the closing appointment!

You may also see POCL, which means "Paid Outside of Closing to Lender." Another example of this term is the YSP, also known as the yield spread paid. This is the fee paid to the mortgage broker by the lender as compensation for bringing the loan package to that lender. This amount is not charged to you, as the borrower, but it must be disclosed.

900. Items Required by Lender to be Paid in Advance:

You may be required to pay in advance certain items, such as accrued interest, mortgage insurance premiums and hazard insurance premiums. These *Prepaids* are often placed into an escrow or reserve account. In other words, the lender requires that you place funds into this account so when the taxes and insurance premiums come due, there is enough money to pay them.

901. Interest. Lenders usually require borrowers to pay the interest that accrues from the date of settlement to the first monthly payment. So, for example, if you close on the May 16, you would then pay for 15 days of interest because there are 31 days in the month.

902. Mortgage Insurance Premium The lender may require you to pay a number of months up to a year of mortgage insurance premiums in advance.

903. Hazard Insurance Premium. Hazard insurance protects you and the lender against loss due to fire, windstorm, and natural hazards. Lenders often require the borrower to pay for one year of insurance in advance. In addition, they require the borrower to pay the first few months for the reserve account. Because of this, you may see hazard insurance posted in line 903 and then again on line 1001.

904. Flood Insurance. Many lenders also require flood insurance.

905. Inspection Fee. This charge covers field inspections, which are often made on newly constructed housing. Employees of your lender or an outside inspector often do field inspections. This fee is usually charged if the lender deems it necessary to visit the property.

1000–1008. Escrow Account Deposits:

These lines identify the prepayment of taxes, insurance and other items that must be paid at settlement. The lender dictates how many months of advance payments he or she wants in this account. However, it is never more than HUD requires. In situations when the individual item deposits are overstated, the *aggregate adjustment*[76] makes the correction in the amount on line 1008. This number will either be zero or a negative amount.

1100. Title Charges:

Title charges cover a variety of services performed by the title company and others doing similar work.

> **1101. Settlement Fee or Closing Fee.** This fee is paid to the title company for administering the closing documents. The seller and buyer usually negotiate who will pay this fee. It's often split 50/50.
>
> **1102-1104. Abstract of Title Search, Title Examination and Title Insurance Binder.** The charges on these lines cover the costs of the title search and examination done by the title company. The title examiner researches the history of the title to make sure it is free of liens and judgments.

---

[76] The *aggregate adjustment* is the amount the lender must credit the borrower at closing, so that the lender doesn't collect more than the initial payment amount, which should be two months, according to RESPA.

1105. Document Preparation. This is a separate fee that the title company charges to cover their costs of preparation of the settlement statement and other documents that come from the lender.

1106. Notary Fee. This fee is charged for the cost of having the escrow agent, who is also licensed as a Notary Public, swear to the fact that the persons named in the documents did, in fact, sign them.

1107. Attorney's Fees. You may be required to pay for legal services provided by the title company for the creation and examination of the title binder.

1108. Title Insurance. The *total cost* of the owner's and lender's title insurance is shown here.

1109. Lender's Title Insurance. This cost is for the lender's policy that protects the *lender's interest.*

1110. Owner's Title Insurance. The owner's title insurance is the title policy that protects the *buyer's interest.* This charge is usually found in the seller's column.

1200. Government Recording and Transfer Charges:

These fees may be paid by you or by the seller, depending on your sales contract. The buyer usually pays the fees for legally recording the new deed and mortgage (line 1201):

- Transfer taxes, which, in some locations, are collected whenever property changes hands. They're set by state and/or local governments.
- You may need to purchase city, county and/or state tax stamps (lines 1202 and 1203).

1300. Additional Settlement Charges:

These are usually self-explanatory.

1301. Survey. The lender may require a professional surveyor to provide a survey of the property so the fee for this service is posted here. It is usually paid by the buyer, but may sometimes be reflected in the seller's column, depending on how it was negotiated.

1302–1305. Pests and Other Inspections. These fees are required by the lender to cover inspections for termites or other pest infestation of the home you're buying. Flood and lead-based paint inspections may also fall under this column.

1400. Total Settlement Charges:

The total of all fees in the borrower's and seller's columns are added to show how much money, as pertaining to closing costs, each party is responsible for paying.

These figures are then transferred to the Summary Page, which is the first page. They're reflected in line 103 in the left column, which is known as the "Summary of Borrower's Transaction."

Summary Page of the Settlement Statement (Page One)

100. Gross Amount Due From Borrower:

Page one is a summary of the fees which are detailed on page two. On page one, the fees are added to the sales price, including any of the seller's personal property you agreed to purchase.

101. Contract Sales Price. This is the sales price you and the seller agreed to.

102. Personal Property. This is the charge for items you may have agreed to purchase, such as a lawn mower, refrigerator or furnishings.

103. Settlement Charges to Borrower (line 1400). This figure matches line 1400 on the second page. It is your total closing costs, which are now added to the contract sales price.

106 – 108. Adjustments for Items Paid by the Seller in Advance. This section will usually be filled out when the seller has paid invoices such as the HOA fee or property taxes *in advance*. The borrower would then have to provide an adjustment or a credit to the seller, starting from the day the borrower takes ownership.

*120. **Gross Amount Due from the Borrower.** This is the actual cost of your property. It includes the sales price of the property, all of your closing costs, any personal property you're purchasing in the home, and the taxes due through the end of the year.*

200. Amounts Paid by or on Behalf of Borrower:

This is where *all* the monies you have paid toward the purchase of the home and where the seller's contribution is reflected:

> **201. Earnest Money.** This is the money you put down to show good faith when you wrote your offer and it was executed. The money was deposited with the title company or attorney.
>
> **202. Principal Amount of New Loan(s).** This is the amount the lender is loaning to you. If you are just getting one loan, that amount will be reflected in this line item. If there is a second new loan it will reflect on its own line.
>
> **203. Existing loan(s) Taken Subject To.** This is where an assumable loan or existing loan amount is reflected.
>
> **204 – 209.** Within this section you may find these items listed:
>
> > **Principal Amount of the Second Loan.** If you have taken out a second loan, this is where it will show up. The title company types this item, and it can show up anywhere from 204 to 209.
> >
> > **Option Fee.** If you paid an option fee, and the seller agreed that you would be credited this money upon closing, it should be reflected here.

Mistake # 53: *Not asking for the seller contributions to be broken out*

207. Seller Contributions.
This is the amount the seller agreed to contribute toward your closing costs. Be very careful with the seller contribution amount, since this credit can also show up in line item 103. This is done by charging *the seller* on page two for the closing costs fees of the borrower. If this is the case, the borrower's fees are added to the seller's side, which is the second column. *This can be tricky so ask the title company to show you a breakdown of how the fees are shown on the seller's column.* Again this is an area where many errors occur. They usually favor the seller, not the buyer. Remember, there may be language in your contract that states the seller will contribute toward your closings costs *up to* an agreed amount. "Up to" means you could be shorted. So make sure you are within the 3% (prime) or 6% (sub-prime) maximum lender requirements and you'll get every penny due to you.

210–219. Adjustments for Items Unpaid by Seller. These items include taxes which are owed – but not paid – by the seller because they are not due until year end. However, these fees are collected for the period of time the seller owned the home. The funds are then credited to the borrower at closing. They will be applied toward:

i.   The borrower's *closing costs,* if you have decided not to escrow. It will then be your responsibility to pay the taxes for the *entire year* since you were *given* the money *from the sellers* for their portion of the time that they occupied the property.

ii. The borrower's *reserve account,* if you have decided to escrow, for the purpose of making monthly payments so the money is available to pay the real estate taxes and homeowner's insurance premium at the end of the year.

220. Total Paid By/For Borrower. *This is the total dollar amount of all items from 201 to 219.*

300. Cash at Settlement from/to Borrower:

This is the section where the subtotals from line items 220 and 120 are subtracted, one from the other, as applicable.

> 301. This is the same number as in line item 120.
> 302. This is the same number as in line item 220.
> 303. Here is where the borrower will:
>
> > i. Bring funds to closing, or
> > ii. Receive funds from closing

Subtract line item 302 from 301. *If the difference between these two line items is negative, this is the amount the borrower brings in certified funds to the closing. If the difference is a positive figure, this is the amount the borrower will get back at closing.* Note: Many lenders will not allow borrowers to receive more than they have contributed. This might include the following paid items outside of closing:

- Earnest money
- Appraisal
- Credit report
- Option fee
- Contributions made directly to the builder for upgrades

So, for example, if the amounts listed above total $3,000, the borrower would not be able to receive more than this amount back at closing. Keep in mind that you, as the borrower, can never get back more than you have actually put into the deal.

Mistake # 54: *Using tax credits toward closing costs and not preparing for year-end taxes*

However, you can be credited the taxes that will be due at the end of the year if you choose not to escrow. This credit will apply toward your closing costs. If the difference exceeds your total closing costs you can receive a check at closing for this.

Have you ever listened to late night TV, where real estate buyers brag about how they received money back at closing? This is how it's done. For example, if you close in the month of June, you will receive from the seller the tax money from January to the day you close in June. That is six months of taxes paid to the buyer. The buyer will then have to use that money to apply toward the balance due for the entire tax year, January-December. The danger comes when the buyers can't pay the tax bill at the end of the year because they used the money toward their closing costs or they simply did not save it for the upcoming tax invoice. This is how people get money back at closing and end up losing their homes the next year!

Keys to Reducing Mistakes in Your Settlement Statement

Your Settlement Statement (HUD-1) comes to you 24 hours before your appointment to close from your loan officer or real estate agent. As previously stated, this document is produced by the title company who provides copies to the lender and to the real estate agent for their comments and/or changes. Normally, HUD-1 statements and your chosen GFE match reasonably well. Problems arise, however, when a HUD-1 is much higher than the buyer anticipated based on the fees shown on the GFE. Because it's not uncommon for the loan officer to *not* be present at closing, it's up to you, your real estate agent and the escrow officer to review the HUD-1.

Most real estate agents are not experts at understanding the numbers on Settlement Statements, and most loan officers don't want them to be! Many loan officers believe real estate agents cause more confusion, and that they interfere with loan officers earning the most they can on loans. This is another reason why it's important for borrowers to understand exactly what they are paying.

The key to reducing mistakes on your Settlement Statement is being organized and prepared. In order to understand why there's a difference between the Good Faith Estimate and your Settlement Statement, you **must** have the following documents:

- Good Faith Estimate
- All amendments to the contract
- Lock-in agreement
- Executed sales contract
- All paid receipts
- Copies of all checks written during the transaction
- Any and *all* documents signed during the transaction

You may not have the luxury of reviewing your HUD-1 very many hours in advance, so you will need to bring your files with you to closing. It's amazing how many buyers come to closing without their documents and then expect their real estate agent or someone else to help them find potential errors. It is even more disappointing to find agents who come to closing without their files.

Some of the errors you may find in your final Settlement Statement could be:

- A transposed[77] number
- An unjustified fee you were never told about
- An incorrect *proration,*[78] *based on an incorrect date, which automatically impacts all of the following:*

---

[77] An example of *transposed* is 56 instead of 65.

[78] A *proration* is the allocation of the property taxes, loan interest and insurance premiums, between the buyer and seller, proportionate to the time of use. For example, if the buyer signs on January 28, the seller is responsible for paying the prorated expenses from the first through the twentieth-eighth of the month while the buyer is responsible for the twenty-ninth through the end of the month – or year, as the case may be.

- Taxes
- Interest due
- Homeowner association fee (if applicable)

- A failure to receive credit for something that was paid in advance, including:

  - Earnest money
  - Option money
  - Upgrades
  - Appraisal
  - Survey
  - A charge the seller should be paying instead of you

- Inaccurate seller contribution amount
- Repair allowance negotiated with the seller
- Incorrectly charging the buyer for something the seller should be paying

Mistake # 55: *Not being prepared to compare the HUD-1 with the GFE*

Even though we've told you a variety of mistakes to watch for, *the most common mistake of all on a HUD-1 is still the one we mention several times in this reference guide: when the broker and lender fees differ greatly from what was originally stated on the GFE.* This is why it's so important that, as a borrower who does not buy property often, you take advantage of the 24-hour period to make corrections.

If you take this review opportunity lightly, it's likely you won't see your Settlement Statement until you walk in the door to sign it. As we've said, the chances are great you *will* find an error on the Settlement Statement! And the correction may not be easy to make, depending on how large or complex it is. You may feel very uncomfortable holding up the deal for what feels like a small problem with the loan documents because to do so might jeopardize the entire transaction, or at least delay the closing by hours or days. Sometimes corrections require the lender to redo some or all of the documents, which can be hundreds of pages. It's easy to see why your closing officer's first inclination may be to try to persuade you to leave matters alone.

It's also very possible the title company will make a mistake, especially if you're closing near the end of the month when everyone else is trying to do the same. Lenders are usually pressed to get complete files and move the buyers onto the next step of the process. This pressure is *very common* and mistakes happen more frequently. Inaccurate information entered in the computer creates inaccurate information on your HUD-1. A similar experience happened to one of our clients:

> *Frances chose to handle her home financing on her own, and she didn't have us help review her Good Faith Estimate. On the day of closing she noticed an error on the Settlement Statement pertaining to the property's title. When she tried to speak with someone at the mortgage office (which was affiliated with the title company) who could address the error, she was given the excuse that the company was in the midst of moving offices and it was difficult to reach them.*
>
> *At that point, our client could either choose to close with the $600 error in place, or wait till Monday and insist it be dealt with then. Since it was a Friday afternoon, Frances signed the paperwork. She wanted the keys because the moving company was scheduled to move her out of her apartment later that day.*

Frances compromised her own leverage by:

- Approaching the mortgage financing process with a lack of knowledge
- Not receiving the Settlement Statement 24 hours in advance so she could review it
- Scheduling movers for the day of closing

The power of choice is your best weapon. You *can* choose to wait until an inaccurate HUD-1 is fixed and, in most cases, you should. Don't think you can't walk away, because you can. Don't make the mistake of thinking the lender has all the power here. Believe me, they don't want to lose the deal, especially at this late stage.

Remember our client who shopped for his loan on the internet, and then couldn't find the loan officer via telephone during closing to resolve an issue? If he had requested and made use of his 24-hour window to review the HUD-1 Settlement Statement, he would have saved a lot of money. Be sure to request and review *your* Settlement Statement 24 hours before closing. You are entitled to this by law.

Your agent should stipulate in your contract that you will require 24 hours to review your Settlement Statement. ***This puts everyone on notice and lets it be known that presenting you with the Settlement Statement on the day of closing is unacceptable.*** You always want to be in the best possible position when you go to close, and you don't want to leave money on the table that belongs to you.

When you sign on the dotted line, the funds are distributed to all parties involved in the transaction. You have now taken possession of this property. Once you have your keys, there is very little chance of questioning or rectifying fees or charges. Congratulations!!! You are now a proud owner.

In Summary, ask questions if the numbers don't make sense to you. The key to ensuring you understand the numbers and that you're not getting ripped off is time and organization. Use your time wisely, especially the 24-hour window you have before your closing appointment to review your Settlement Statement. Let it be known that, until the numbers make sense and are correct, you will not sign. It is much easier to address any issue on your Settlement Statement when you show that you were organized with copies of checks and *all* documents. Also pay close attention to the *date of settlement.* This is the date used to calculate and prorate your Prepaid expenses. It is imperative that the taxes are handled correctly and that you understand your responsibility when the invoice becomes due.

Pass The Knowledge On!

CHAPTER 22

THINGS TO DO AFTER CLOSING

In this chapter we will discuss a few tasks you should consider noting on your calendar to complete within the first 30 to 90 days of ownership.

Of course the most obvious is to change all the locks and alarm codes in the home. You'll want to do this before you move in, if at all possible. Ask your real estate agent if you need advice on how to arrange this.

The second is to get settled in with what you already own. Most homeowners are so excited that they go overboard shopping for new furnishings and accessories for the home. We aren't saying don't enjoy the process of decorating and making it your own but you should be realistic about your finances. You've just made one of the largest investments in your life and everything does not have to be done immediately. Stick with the plans you wrote on your *Budget Spreadsheet* and stay the course.

Remember, if your goal is to live in the home for a relatively short while, watch that you don't over-improve the home. Sometimes sellers want to recoup the money they invested in improvements in their houses, which often means the house is overpriced for the neighborhood. It's much more difficult to sell at the price these homeowners believe it should sell for. This is why having that relationship with your real estate agent is so important. *Every six months send your agent an email asking them to provide you with the latest sales in your neighborhood. This way you stay current and you can see how the neighborhood is appreciating.* Perhaps adding that pool to the backyard will increase the value of your property; then again, maybe not. Remember, your home is your safe haven, but it's still an investment. It's prudent to not lose sight of this. So when it's time to sell, make sure you've profited!

Here are some other tasks to consider:

Appraisal District

- Be sure to request the correct name and/or address change on your property tax account. New owners often forget this step. The title company will always say that it's the real estate agent's job to remind you, and the real estate agent will always say it's the title company's responsibility. The bottom line is *annual property taxes are due no later than December 31,* and it's your responsibility to make sure they are paid on time. If you forget, the taxing authorities will have no compassion. You will be required to pay the late fees and penalties associated with *not knowing* you had to change your name on the property tax records.

- Apply for your Homestead Exemption after living in your home past January 1 of any given year. Many states provide a discount on your taxes if the property is your primary residence, also known as your homestead. You can acquire this form by going to your county's appraisal district website or by contacting the title company.

Lender

- Be sure to check the mail for any changes in your mortgage bill. The chance your loan will be sold to another lender is greatest within the first six months. It might be referred to as *loan servicing* in any new paperwork. You agreed to this possibility when you signed the Servicing Transfer Disclosure. So be on the lookout; you don't want any payments to be late.

- If your loan is sold, be sure to contact the old lender to confirm the change. There are companies who prey on new borrowers' ignorance. You would NOT want to send a mortgage payment to the wrong company – or a scamming company.

- Consider making one extra mortgage payment a year. On a 30-year note, doing this will reduce the number of payments down to 23 or 24 years' worth. Contact your lender about making payments every two weeks, if this is how you are paid by your employer. This exercise will easily create an extra payment each year. The key here is to make sure that the extra payment is applied to the *principal* portion of the loan amount. Be sure to note this when you send your extra mortgage payment in by stating, "Please apply toward principal."

Title Company

- You should receive a copy of the title policy within six weeks. Contact your title company if you don't.

Homeowners' Association

- Within the first 30 days, verify with the homeowners' association management company that they have your correct information, especially if you purchased an investment property in the community. Pick up any necessary pool tags, community access keys, gate openers, and access codes to websites.

Home Warranty

- You should receive a copy of your home warranty package in the mail. At closing, you should have received a receipt showing it was ordered and paid for.

Taxes

- If you decided to pay your own property taxes, be sure to watch for the tax bill(s).
  - You may have more than one invoice and they may show up at different times. These envelopes may come from the school district, MUD district, city, county, etc.

- Be prepared to pay your property taxes as they're due. In some areas, homeowners pay them once a year, with a due date of December 31. Understand that if, for some reason, you pay them after December 31, you will not be able to deduct the property taxes for the year paid until the next year. Talk with your accountant about this rule. Other geographic areas send out tax bills twice a year. In Washington State, for example, several counties bill semi-annually, with property taxes due April 30 and October 31. Know which taxing authority bills you for property taxes, how regularly and when they're due.

- You should also have received the seller's portion of property taxes at closing. If you see that the seller has not contributed enough for their portion while they lived in the home, contact them immediately. Chances are if you closed prior to the tax bill being issued, *the seller may owe you some tax dollars for the period while they owned the home.* This can also work in reverse. The seller may have paid you too much and you owe them a refund at the end of the year. Hopefully this amount is not worth addressing, but you never know. You have signed a document at the title company that states that both the seller and buyer will cooperate with each other in this matter. You can also contact the title company and ask if there is a significant enough difference to warrant contacting the seller.

- It is always wise to set up a separate savings account to hold the money you'll later use to pay your property taxes.

Legal

- Contact your attorney with the news that you have purchased an asset which needs to be added to your will.

- Consider purchasing additional life insurance or mortgage protection insurance to cover the cost of the mortgage note in the event of death.

Something that all homeowners look forward to is the day when their debt to the lender is paid. This paragraph tells you what is supposed to occur. It's found in your Deed of Trust in a section called "Release."

Release. Upon payment of all sums secured by this Security Instrument, Lender shall request that Trustee release this Security Instrument and shall produce for Trustee, duly canceled, all notes evidencing debts secured by this Security Instrument, Trustee shall release this Security Instrument without further inquiry or liability, Borrower shall pay any recordation costs and the statutory Trustee's fees.

In Summary, take your time and enjoy the journey of home ownership. Follow the plan you set up in the beginning when you were budgeting, and don't over-improve your property while you live in it. Immediately after closing, pay attention to your mail, particularly the tax bills since they come with hefty penalties if you're late. More importantly, never lose sight that your home will always be your home, but it's your largest investment too. So take care of it and keep up with what's going on in your neighborhood by checking on home sales twice a year.

Pass The Knowledge On!

CHAPTER 23

WHY YOU NEED A WILL OR LIVING TRUST

It's inevitable that one day we'll all die. Yet, more than 60% of Americans will not bother to draft wills, which often leaves a legacy of financial hardship and family feuding for their loved ones. When real estate is involved, the situation can be even worse.

Keep in mind, if you die without a will, which is referred to as *intestate*, the state in which you lived would determine who receives your assets (those left solely in the decedent's[79] name). *In other words, the state court system – not you or your family – will determine who gets what!* Thus, complete strangers will make decisions having a huge impact on your family members' lives.

In this chapter we encourage you to talk with an attorney about the benefits of a will and/or a living trust *now that you own real estate*.

Mistake # 56: *Not drafting a will*

The purpose of a will is to provide you with a way to distribute your property at the time of your death in any manner you choose. This

---

[79] *Decedent* is the person who passed away.

document is filed as a *public record* after death for anyone who is interested in seeing it. It's one of the most important steps in protecting your loved ones and ensuring your wishes are followed after your death.

There are specific rules, however, about how the real estate you own can be willed. It depends on the form of ownership you listed when you purchased the real estate. If you are a homeowner, the title of your property *does not* automatically go to your family, unless you are a surviving *spouse*. This type of ownership is defined as *joint tenancy.* Or, if you own this property with another person as *joint tenants with right of survivorship,* the property will pass directly to the remaining person or entity upon your death, avoiding the probate process, which we describe below. With joint tenants with right of survivorship, it doesn't matter if the other owner is your spouse – whoever it is will receive ownership of the property.

If you die intestate, your assets will need to go through *probate.* Having a will or living trust means your family can likely avoid the time, expense and hassle of going through probate. But as we said earlier, 60% of Americans don't have wills. Let's look more closely at what happens in this situation.

Real property valued over $20,000 is subject to probate. The probate process is a court procedure during which the state court:

1. Inventories the deceased person's assets
2. Gathers information about claims made against the estate from creditors
3. Investigates all claims for their validity
4. Pays off any outstanding debts, including taxes
5. Decides, based on state law, who gets what

If there was a will, the **executor** is the appointed individual who carries out the instructions and wishes of the deceased. If there was *no* will, then the court appoints an **administrator**. The executor and administrator functions are the same and can be almost anyone, but are usually a lawyer, accountant or family member who is of legal age and has no prior felony convictions. The probate process can take months or years, and become extremely expensive depending on how complex and large the estate was. For example, a home valued at $300,000 could easily incur over $25,000 in fees before the deceased person's heirs inherit the net proceeds from the sale of the property. Not to mention the family squabbling between family members.

There are *other assets* that can avoid the probate process. These assets are most life insurance policies, annuities, and retirement accounts that name *beneficiaries* in the event of death, known as *payable on death accounts, or POD.* At your death, your beneficiary simply needs to go to the bank, show your death certificate and his or her identification, and collect whatever funds are in the account. The probate court is never involved, and it doesn't matter how large the sum is. If any of these accounts were jointly owned, however, the beneficiary would not be able to take possession until the other spouse died.

Problems can occur when there is no will and no surviving spouse and it was *the intent* of the deceased to leave the property to children, other family members, a friend or charity.

There is, however, a tool to use to avoid probate, called a "living trust." The living trust can take many forms. The most common are *revocable* and *irrevocable trust.*

A revocable living trust is a document stating who controls your assets while you're still alive; normally, that's you. You decide what you want to happen to those assets once you're gone. The reason it's revocable is because you can revoke it at any time while you are living. You create and fund it while you are alive. The biggest mistake people make is that they don't take the time to fill out the necessary paperwork to fund the trust.

The objective of a revocable living trust is to allow assets to transfer without going through probate. Your estate proceedings remain private, unlike a will, which is public. As a result, a will can be challenged, mainly because the deceased's heirs believe they know what their loved one intended for them to have. These opinions often conflict. You've probably heard this act as "contesting" the will. This is why *wills do not go into effect immediately* and the deceased's wishes are not administered until they are court ordered.

The difference between a revocable and an irrevocable trust is *the irrevocable living trust cannot be changed once it has been*

created. Whatever assets are placed in that trust cannot be withdrawn by the Grantor – the person who made the trust and to whom the items belong – at any time, no matter what.

In Summary, don't be one of the 60% of Americans who don't have a will or a living trust. You're condemning your heirs to the hassles of probate if you don't get organized on this. There are many details regarding wills and living trusts that we didn't cover here. Ask a tax advisor, attorney, or estate planning professional if some kind of living trust is best for you. Be sure to select an attorney with experience in estate planning, specifically in establishing living trusts, if that's the route you want to go. Vow to leave a legacy your family can build on and use to get ahead!

Pass The Knowledge On!

Section VII:
How To Keep Your House, And Other Tips

CHAPTER 24

REFINANCING – DOES IT MAKE SENSE?

In this chapter, we'll cover the reasons why you might want to refinance and what criteria you must consider in today's real estate market. It's a great time to refinance because mortgage rates are still relatively low.

If you do refinance, the process and the *costs* are very similar to purchasing your home again. You may be looking at title company fees, lender fees, the cost of an appraisal and a survey (if they won't reuse the one you have) and title policy fees.

When you purchased your home the seller may have paid for many of these closing costs. Now you will have to pay for them. There's no way of getting out of it even though there has been no change in ownership. The title company and lender simply want the reassurance that the property being financed is clear of any title issues at the time it's financed. Some examples of what would cloud a title are a mechanics lien, a judgment due to unpaid taxes, homeowner association dues or child support, for instance.

The best that any title company can do is to reduce the charge by a certain percentage. This discount is known as a *reissue rate*. This is something you *must ask* about since every state is different and it's not an automatic discount. *Refinancing is not free, so you will have to determine how much you'll save on your monthly payments with a lower rate and how long it will take, given those savings, to repay the cost of getting a new loan.*

One of the first factors you must look at is the term of your current mortgage. If you are 23 years into a 30-year note, would you want to start all over again, just to have a lower monthly payment amount? If so, perhaps you should consider a 15-year note. You may find that your monthly payment is slightly higher, but you've not started over again with a new 30-year note.

Here are questions you need answers to before you commit to refinancing your home:

- **Is there a prepayment penalty involved with your existing loan?** A prepayment penalty may make refinancing cost-prohibitive. Look at your Notes Payable document to see if one exists and, if so, how much the penalty is. Then decide if adding the penalty amount to the balance owed is worth it.

- **What is your current interest rate?** It is usually stated that a difference of 1% may warrant refinancing. However, the loan amount you're refinancing and the length of the term should also contribute to your decision. Replacing an ARM with a fixed-rate product is another good reason to refinance, but you still have to qualify for the loan. Knowing your rate will stay fixed for the long haul is certainly more comforting than the unknown of an adjustable-rate product, so some people choose to refinance away from an ARM even if they're not saving a lot of money with a lower interest rate.

- **What do you currently owe on the property and what is the current market value of your property?** There are certain areas in which home values are rapidly deteriorating and you will find it almost impossible to get your home refinanced. In order for a home to be refinanced the lender must see that the new appraised value meets or exceeds the new loan amount, which is the current loan amount plus closing costs. Lenders often conduct reviews of all appraisals.

They'll have an independent third party go over the appraisal to make sure the property's market value is accurate.

- **How much longer do you expect to continue owning the property?** Obviously, the longer you plan to stay in the property, the better. It would not make too much sense to go through the expense of refinancing if you plan to stay in the home for only another year or two. You should calculate the payback period for all out-of-pocket costs by dividing the monthly mortgage payment savings into the total cost of refinancing. For example, if your new loan reduced your payments by $100 per month and the total cost to refinance was $4,800, the payback period would be 48 months, or four years. There are tons of mortgage calculators on the internet that can help you with this decision from a financial standpoint.

Most of us get caught up in chasing the lowest rate. But remember, just because there's a lower rate, it doesn't mean you qualify for it. The market has changed recently and it may not be as easy to refinance as it was in the past. The good news is that rates have dropped, but the bad news is many homeowners can't meet the new lender guidelines for refinancing.

In Summary, make your refinance decision based on what you stand to gain at the time you take out the loan, since no one can tell you which way the rates will go. Look at all of the factors: How long you plan to stay in the home, calculate how long it will take you to payback the cost of refinancing based on the proposed monthly savings, and then decide.

Don't be fooled by the offer of a "no-cost" refinance. What this really means is that the costs have been rolled into either the new interest rate or into your new loan balance. You'll have to pay the same fees that you paid when you bought your home the first time. In addition, you'll pay for the cost of the title insurance which the seller more than likely paid on your behalf when you purchased the house.

However, you may be entitled to a "re-issue" rate which would bring down the cost significantly, so be sure to ask.

Pass The Knowledge On!

CHAPTER 25

FORECLOSURE OPTIONS

In this chapter you will learn about your options if you are facing foreclosure. We'll show you exactly what to do, and why it's so important to deal with your situation as soon as possible, even though it may be painful or embarrassing. In the end, you'll have fewer problems, and recover from them faster, if you act now.

The American Dream is coming to a devastating end for many. Thousands have lost their homes and more will lose them in the future. If you keep up with the headlines, you are well aware of the main reasons for all these foreclosures. Some sources blame the sub-prime lenders, while others blame the borrowers. Even Wall Street has been blamed for creating the greatest mortgage meltdown in history.

One fact we cannot escape is sub-prime lenders sold the most dangerous loans to the most vulnerable borrowers, which created the largest number of foreclosures in modern history. These lenders created and worked a formula that could produce nothing but an absurdly high number of foreclosures. The lenders simply took the highest-risk loan features, packed them into adjustable-rate mortgages with temporarily low monthly payments, advertised them, and then approved the ensuing flood of loan applications without considering whether the borrowers could afford the loans after the payments increased. Some interest rates on the loans jumped by 30% to 40%.

Could you afford such a jump? Most American families cannot, so the economy ends up with another foreclosure. Fortunately, many of these lenders are no longer in business or have been purchased.

To make matters worse, most of these loans came with an expensive prepayment penalty. This means the homeowner would have to pay a penalty to get out of the existing loan if he or she tries to sell or refinance the property before the penalty period is up. The penalty could be hundreds – or even thousands – of dollars.

If you are faced with the possibility of foreclosure, you have to act now! Procrastination or denial will only make your situation worse as time passes.

Mistake # 57: *Facing foreclosure with no plan*

If you find yourself facing a monthly mortgage payment that will soon increase to an unaffordable level, act now! You are not alone in this. You do have resources that can help, including this reference guide.

Refinance *Before* the Payments Increase

If you can, refinance your home before the increased payments become a problem. The first thing you need to do is learn about and understand the details of this mortgage payment increase.

- *Look at your credit six months in advance.* This should give you time to correct or improve your credit score. Don't be like the thousands of people who wait, meanwhile destroying their credit trying to make payments they can't afford. An increase in your mortgage payment can change everything. When you're struggling to make monthly mortgages payments, you have less to spend on everything else. You'll feel squeezed and stressed at a time when you will need to make decisions that impact the quality of your life. You don't want to make a decision while you are at your weakest. *Act while you have time to strengthen your position, not when your mortgage is already increasing.*

- Understand what type of loan you have and its terms. Is it an ARM (adjustable rate mortgage) or is the interest rate (and thus the payment) fixed for 2, 3 or 30 years? If you don't know what type of loan you have, call your lender to find out.

- You need to know when your fixed period ends, when the new rate adjusts and by how much. This is important because it will tell you when your payments will start to increase and give you time to plan. A large percentage of borrowers who get into trouble with adjustable rate mortgages don't see it coming until they receive an increase notice in the mail. Don't let this happen to you! Increase your options by being *proactive!*

- What interest rate did you commit to? Are rates lower now? Would refinancing decrease your monthly payment enough to justify paying the closing costs?

- Do you live in an area where you suspect property values decreased? ***It may be impossible to refinance without having to bring money to the closing in order to cover the closing costs.*** Contact your mortgage company and request a payoff. This will tell you how much you owe on the property. Ask a real estate agent who markets to your area to provide you with a list of comparable properties that sold within the last 6 months, before you spend money on a formal appraisal. If property values have dropped you will need to know if you owe more than your property is worth. This situation is often referred to as "being upside down." Many people who go into foreclosure do so because their property is worth less than they paid for it and refinancing is not an option.

- If you have an ARM, this is the time you should consider a fixed rate loan. One good thing about a fixed rate payment is that it stays fixed over the life of the loan; your principal and interest payments will *not* increase. Only your insurance and taxes increase as time goes on, regardless of whether you have a mortgage note.

- Consider looking at significant changes in your spending and lifestyle. Perhaps you could take on a second job or bring in a roommate to contribute extra money toward the mortgage payment.

- Also consider liquidating other assets, such as cars or boats. The key is to reduce debt as much as possible and not add to your problems by spending money on unnecessary purchases.

Your goal is to investigate and gain knowledge of all your options in advance so you can work from a position of strength.

Talk to Your Lender

The further behind you become, the harder it is to reinstate your loan, which increases the chance you will lose your house. Call your lender as soon as you realize you have a problem. Even if foreclosure is at your doorstep, you may still have a way to negotiate with your lender. As foreclosures are hitting their highest levels in decades, none of the lenders want to be stuck owning yet another house. They are not in the business of owning foreclosed homes, and they especially don't want to own one in an area surrounded by other homes in foreclosure.

So give your lender a call and try to arrange to pay a more manageable monthly amount. This concept is often referred to as a *loan modification*. *In most cases, the larger the loss the lender is faced with, and the greater the possibility the loss will occur, the more flexible the lender will be with you.*

Usually the first notices you receive from your lender offer help in the form of good information about foreclosure prevention options. If you don't respond at all, the lender will become increasingly more demanding, and will send notices at an accelerating rate about pending legal action. If you don't open the mail you will only set yourself up to be blindsided by the legal action that will take away your home.

Contact your state government's housing office to learn about the foreclosure laws and timeframes in your state. They are different in every state. Read your loan documents and Deed of Trust to learn what your lender can do if you can't make your payments.

Mistake # 58: *Giving up too easily when the answer is no*

If your lender is not flexible then you need to remind that person about the losses the lender faces. Sometimes it is not the lender but the investor who dictates how much a loan can be modified. Also, if you get someone on the phone that is not helpful, hang up and try again. Keep trying until you get someone in the organization that will help you. Sometimes persistence will pay off.

In the past, lenders have always modified loans for borrowers facing job loss, illness, divorce or a death in the family. There is no reason they should not modify your loan. No legitimate lender wants to foreclose and lose money; it is worth a phone call and a conversation with your lender.

Mistake # 59: *Not understanding your foreclosure prevention options*

If you don't understand your foreclosure prevention options (also called *loss mitigation*) they can be found on the internet at:

www.portal.hud.gov/portal/page?_pageid=33,717348&_dad=portal&_schema=PORTAL

Some of the options that are available to you are:

Repayment Plans - Based on your financial situation your lender may consider you for a repayment plan. They will work with you and could offer you a reduction or suspension of your payments to help bring your account current. You have to be able to show that you have the income to make the new payments.

Loan Modification - If you qualify, you may be able to refinance the debt and/or extend the time period over which you pay back the past due amount. In some instances, you may have a pay-back period that extends as long as the remaining term of the loan. You may qualify for this if you no longer have the financial problem and can afford the new payment amount. This option should be the first you seek if your intent is to still live in and pay for the home. But beware, not too many loan modifications are working for struggling homeowners who need foreclosure prevention. And in many cases, the loan modifications backfire on the homeowners they are meant to help. Here's why:

- More than 50% of these loans are packaged with increased payments.
- Fewer than one in ten of the current loan modifications result in a reduced principal loan balance.
- During the housing boom many borrowers were sold on the benefits of a second mortgage in order to avoid paying mortgage insurance. Not many first lien mortgage holders are willing to help borrowers with payments on second mortgages. Similarly, the second mortgage holders would rather not waive their rights in a loan modification situation that could result in a 100 percent loss. They'd rather try collecting a few more payments before the borrower goes into foreclosure.
- Overwhelmed loan servicers have set up an automated foreclosure process that has built-in financial incentives. They are *not* set up for the case-by-case negotiation process necessary for modifications.
- Many loan servicing companies are set up to receive monetary incentives to foreclose – rather than modify – your loan.
- Many of the loans that were purchased by private investors rather than the secondary market can't be found and brought into the process. Because the loans have been divided so many times, they would all have to agree to the modification.

As of this writing, loan modification is not truly working for all those who need it. Instead we are seeing fraud from a largely unregulated industry of private loan modification service companies popping up to take advantage of those in need of real help. They are apparent when they charge thousands of dollars in upfront fees. We ask you to keep updated by checking our blog on our website at www.MakeNoMistakes.com and click on loan modification. It is our goal to always have the most current and helpful information available to you.

Partial Claim – Sometimes setbacks are temporary, and if you can now make your regular monthly payment, this plan will help bring your account current. It works by creating a second lien on your property for the delinquent amount.

Pre-Foreclosure Sale – This option allows you to sell your home to avoid foreclosure. The lender may allow you to sell your home for less than what is owed on the mortgage loan, which is often referred to as a "short sale." *This will also keep the derogatory credit rating of a foreclosure off your credit report.* However, it is not uncommon for a lender to forget to update the *zero balance* option on the credit report due to their financial loss. And, you must meet the lender's guidelines to qualify for this option.

Deed-in-Lieu of Foreclosure – When there is no other option, tell your lender you want to voluntarily give the property back or transfer over your interest in the property to the lender. You won't destroy your credit rating since this is not as damaging as a foreclosure. This option is usually available with one loan, but not two loans.

FHA Loans – In 2008 new legislation was passed to help distressed homeowners facing foreclosure. The Hope for Homeowners Act of 2008 creates a new, temporary, voluntary program within FHA to back FHA-insured mortgages for borrowers at risk of losing their homes to foreclosure. In exchange, homeowners will share future appreciation with FHA.

- Only owner-occupants who are unable to afford their mortgage payments are eligible for the program.

- No investors or investor properties will qualify.
- Must have a mortgage debt-to-income ratio greater than 31 percent as of March 1, 2008.
- Lenders must document and verify borrower's income with the IRS.
- Loans must be 30-year, fixed rate loans.
- The new loan amount will be 90% of the current value of the home.
- The program began October 1, 2008 and will end on September 30, 2011.

VA Loans – Call the VA Regional Loan Centers at 1-800-569-1000 if you have a VA Loan and are facing foreclosure. They offer financial counseling designed to help you avoid foreclosure. Ask for the phone number of the loan service representative in your area.

Mistake # 60: *Not taking advantage of free mortgage counseling*

If you need assistance interacting with your lender, a housing counseling agency can help. These agencies usually have information on services and programs that can assist you with not only talking with your lender, but determining an appropriate course of action for *you*. Some also offer credit counseling. Hope Now is an example of the government bringing together members of the private sector, lenders, counselors, investors and HUD-approved counseling agents to provide free foreclosure prevention assistance. You can find them at Hopenow.com or call 1.888.995-HOPE to speak with a counselor. Services from these agencies should be free of charge. If they ask for a fee to perform certain services, consider it a big red flag waving at you. If you don't feel right about the agency, call a HUD-approved housing counseling agency at 1-800-569-4287 or TDD 1-800-877-8339. Call *before* you pay anyone or sign any paperwork promising to pay.

In Summary, if you find yourself with a mortgage payment that's increasingly out of control, or you're facing foreclosure, your lender is the first person to call. Remember, your lender would prefer to work with you rather than foreclose on your property.

Only your lender can determine what you qualify for, so be wary of investors and scammers who prey on people in circumstances such as yours. More importantly, ask questions. If you do not qualify for any of the programs discussed above, you must create new strategies for yourself and your family to position yourself to recover from the loss.

We know many people who recovered from the loss of their home. They didn't do so by buying into a magical quick fix, but rather, they learned from their mistakes, made some changes, and knew what to look for the next time they considered buying a home. It took real commitment on their part to create this positive transformation, but they stuck with it. Keep in mind you can turn negative consequences into positive rewards simply by not making the same mistake twice.

Pass The Knowledge On!

CHAPTER 26

AVOIDING SCAMS

In this chapter we discuss one of the biggest problems in the mortgage business – scams. While thousands of Americans are in danger of losing their homes during the current housing crisis, they also have to guard against scam artists. The problem is most stressed-out homeowners welcome scammers into their homes because they offer a way for people to save their homes. Other scam artists will just wait for foreclosure proceedings to start, and then they will come out of the woodwork with rescue offers.

In this business, the scam artist knows *far more* than the borrower, so a lack of knowledge can cost you your home and/or a considerable amount of money. What's worse is borrowers may *never* know they were scammed until they try to sell or refinance their property.

So in an attempt to level the playing field, we will share with you some of the scams borrowers fall for everyday, all the while believing they are getting the best deal at the time.

Foreclosure Scams

Keep in mind that if you are facing foreclosure, you are probably very emotional about the situation, and thus susceptible to falling for false promises. If it seems too good to be true, chances are, it is.

Mistake # 61: *Trusting too easily*

We all want to trust someone when we need help, but people trust too easily when they're already suffering or are vulnerable. Beware of any individual or company proclaiming the following:

- Calls itself a "foreclosure service," or some similar name. If they are truly in the mortgage business they should have a mortgage license, which is easily found on the internet under the mortgage lending licensing department for your state.
- Specifically targets homeowners whose homes are listed for foreclosure.
- Tells you or makes arrangements for you to make your home mortgage payments directly to them or their company.
- Says you must transfer your property deed or title to the individual or company.
- Asks for an up front fee.

If anyone asks you for a fee up front, RUN!!! There should not be an upfront fee associated with negotiating any kind of new financing deal for you, and certainly not when you're facing foreclosure. This is almost always a scam.

> **Tip:**
> *Let the scam artist know you will have an attorney review the paperwork first and take notice of their response.*

This "upfront fee" scam works because scam artists convince homeowners that they can "negotiate" lower payments or better payment plans with the lenders, but that there is a charge to do so. To save a home from foreclosure, it will cost between $500 and $1,000, the scam artists typically say. It is not uncommon for the scam artist to come back for an additional payment to close the deal.

Don't deal with anyone asking for money upfront. There are agencies that will help you if a foreclosure looms on your near horizon. Start with a HUD counselor who can look at your specific situation and recommend routes to take or agencies to contact. Or, check with Neighbor Works America, a nonprofit organization. Either one of these agencies should be able to put you in contact with somebody who can help.

The key is to have your attorney or an experienced real estate professional look over any foreclosure documents. You might hesitate to contact an attorney due to the cost, but consider the cost of losing your home if you make a mistake. A scam artist will undoubtedly resist having other eyes look at the proposed deal and its paperwork, so this alone should be a sign you're dealing with a scam.

Also, don't sign anything with blank lines or spaces, since other information could be added later without your knowledge. If the sentence does not apply simply add **N/A** (Not Applicable) in the blank space.

If you believe you are being targeted by an individual or company running a foreclosure scam, contact the local office of the United States Trustee at www.usdoj.gov/ust.

Equity Skimming

Equity skimming is the most common foreclosure scam. Equity skimming is fairly easy to understand if you're clear on the two terms, equity and appreciation.

Equity is usually defined as the difference between what is currently owed (also known as the payoff or principal balance) and the original sales price.

Then there's appreciation (also known as profit), which is the amount for which the property can be sold minus the original sales price.

Following is a short example to best explain *equity* and *appreciation*. Mark and Sara recently sold their home. When they bought it five years ago they made a $40,000 down payment. See what's happened to the value of their investment, as defined by equity and appreciation:

1.	Home recently sold for	$250,000
2.	Original purchase price of the home was	$200,000
3.	Original loan amount was	$160,000
4.	Remaining balance amount is	$154,000

Line 2 minus Line 4 = *Equity*
      $200,000 minus $154,000 = *$46,000*

Line 1 minus Line 2 = *Appreciation*
      $250,000 minus $200,000 = *$50,000*

Mark and Sara had $46,000 of *equity* in their home when they sold it. The house had *appreciated* by $50,000.

This review of equity and appreciation is necessary so we can better explain the scamming term *equity skimming*. **When someone says "equity skimming," that person is actually referring to both the equity and the appreciation in any given property, and not just the equity.**

Equity skimming is accomplished in many ways. The two most common methods are:

- **Signing Over of the Deed**: A person claiming to be an "investor" persuades the homeowner facing foreclosure to sign over the ownership of the home by signing over the deed to the home. Remember, the title deed (also known as the deed of trust) and the mortgage loans are two completely different things! This investor promises that, because the homeowner is signing over the deed, the investor is now liable for the monthly payments. What's more, the investor proclaims, he will let the homeowner pay a reasonable amount of rent to the investor. Because people don't want to move, and they *do* want to get out from a mortgage they can't afford, they agree to rent back their own home from this investor.

a. The problem with this concept is that the names on the loan never changed. *The homeowner is still liable for the loan.* The names on the property's deed did change which gave ownership of the house over to the scammer.

b. The investor never makes a payment to the lender.

c. This scammer accepts rent money or a lease payment each month from the homeowners, who now believe they're renters, or from other tenants who move in after the original homeowners move out. So, in the interim, the investor has a stream of cash flow.

d. The lender, of course, continues the foreclosure process and, usually sooner rather than later, the lender forecloses on the house and it's legitimately sold to a new buyer.

e. The original homeowner finds out his house has been sold out from under him and he must now vacate the property he thought he was renting. Plus, his credit is now in much worse shape.

There are a number of other routes the scammer can take:

- **Straw Buyer:** The investor introduces another unsuspecting person into the deal. This new buyer is known as a straw buyer who is anxious to take advantage of *an investment opportunity.*

  a. The investor charges the straw buyer a purchase price higher than what's owed.

  b. The investor commits to giving a few thousand dollars to the straw buyer. This serves as the incentive to do the deal along with the added benefits:

     i. Of knowing there is already a tenant in the property who will pay the mortgage,

     ii. Of having acquired an investment property in his or her name.

c. The investor usually refers a loan officer to work with the straw buyer who handles the mortgage logistics of the deal.

d. At closing, the scammer keeps the equity and appreciation himself because he is the owner of the property.

e. The mortgage is now off of the backs of the original homeowner, but they have lost their equity and appreciation.

The straw buyer, on the other hand, finds out that:

a. The rent the current tenants are paying is not enough to cover all the costs of the mortgage payment, i.e. taxes.

b. The straw buyer now has a big challenge because there's no equity left in the home to cover the closing costs if he wants to sell the property, since the home is not worth what he paid for it.

c. The straw buyer doesn't usually figure out he was lied to by the investor until all the investor's promises are broken and the straw buyer is left with the responsibility of having to sell or lease the property by himself.

d. And while the straw buyer is figuring all of this out he's made the first few monthly mortgage payments which has now dipped into the few thousand dollars he or she received from the investor at closing. The straw buyer gets stuck holding the bad investment, and his good credit is at risk, too!

Be Wary of Street Corner Signs

Exercise caution if you call a number on a street corner or yard sign that reads something like this:

- Avoid Foreclosure
- We Buy Houses
- Stop Foreclosure

The people behind these signs may be legitimate, but how do you properly check them out before you do business with them? In most cases, you only have a phone number and a sign that claims they are real estate investors or something similar. You would not call any other professional based on a street corner or yard sign, so why would you risk calling someone you can't check out when your home is at stake? We realize it's tempting when you're desperate to keep your house. The carrot they offer is to help you avoid losing your home to foreclosure. If you still can't resist calling, here are indications you're speaking with a scammer:

- If they urge you to not talk with anybody else about what they have offered you. This should be your first sign to run. The only reason they're asking you to keep it a secret is because they don't want anyone to tell you the truth. And if they were making money legitimately, what kind of company doesn't want word-of-mouth advertising? An illegal one.
- If they ask you to pay money up front, this is a huge red flag.
- If anyone asks you to sign documents but doesn't give you the necessary time to read them or to have them reviewed by someone else, this is another red flag. The reasons for the rush may sound legitimate, so don't be taken in.
- If the deal "has to be done today," walk away from it.

No Closing Cost Scam

We have all read the ads proclaiming, "NO CLOSING COSTS." The ads then state the following fees will not be charged at closing: survey, title insurance, processor, attorney, flood certification, appraisal, credit report, underwriting, and loan origination. Have you ever met an attorney who works for free? What about a surveyor or loan processor? I don't think so! Somebody is paying for it and that somebody is the borrower. The fee might not be labeled as something listed in the ad, but the borrower is definitely paying it, probably by paying a higher interest rate to cover the cost of charging no closing costs.

This concept may not be considered a scam but it's definitely misleading and so worth noting. If you're in this situation, try asking the loan officer to let you pay the fees and then a lower interest rate. See what response you get!

Don't forget to use your Lender Comparative information so you're comparing apples to apples.

In Summary, these are just a few of the scams – and the mistakes they steer you to make – that exist today. Both prospective borrowers and homeowners having difficulties making their payments are targets for scammers.

If you're a homeowner facing an increased mortgage payment or foreclosure, you could be scammed by a so-called investor. Never sign your title over to someone else except in the presence of knowledgeable and trustworthy professionals who come well-recommended. Keep in mind that no one, no matter what promises or offers are made, has any responsibility for your mortgage payments except the people named on the actual loan papers.

Remember to ask questions. Don't be rushed into signing something you don't fully understand. Don't include anyone whom you can't fully check out in a transaction as important as one that affects your home. Keep in mind that a lack of knowledge is not an excuse in the court of law, and could cost you dearly!

In the next chapter we will look at how fraud can separate you from your money and home, and possibly even land you in jail.

Pass The Knowledge On!

CHAPTER 27

HOW TO AVOID FRAUD

In this chapter you will learn about one of the fastest-growing white-collar crimes in the US. This crime can land the borrower and all those involved in jail, and it's called mortgage fraud. There are many forms of mortgage fraud, but we will only discuss the ones that are having the biggest impact on the industry: fraud for profit and fraud for housing.

Fraud is defined as a "knowing misrepresentation of the truth or concealment of a material fact. The information, no matter how true or false, is used to induce another to act to their own detriment." The flip side to this issue is "ignorance is not an excuse," so saying, "I didn't know," may not help you in a court of law. If you signed off on paperwork with fraudulent or incorrect information because you failed to review it, you could face federal prosecution. So be sure to read *everything* that you sign because *you* are responsible for your actions.

Who's Involved in Mortgage Fraud?

Most anyone can be involved in mortgage fraud, from your broker to your real estate agent, to your banker, appraiser, loan officer, processor, underwriter or any employee of the lender. You can be suckered in by a church leader, relative, friend or acquaintance. When it comes to money and business, trust no one without checking them out first. People who run these schemes have often earned your trust in the past. They target people with good credit, college students, hard-working people in need of cash, and people looking to invest in real estate. Anyone could become a victim, and we do mean *anyone*. Ask questions, and check with the agency that polices the mortgage industry in your state. If it's too good to be true, it is most likely not true.

Read your loan application!!! When you sign off on your loan application you are signing a statement swearing everything you said was true. If it's not, you're subject to criminal, civil penalties and imprisonment.

You will find the following statement on page four of your mortgage application, right above your signature lines: *any information you provided is true and correct and that any intentional or negligent misrepresentation of this information in the application may result in civil liability to any person who may suffer loss... the property will be occupied as indicated in the application... no lender, nor its agents, brokers or insurers has made any representation or warranty, express or implied regarding the property or the condition or the value of the property.*

When you sign your HUD-1 Settlement Statement, you see similar language: ***WARNING: It is a crime to knowingly make false statements to the United States on this or any other similar forms. Penalties upon conviction can include a fine and imprisonment.***

So think twice before engaging in any fraudulent activities. Lenders take mortgage fraud seriously. Law enforcement and the courts are sending people to jail. Fraud comes in a variety of forms. Some forms are intentional and others come from ignorance or carelessness. Either way, by law, it's fraud and is punishable – starting with the borrower and continuing to all of those involved with the property.

As we discussed earlier, fraud in the mortgage industry can be divided into two broad categories: Fraud for Housing and Fraud for Profit. Let's look at several of the most common forms.

Fraud for Profit

Fraud for profit is when the *intent* of the act is to make a profit by selling or buying property in order to generate cash proceeds from the transaction, often referred to as taking "cash out." Mortgage fraud for profit will typically involve falsified loan applications, an inflated appraisal, property flipping, equity skimming, and even identity theft.

Fraud for profit can also be referred to as "Industry Insider Fraud." It involves collaboration between industry insiders to override lender controls and guidelines. These acts may include overstated income, altered credit histories, overstating the appraisal value, length of a fictitious employment, and/or not fully disclosing the borrower's debts.

Who are these industry insiders? They are people who are often well-versed in mortgage finance and know how to exploit the system. It typically involves a mortgage broker or loan officer, an appraiser, an outside investor and a straw buyer. As we discussed earlier, a straw buyer is someone who has good credit or a falsely inflated credit score and who will pose as a buyer for the purpose of buying a property or properties for someone else – usually for someone who can not qualify for the loan himself. In some cases, a straw buyer can even be someone whose identity has been stolen and knows nothing about the transaction until other credit is denied or the mortgage appears on his credit report. In other cases, a straw buyer is a willing participant in the scheme and receives compensation for being involved. But in many cases, a straw buyer is a person who is introduced to the crime by a family member, a church member, their friends or co-workers. They are simply told how they can make quick money by just letting someone use their credit and/or identity. Many people would be tempted by the chance to make up to $10,000 with apparently no negative repercussions. But as we both know, nothing is free, easy or without risk. In most cases, the straw buyer's credit is destroyed because no payments are made on the mortgage. Also, the FBI may come knocking because they tend to get involved in fraud and conspiracy, which is what this is.

In a typical mortgage fraud for profit scheme, a mortgage broker, loan officer, title company employee and an appraiser are the key participants. Usually, they receive money for falsifying documents. The appraiser will report an inflated value on the property and the broker or loan officer will help falsify the loan package that will be sent to the lender. A title company employee will create the closing documents and disburse funds after the sale is completed.

Fraud for Housing

Fraud for housing or "fraud for property" generally occurs when a borrower wants to purchase a house he or she could not afford without submitting false information about their income, assets or employment in order to qualify for a mortgage loan. Usually, the buyer intends to repay the loan so it typically carries a lower financial risk to lenders because the fraud is a one-time occurrence on a loan. ***The difference between fraud for housing and fraud for profit is the intent behind the fraudulent act.***

Most people who commit this type of fraud often don't know they are breaking the law or defrauding lenders. The borrower can be coached by the mortgage broker/loan officer or real estate agent to give the lender what they want to see on the application. In the eyes of the borrowers, they simply bent the truth in order to qualify for a loan that they feel they are entitled to. In most cases they are not entitled to the property under the lender's guidelines without making a few misrepresentations, usually regarding income, personal debt, and property value. The borrower wants the property, intends to occupy it, and has every intention to repay the loan. But this does not excuse the fact that making a false statement to a lender is mortgage fraud. Each mortgage fraud scheme entails some kind of deception and misrepresentation or omission of information; the following are some of those ways.

> **Falsifying "Stated Income"** - The "stated income" loan is the perfect vehicle for fraud. These loans have earned the nickname "liar loans" in the mortgage industry. Borrowers just need to state their income level and don't need to provide any documentation to support it. No one knows how many "stated income" loans were given during the mortgage boom of the

early 2000s, but mortgage industry experts suggest these loans made up a significant portion of all mortgages. It is almost impossible to get a stated income loan due to the high foreclosure rate associated with these loans. In fact, many lenders are now using comprehensive systems for detecting and preventing mortgage fraud that involves misrepresentation of the borrower's income. As a result, borrowers must complete the IRS form 4506T which gives the lender permission to request a copy of your submitted tax returns from the IRS. The loan will not be processed without one. Other services include verification of the borrower's social security number and the elimination of broker-ordered appraisals (which reduces the risk of appraiser coercion by the loan officer).

Rebates and Credits - All information, which includes rebates and credits to any individual as a result of a real estate transaction, must be disclosed on the Settlement Statement. If it's *not disclosed*, but paid outside of the closing, it's considered loan fraud. The lender is making the loan based on all information supplied, and is relying on the final Settlement Statement and its information to be correct. For this very reason, all information must be disclosed. In fact, during the closing it is now required that both buyer and seller sign a document that has specific language that states that neither side is involved in any agreements outside of the closing table. This includes real estate agents giving back a portion of their commissions to either side – seller or buyer. Any transaction outside of the day of closing that was not documented prior to the closing date and approved by the lender can and will be viewed as fraud.

Secret Second Mortgages - This occurs when someone loans money to the buyer so that the buyer can close on the home, but the second loan is not disclosed to the primary lender. A second mortgage is usually recorded a few days after the first, securing the debt by placing an additional lien on the property. This secret second mortgage is usually drafted by the seller of the property or some other person who has made an agreement with the borrower in order for them to get the first loan from the lender. As stated above, the lender is making the loan based on all information supplied, and is relying on the final Settlement Statement and its information to be correct. For this very reason all information must be disclosed. If they are making this loan based on information that is not disclosed anytime during the loan process, it's fraud.

Bogus Earnest Money Deposits - An example of a bogus earnest money deposit is when the purchase contract states that the buyer has deposited a larger down payment amount than was really made. The Settlement Statement might show the bogus funds as "POC," paid outside of closing. Proof is often required by the lender, so the borrower and perhaps even the seller create false documents showing that deposits and monies were exchanged.

Falsifying Gift Letter - Buyers close with money that was given to them as a gift all the time. Lenders verify that the money is not a loan, but a gift. They provide the donor with a document to sign stating repayment is not required. Donors and recipients commit loan fraud when they falsify any aspect of the gift letter, for example, making a deal after the closing that alters the original gift letter.

Falsely Claiming Owner Occupancy - Some loans are only intended for owner-occupants, *not* investors. Owner-occupied loans come with better rates and terms and if you obtain one of those loans, you'll be asked to sign a statement that you intend to occupy the home. Some loans ask that you'll be an owner-occupant for a specific length of time. Falsifying any documents when you have no intention of living in the home is fraud.

Over-Inflated Appraisal – Over-inflated appraisals were common when lenders and loan officers put pressure on appraisers to raise the valuations of the property to allow the mortgage deals to work. Many appraisers who depended on the brokers' business did this to continue earning their business. Sometimes it involved the real estate agents who would change the list price in the Multiple Listing Service (MLS) in order for it to match the artificially inflated offer price.

What can you do about an inflated appraisal loan after you have closed on the house? Again, most people don't realize they have bought a house with an inflated appraisal value until they try to sell or refinance. An inflated appraisal is hard to detect unless the value is so out of line with other similar houses in the area. Not too many borrowers are questioning the value when the appraisal comes in a few thousand above the asking price. But if you're concerned, contact a local real estate attorney. The original appraisers may be in violation of the state's consumer practices acts. The attorney may be able to sue them for negligence. Also, contact the agencies or boards responsible for overseeing appraisers in your state and file a complaint. Even if you didn't financially suffer because of the inflated appraisal loan, you still have a moral obligation to report the offenders. Besides, if you don't, you could be named as one of the fraud perpetrators if appraisal inflation is brought up!

In Summary, making a false statement to a lender or on any of your paperwork is a federal crime. Don't do it on your own, and don't do it because someone encourages you. If someone asks you to do something that doesn't seem right, start asking questions and don't stop asking until you are sure you have uncovered the truth. Ignorance of the law is no excuse.

Fraud is on the increase, so your chances of crossing paths with a fraudster have also increased. Simply looking to refinance or buy a home can bring you into contact with someone committing fraud. Remember, anyone can be involved in mortgage fraud. In today's world of mass foreclosures, be aware of offers to "save" your home from foreclosure. Understand what you are signing and make sure the name on your application is yours and it matches your social security number. Be suspicious of "get rich" investment property schemes promising extraordinary profits by simply buying a specific home or piece of property.

Before you buy a home, get a real estate professional to pull the comparable sales in the area and look at the tax assessments to verify the home's value. If you don't understand the terms of your mortgage, get someone who does, or seek the assistance of a real estate attorney before you sign your loan documents. Ask lots of questions before you buy. Remember, if it sounds too good to be true, it probably is.

Pass The Knowledge On!

CHAPTER 28

DON'T BE A VICTIM OF PREDATORY LENDING

In this chapter you will learn about predatory lending and how, even though many of these practices are legal, they're not in the best interest of the borrowers. Predatory lending is the term used to characterize fraudulent or legal – but always unfair and deceptive – mortgage lending practices directed at homeowners.

Predatory lending can involve fraud, but it is different from mortgage fraud in that mortgage fraud typically involves falsified loan documents, equity skimming, property flipping, inflated appraisals, and maybe even identity theft. Predatory lending, on the other hand, typically involves a single home loan for the purchase of a new home or to refinance an existing one. These loans come with extremely high fees, prepayment penalties for paying off the loan early and a high interest rate, even if the homeowner has great credit.

A predatory mortgage lender will refinance loans to generate a commission for the company without providing any net tangible benefit to the borrower. This practice steals a family's home equity, and increases the likelihood they will join the ranks of those already on the foreclosure rolls. You can see the effects of this practice across America by looking at the increased number of people losing their homes. A chunk of those foreclosures are because of predatory lending tactics.

Additionally, predatory lending also destabilizes our communities by decreasing the value of the homes because of the increased number of foreclosures.

How does this happen?

A large percentage of the foreclosures are a result of predatory lenders, who knowingly lend more money than borrowers can afford to repay. A lender does this by making a loan based on a percentage of the equity the borrower has in the home: usually 80% or less. The lender gives little to no regard to the borrower's ability to repay the loan, which is more common in a refinance scenario. In this case, the lender realizes a home with a minimum of 20% equity can be used as collateral to protect the lender from a loss.

Predators are good at getting *homeowners* to trust them. Unfortunately, this isn't too hard to accomplish. The borrower wants to be sold a loan product, especially if the homeowner is falling on hard times and sees this as a solution. Then, once the lender has the borrower's trust, the predatory lender convinces the homeowner that some form of refinancing or cash-out loan is best.

Who does this commonly happen to?

Predatory mortgage lending takes wealth from families by destroying the benefits of homeownership, and sometimes leaving its victims homeless after foreclosing. They find their victims among the poor, elderly, minorities, women, the sick, and those seeking desperate measures because they may not qualify for conventional Fannie Mae/Freddie Mac mortgages. The one thing all of these victims have in common is a lack of knowledge. They don't understand the financial implications of what they are getting themselves into.

Also at risk, not surprisingly, are people seeking to buy in neighborhoods that have been red-lined by banks. These are areas where banks choose to not make loans, often because the areas are considered bad investments because property values are on the decline. Buyers in these areas are, by default, placed at the mercy of predatory lenders because lenders with more upstanding lending practices have chosen not to lend in these areas. Recently, because of tighter, tougher credit guidelines, predatory lenders are now able to prey on middle-class, working-class suburban and rural homeowners as well. Acquiring a home loan is not as easy as it once was due to what has happened to the banking industry.

There is another side effect of predatory lending that people don't talk about – the psychological effects of losing one's home. This can leave families feeling defeated, causing many to break up after losing all hope. It's extremely demoralizing to own a home and then lose it; to have a taste of the great American dream of home ownership, and then have it taken away.

Unfortunately, many of these loans are perfectly legal. But the result is almost always the same: the lender makes money and the homeowners have the undue stress of trying to save their homes from foreclosures.

How do I know if I am a victim?

Many lending practices are called "predatory lending," and there is a great deal of dispute as to exactly what constitutes "predatory" practices. There are some obvious clues, however, to help you identify if you are working with a predatory lender:

- Paying Excessive Fees

Compared to a regular mortgage, which usually has fees about 1% of the sales price, a predatory loan can have fees in excess of 5%. These fees are often disguised in the loan amount by bundling several charges under one fee. These fees are unnecessary, and serve only to put large sums of money into the predator's hands.

- Higher interest rate

You should ask the lender to explain all fees, including the origination fees and any fees the lender receives for giving you the loan. A predatory lender will often receive a higher YSP, which is the commission the lender earns for giving you a high interest rate. Always ask what is par on the loan. Remember, "par" is the rate before the lender or mortgage broker earns a commission, or makes money "on the back." Always shop and ask for par rates so that you will know how much each lender is marking up the interest rate, and so you can compare par rates between lenders.

- Steering and targeting

Not all borrowers who can qualify for a great loan end up with one. Predatory lenders may steer borrowers into sub-prime mortgages. All borrowers with sub-prime mortgages don't have bad credit. *According to Fannie Mae, almost half of the borrowers with sub-prime mortgages could have qualified for better loans with better terms.* Without the right knowledge you cannot protect yourself. You are more likely to believe the promises and sales tactics of the predatory lender if you do not truly understand what you're being offered.

- Insurance products added to your loan

Most predatory loans will have unnecessary insurance added to the loan amount, which means the cost of this insurance is difficult to spot. Unnecessary insurance covers more than just homeowner's insurance. Some examples are disability and life insurance, and these policies can include the whole family, not just the borrower, which further increases the price. A loan officer manages to tuck this superfluous insurance purchase into the loan, and then collects premiums as long as the policy is in effect. We're not recommending that you do not buy disability or life insurance, but that you shop around and make your own decision. It's not right for a loan officer to add it without your knowledge, or to not give you an opportunity to comparison shop.

- Abnormal prepayment penalties

Borrowers who pay off their loans early may have to pay prepayment penalties to their lenders. The good news is this particular penalty is usually in place for only the first two or three years of a loan. The penalty may vary, but it is usually 6 months' interest, which is almost as much as six months' mortgage payment (six months' mortgage payments minus the monthly taxes and insurance). Also, it usually doesn't matter if the homeowner is selling or refinancing the home; the prepayment penalty still applies.

For example, the homeowner of a $200,000 loan with 6% interest and a prepayment penalty based on 6 months' interest would pay a $6,000 penalty fee.

Prepayment penalty fees are expensive. They eat up any equity the homeowner has built if the borrower tries to refinance the loan or sell the home within the prepayment penalty time period. This is why many borrowers are trapped in high interest rate loans that they can't get out of until the prepayment period expires.

- Hidden "mandatory arbitration" language

Predatory lenders will hide language in the fine print that makes it illegal for the borrower to take legal action against them. The borrowers unknowingly sign away their rights to sue the lender for any predatory actions or illegal actions, including fraud. Borrowers can only take their complaints to arbitration, which is totally controlled by the lender. Furthermore, borrowers usually don't have adequate representation by hiring an attorney, and borrowers cannot appeal the decision because most arbitration decisions are binding. The fees for arbitration are also a deterrent since it can cost more than going to small claims court. Some lenders keep their right to go to court but prohibit the borrower from doing the same. Overall, this is a lopsided contract that rarely is in the best interest of the borrowers.

Get an attorney to help you understand the fine print, and don't sign anything that takes away your rights to go to court.

In Summary, predatory lending is very profitable, so be careful whom you trust. *Remember that our blog, which you can access through our website, discusses various subjects, updates and* *current events related to real estate, including predatory lending. It also shares other mistakes we've come across since writing this edition of our book. Our goal is to always keep you current.*

We provided this information to help educate you, so you can make an informed decision about the financial services and providers with whom you choose to do business. We realize there are real limits to the extent we can help vulnerable households who are the focus of fraudulent professionals. To expect a borrower to understand the extremely complex mortgage documents and challenge specific provisions is a highly unreasonable expectation – and predatory lenders know it. This is another case of a lack of knowledge costing you money or even your home.

Do your homework, ask questions and tread carefully. Remember, don't let anyone persuade you to borrow more money than you can afford to repay. Don't sign the loan documents at closing if the terms have changed and are not what you agreed to. If you don't understand the terms of your mortgage get someone who does, or seek the assistance of a real estate attorney *before* you sign your loan documents. Beware of mortgage professionals who ask you to make false statements, such as overstating your income so you can qualify for the mortgage loan. If this happens, you will probably be taking on more debt than you can repay.

Pass The Knowledge On!

Section IIX:
Pass The Knowledge On

CHAPTER 29

PASS THE KNOWLEDGE ON: ESTABLISHING MULTIGENERATIONAL WEALTH THROUGH REAL ESTATE

By now many of you have noticed that at the end of each chapter we encouraged you to Pass the Knowledge On. Our vision is to increase homeownership and revitalize America's communities for future generations through real estate literacy and by creating a grassroots movement to 'Pass The Knowledge On.' Real prosperity is multigenerational. Our beliefs about money and wealth are often passed down from our parents to us at a very young age, and then influenced by our experiences, friendships and media.

In our business, we encounter many people of all races and financial backgrounds. Yet we notice one thing common to everyone. When our clients bring their children with them while searching for real estate, the children all take an interest! From the 4-year-old who insists on finding his or her new room to the 14-year-old who has a comment about the offer price. All children know what they like and whether or not that home makes sense for their family.

Yet so many parents leave their children at home because they view it as adult business and the kids will only slow down the process. When, in fact, *one of the most important gifts parents can give their children is teaching them the process of buying real estate and what it takes to own a home.*

Ask children to point out homes they would love to live in and they all will answer with enthusiasm. Would this not be a great time to discuss what this dream home would cost and what they would have to do in life to get it? As parents, we want to teach responsibility to our children and how to become self sufficient in life. However, as parents, many of us are limited to the knowledge and experiences our parents passed on to us.

Almost everywhere you turn, you can find books, articles, lectures, blogs, workshops and courses on real estate. Never before have we had such a variety of resources available to us in real estate. But at the same time, many parents have neglected to "Pass the Knowledge On" to their children. The question is, why?

- They think the kids will not understand it.
- They believe its adults' business, not kids'.
- They don't know how to communicate it to their kids.
- They don't remember what they learned about real estate so they can't share it.

Let's give them the knowledge that will help prevent future real estate mistakes. Start the process with just allowing them to follow your purchasing process and learn from your positive experience. Trust us when we tell you they'll ask questions and want to learn about it.

Even if you are not in the market right now to purchase a home, ask your child to go online to MLS and find a house for sale that he or she would want to live in one day. Then, make an appointment to visit the house during an open house. See what types of questions your children ask and encourage them. Use your reference guide to answer any questions and, more importantly, let them know it's possible!

Pass the Knowledge On!

# Final Words

If you have read this reference guide all the way through, *congratulations*! There are no shortcuts to purchasing real estate without increasing your risk of making a costly mistake. It is a process and we encourage you to utilize the tools and checklists discussed throughout the reference guide and at our website. The forms will always stay updated! So if you plan to purchase real estate tomorrow or five years from now, know your checklists and tools will be current when it matters.

In reality, *YOU* are the only one who can truly look out for your best interest. And when the transaction is complete, you are the one who is *ultimately* responsible for the property and paying the mortgage loan. Yet, many place their trust in others, which can be costly.

That's why, in addition to this reference guide, we have devised a **Make No Mistakes™ System**. So, in the event you don't want to get tied down to the details of reading *all* the chapters, the Make No Mistakes™ System will provide you with email reminders telling you what you have to do next in the process, taking you through your closing date, and beyond. In addition, you'll be provided with your Make No Mistakes™ *Home Buyer's Checklist* workbook which will allow you to follow each task to ensure that all parties involved in your real estate deal are doing what they are supposed to do on your behalf. Remember, you need to be the one driving this ship since you are the one who will be ultimately responsible. You can get more information on this system by going to www.MakeNoMistakes.com, clicking on the Make No Mistakes™ System. Follow the directions on the first page so you can begin receiving your automatic emails.

Everything we have shared with you came from someone making a mistake and paying the price *already*. Certainly, there are no absolute guarantees, but being willing to learn from others' mistakes will go a long way to ensure that your real estate experience is successful.

We have educated you on the process and shared with you the inside scoop behind everything involved in your transaction, which gives you that *edge* in knowl*edge*. Now is the time to do something that most people don't do: *Use* the information you gleaned from investing so much time in reading, instead of putting the reference guide on the shelf.

Remember that our blog, which you can access through our website, discusses various subjects, updates and current events related to real estate. It also shares other mistakes we've come across since writing this edition of our book. Our goal is to always keep you current.

We are all faced with decisions when buying real estate. We encourage you to keep the emotions out of your decision-making process and look at the transaction as an investment in your future. Take this journey, as it can produce *extraordinary* results! We wish you the best of luck, good judgment and great happiness!

Pass The Knowledge On!

APPENDICES

Appendix 5.1:   Buyer Services

Appendix 10.2:   Borrower's Paperwork Checklist

Appendix 13.3:   Lender Comparative

Appendix 13.4:   APR Calculation Table

CHECKLISTS, FORMS AND TOOLS LOCATED ON THE WEBSITE

After-Closing Checklist

APR Calculation Table

Borrower's Paperwork

Budget Spreadsheet

Comparative Market Analysis   (CMA)

Good Faith Estimate (APR Checked Off)

Home Search Criteria

How to Identify a "Good" Loan Officer

How to Identify a "Good" Real Estate Agent

HUD-1 Settlement Statement

Identify Your Leverage

Lender Comparative

Make No Mistakes ™ Home Buyer's Checklist

Mortgage Loan Application

Moving Checklist

Murphy's Law

Pre-Inspection Checklist

Property Viewing Checklist

Settlement Statement (HUD-1)

Taking Possession of Your Home

Tax Credit Chart

Things Not To Do When Applying for a Mortgage

Things to Ask For At Closing

Utility Checklist

OTHER LINKS
THAT WILL KEEP YOU INFORMED

www.consumeraffairs.com

www.dol.gov

www.equifax.com

www.experian.com

www.fanniemae.com

www.fha.gov

www.freddiemac.com

www.freecreditreport.com

www.housingprograms.org

www.hud.gov

www.irs.gov

www.irs.gov/publications

www.makenomistakes.com

www.metrostudy.com

www.onecalloneteam.com

www.realtor.org

www.recovery.gov/

www.salary.com

www.transunion.com

www.treas.gov

www.va.gov

www.whitehouse.gov

Appendix 5.1

BUYER SERVICES (Part 1)

What a Good Real Estate Agent Can Do For You:

1. **Analyzes the client's wants and needs**
    - Asks questions based on the type of property client requires
    - Determines price points
    - Determines if there are obstacles, such as the sale of an existing home
    - Determines if there are any special needs, special financing concerns
    - Identifies appropriate areas of town
    - Familiarizes client with area/city/schools

2. **Assists with the client's Loan Pre-Qualification**
    - Reviews financing options
    - Provides a list of good loan officers
    - Assists in providing necessary information to loan officer
    - Provides solutions for challenges that arise from conditions listed by the underwriter
        - Reviews and makes sure the property appraises correctly and compares it to the MLS listing
        - Reviews and follows the process to a quick close
    - Reviews Good Faith Estimate to determine how to structure your sales contract

3. **Locates potential properties**
    - Conducts MLS searches
    - Researches new home builders (for new construction)
    - Analyzes value for price growth potential

BUYER SERVICES (Part 2)

4. **Prepares the offer**
   - Presents research found on property, such as historical pricing (Comparative Market Analysis) and sales
   - Determines favorable terms for client
   - Presents the offer to seller and/or seller's agent

5. **Negotiates the deal**
   - Uses knowledge of other properties available (competition)
   - Obtains the best deal possible for the client
   - Recommends price and terms
   - Protects client's earnest money
   - Advises on taking possession / moving in

6. **Facilitates inspections / negotiates repairs**
   - Provides a list of good inspectors: mechanical, structural, termite and environmental
   - Attends the home inspection
   - Reviews inspection report
   - Provides a list of good contractors to make repairs
   - Provides a list of good insurance companies for hazard insurance
   - Provides a list of good home warranty companies

7. **Reviews closing documents from title company and mortgage lender**
   - Insures and reviews title commitment
   - Checks HUD–1 Statement for errors or omissions
   - Reviews and provides solutions to last-minute items
   - Ensures survey is ordered
   - Schedules closing date and time
   - Attends closing and reviews all documents placed before buyer

BUYER SERVICES (Part 3)

8. **Utilizes the Make No Mistakes™ System checklists**

9. **Communicates with buyer every step of the way**
    - Email
    - Voicemail
    - Mobile
    - Text messaging

10. **Is time sensitive to:**
    - Acquiring and reviewing financial papers
    - Signing amendments
    - Making deadline dates

Appendix 10.2

Borrower's Paperwork Checklist (Part 1)

EMPLOYMENT INFORMATION

____ If relocating, letter from employer stating you will be employed with the current company in _____ (city)
____ Completed application –
____ Current pay stubs for last 2 months
____ W-2's for the last 2 years

Self-Employed only:

____ Tax returns for last 2 years, with all schedules
____ Year-to-date profit and loss statements
____ Corporate tax returns for last 2 years with all schedules

INFORMATION ON YOUR ASSET ACCOUNTS

____ Last 2 months' statements for checking, all pages
____ Last 2 months' statements for savings, all pages
____ Last 2 months' statement for investment accounts, all pages
____ Last statements for 401-K/IRA, etc. (all accounts) all pages
____ 2 months' worth of PITI (Principal + Interest + Taxes + Insurance) in checking or savings accounts

INFORMATION ON YOUR LANDLORD OR MORTGAGE COMPANY

____ Name and address of landlord, leasing office, or mortgage co. (phone number, fax number, account number)

Borrower's Paperwork Checklist (Part 2)

ADDITIONAL ITEMS NEEDED IF YOU ARE PURCHASING

____ Copy of fully executed sales contract, signed by all parties
____ Copy of cancelled earnest money check or receipt from the title company

ADDITIONAL ITEMS NEEDED IF YOU'RE REFINANCING

____ Copy of survey of subject property
____ Declaration page from hazard/homeowner's policy showing coverage and premiums

ADDITIONAL ITEMS THAT MAY PERTAIN TO YOU

____ Copy of fully executed divorce decree
____ Green card
____ Copy of bankruptcy papers
____ Lease agreements on rental property you own
____ Certificate of eligibility (VA)
____ Property you own
____ Copy of social security card
____ Copy of driver's license

Appendix 13.3

Lender Comparative (Part 1)

LENDER COMPARATIVE				
LENDER	Lender #1 ABC	Lender #2 DEF	Lender # 3 GHI	EXPLANATION
TERM	30	30	30	
PROGRAM	FIXED	FIXED	FIXED	
Sales Price	$ 313,183.00	$ 313,183.00	$ 313,183.00	
% Down Payment	20%	20%	20%	
Down Payment	$ 62,636.60	$ 62,636.60	$ 62,636.60	
1st Loan Amount	$ 250,546.40	$ 250,546.00	$ 250,546.00	
2nd Loan Amount				
1st Interest Rate	6%	5.75%	5.875%	
2nd Rate				
1st Principal & Interest	$1,502.15	$1,482.07	$ 1,483.61	
2nd Principal & Interest				
Monthly Principal & Interest	$1,502.15	$1,462.12	$ 1,482.07	
Hazard Insurance	$ 143.92	$ 143.92	$ 143.92	
Taxes	$ 629.00	$ 629.00	$ 629.00	
PMI				
HOA	$ 83.33	$ 83.33	$ 83.33	
Monthly Mortgage Amount	$2,343.53	$2,318.37	$2,338.32	
ITEMS PAYABLE IN CONNECTION WITH THE LOAN				
LOAN AMOUNT	$ 250,546.00	$ 250,546.00	$ 250,546.00	
Origination Fee	$ 2,505.46	$ 2,505.46	$ 2,505.46	
Loan Discount**		$ 1,252.73		
Appraisal Fee	$ 300.00	$ 350.00	$ 350.00	Lender #1 requires $300. What company are they using?
Credit Report Fee	$ 17.00	$ 35.00	$ 35.00	
Flood Certification	$ 20.00	$ 26.00	$ 26.00	
Lender Inspection Fee	$ 100.00			Why is there a difference in fees?
Tax related Service Fee	$ 77.00	$ 105.00	$ 105.00	Why is there a difference in fees?
Processing Fee	$ 200.00	$ 200.00	$ 400.00	Why is there a difference in fees?
Underwriting Fee	$ 250.00			Why is there a difference in fees?
TOTALS	$ 3,469.46	$ 4,474.19	$ 3,421.46	

Lender Comparative (Part 2)

LENDER COMPARATIVE						
TITLE CHARGES						
Closing/Escrow	$	250.00	$	250.00	$	250.00	Should be the same
Doc. Prep-Title/Closing Agent			$	150.00	$	150.00	Should be the same
Attorney Fee	$	365.00	$	150.00	$	150.00	Should be the same
Title Insurance			$	1,649.00			Seller pays for the title policy - Buyer only pays for the lender policy
Courier /Express Mail			$	30.00			Lender #1 and #3 are not charging?
Lender Title Insurance	$	280.00	$	225.00	$	225.00	Should be the same
TOTALS	$895.00		$2,454.00		$	775.00	
GOVERNMENT						
State Tax Stamp	$	70.00	$	70.00	$	70.00	Should be the same
Recording fees	$	120.00	$	120.00	$	120.00	Should be the same
TOTALS	$	190.00	$	190.00	$	190.00	
ADDITIONAL SETTLEMENT COSTS						
Survey	$	514.19	$	380.00	$	380.00	What is Lender # 1 including in its survey that lender 2& 3 are not?
Termite/Pest Inspection	$	100.00	$	75.00	$	75.00	Why is Lender # 1 not requiring a Termite Inspect?
HOA Transfer Fee	$	125.00					Lender #2 & #3 forgot to charge HOA fees
HOA Pro Rates	$	200.00					Lender #2 & #3 forgot to charge HOA fees
TOTALS	$	939.19	$	455.00	$	455.00	
ESTIMATED CLOSING COSTS	$	5,493.65	$	7,573.19	$	4,841.46	
ESTIMATED PREPAID ITEMS / RESERVES						
Prepaid Interest	$	417.58	$	400.18	$	408.88	Should all be based on the same number of days till closing
Hazard Insurance - 1 year	$	1,727.04	$	1,727.04	$	1,727.04	
Hazard Insurance in Reserve Account	$	431.76	$	431.76	$	431.76	
County Taxes	$	1,887.00	$	1,887.00	$	1,887.00	
ESTIMATED TOTAL PREPAIDS/RESERVES	$	4,463.38	$	4,445.98	$	4,454.68	

Lender Comparative (Part 3)

LENDER COMPARATIVE				
PURCHASE PRICE	$ 313,183.00	$ 313,183.00	$ 313,183.00	
LOAN AMOUNT	$ 250,546.00	$ 250,546.00	$ 250,546.00	
DOWN PAYMENT	$ 62,637.00	$ 62,637.00	$ 62,637.00	
ESTIMATED CLOSING COSTS	$ 5,493.65	$ 7,573.19	$ 4,841.46	
ESTIMATED TOTAL PREPAIDS/RESERVES	$ 4,463.38	$ 4,445.98	$ 4,454.68	
TOTAL ESTIMATED SETTLEMENT CHARGES	$ 9,957.03	$ 12,019.17	$ 9,296.14	
SELLER CONTRIBUTION (AMT. PAID BY SELLER)	$ -	$ -	$ -	
OPTION MONEY	$ -	$ -	$ -	
EARNEST MONEY	$ (3,000.00)	$ (3,000.00)	$ (3,000.00)	
TOTAL ESTIMATED FUNDS NEEDED TO CLOSE	$ 69,594.03	$ 71,656.17	$ 68,933.14	
INFORMATION YOU MAY NEED TO INQUIRE ABOUT				
Escrow Required	no	no	no	
Tax Credit *	n/a	n/a	n/a	
Prepayment Penalty	no	no	no	
APR	6.138%	5.922%	6.009%	
Lock Code				
Expiring Date				
Lender	ABC FUNDING	DEF FUNDING	GHI MORTGAGE	
Telephone #	713-111-1100	281-111-2600	704-555-1212	
Contact	JOE SMITH	MARY JONES	JOHN DOE	

* Tax Credit Given by Seller but due by the end of the Year from Borrower

** Interest Rate was lowered. As a result there was a buy down cost of .025%

Appendix 13.4

APR Calculation Table (Part 1)

Fees Paid By Borrower	Exclude	Include
	Does Not Affect APR	*Does* Affect APR
	Not a Prepaid Finance Charge	Prepaid Finance Charge
Amortization Schedule		X
Application Fee		X
Appraisal Fee	X	
Assignment Fee		X
Assumption Fee		X
Attorney Fee	X	
Commitment Fee		X
Courier Fee		X
Credit Line Insurance (exclude if optional)	X	
Credit Report Fees	X	
Document Preparation	X	
Escrow Waiver Fee		X
Escrow Fees (Hazard Taxes, etc.)	X	
Final Inspection Fee	X	
Flood Certification Fee	X	
Flood Certification w/ life of loan		X
Funding Fee		X
Homeowner's Insurance (include if agency is not third party)	X	

APR Calculation Table (Part 2)

Fees Paid By Borrower	Exclude	Include
	Does Not Affect APR	Does Affect APR
	Not a Prepaid Finance Charge	Prepaid Finance Charge
Inspections for Construction		X
Interest		X
Loan Discount Fee (paid by Buyer)		X
Loan Origination Fee		X
Mortgage Broker Fee		X
Mortgage Insurance Premiums		X
Notary Fees	X	
Per Diem Interest		X
Pest Inspections	X	
Points / Fees Paid by Seller	X	
Processing Fee / Administration / Underwriting		X
Recording Fees		X
Settlement/ Closing Fees/ Escrow	X	
Survey	X	
Tax Life Loan Certification		X
Tax Service Fee		X
Title Endorsement Fee		X
Title Insurance	X	
Verification Fee		X
Well and Septic Inspection	X	
Wire Fees		X

Index

ABOUT THE AUTHORS

Melissa Walters

 A real estate investor for more than 18 years, Melissa Walters is also a business owner and a top-producing broker agent with Keller Williams Realty in Houston, Texas. She's consistently achieved top agent recognition for productivity in sales and has garnered many honors for business contributions to such companies as Keller Williams Realty, Xerox, and West Publishing. She's originally from New York and a graduate of Hofstra University, with a BBA in Marketing. She co-founded One Call-One Team, LLC, whose main objective is to provide viable solutions to the many facets of real estate, from marketing to financing. Her professional background skyrockets clients' success in real estate, sales, management, negotiations and marketing multi-million dollar projects. She has accumulated many accolades throughout her career due to being knowledgeable, loving what she does and surrounding herself by a team of people who are mutually focused on achieving.

One Call – One Team, LLC
1650 US Hwy 6 # 350
Sugarland, Tx 77479
Email: Melissa@MakeNoMistakes.com

Rudy Silmon

 Rudy Silmon is an entrepreneur, coach and loan officer. He co-founded One Call-One Team, LLC, where the main objective is to provide viable solutions to the many faceted needs of real estate, from marketing to financing. A regular speaker at seminars, he focuses on leveling the playing field between the borrower and the mortgage industry. He spent over 25 years with such companies as IBM, Exxon and Wiltel, where he learned how to identify mistakes and develop solutions that earned him success. His focus has always been on how to get the maximum return from the decisions you make – when it counts the most. He realized early in his career that you have to minimize the mistakes through increased knowledge if you want to achieve maximum return and have a successful outcome. He has dedicated his life to helping people achieve success, and now, with this reference guide, he will help many, many more. He resides in a suburb just outside of Houston. To contact Silmon, or to obtain information about volume discounts, coaching programs, speeches, seminars or other offerings contact:

One Call - One Team, LLC
1650 US Hwy 6 # 350
Sugarland, Tx 77479
Email: Rudy@MakeNoMistakes.com

We Want to Hear From You!

If you have a real estate mistake that you would like to share with our readers please send it to us. You may prevent someone from making the same mistake that you made. So "Pass The Knowledge On" and we look forward to hearing from you.

You can reach us online at www.MakeNoMistakes.com

Email Address:

Melissa@MakeNoMistakes.com

Or

Rudy@MakeNoMistakes.com

NOTES

ISBN: 978-0-9795604-3-9

www.MakeNoMistakes.com

Printed in the United States
144721LV00003B/2/P